About the author

Jonathan Steele is Senior Foreign Correspondent and in-house columnist on international affairs for the *Guardian*. Educated at Cambridge and Yale, he has reported for the *Guardian* since 1965. He was the only English language reporter to reach Mikhail Gorbachev's prison dacha during the August 1991 coup, and the subsequent interview he gained with the Russian President won him the London Press Club's Scoop of the Year award. In his present role he travels frequently to the Middle East and has contributed to the *Guardian*'s coverage of Iraq since the start of the war. He has won numerous prizes for his foreign news reporting, including the James Cameron and Martha Gelhorn awards. He has twice been named International Reporter of the Year at the British Press Awards. A frequent broadcaster on the BBC and CNN, Steele has written several books on international affairs.

'This is a superb book – the best account so far of what went wrong in Iraq, and why. Measured, highly intelligent, and written from personal observation by perhaps the best foreign correspondent working in British journalism, it examines why the occupation of Iraq turned into the disaster it did, and not simply how it happened. With immense care and first-hand knowledge, Jonathan Steele has written the one indispensable account of the whole disturbing, thoughtless, cynical process.'

John Simpson, World Affairs Editor, BBC

'For many years, it has been a remarkable experience to watch history unfold through Jonathan Steele's discerning eyes. This wrenching analysis of the suffering of Iraq is written with penetrating intelligence and deep knowledge, drawing on his own courageous reporting from Iraq and the region and genuine comprehension of the rich and complex historical background of the awful events taking place before our eyes.'

Noam Chomsky

'A splendid contribution.'

Amartya Sen

'This exquisite prose resonates with integrity and compassion. Amongst the many volumes that will record and unpick this catastrophic war, this book will stand the test of history. A classic of our times.'

Helena Kennedy, QC

'The violence in Iraq has begun to fade from our press reports, which is why Jonathan Steele's new book is timely … A dangerous complacency is creeping into our attitude. I hope it will be shaken by Steele's book … Jonathan Steele finds the right answer to the question of how this disaster came about.'

Douglas Hurd, the Guardian

'useful and important'

Mark Thomas

'impressively written and powerful'

Charles Tripp, the New Statesman

'impeccably written and thoughtful'

Paul Rogers, the Independent

DEFEAT

WHY THEY LOST IRAQ

JONATHAN STEELE

I.B. TAURIS

LONDON · NEW YORK

New edition published in 2009 by I.B.Tauris & Co Ltd
6 Salem Road, London W2 4BU
175 Fifth Avenue, New York NY 10010
www.ibtauris.com

First published in hardback in 2008 by I.B.Tauris & Co Ltd

ISBN: 978 1 84885 077 4

A full CIP record for this book is available from the British Library

Typeset in Minion Pro by Sara Millington, Editorial and Design Services
Printed and bound in India by Replika Press Pvt Ltd

For Sumaya, Pravin, Leah and Amos

They shall overcome

Acknowledgements

I gathered some of the material for this book while on various assignments for the *Guardian* in Iraq and I am grateful to Alan Rusbridger, the paper's editor, and Harriet Sherwood, the foreign editor, for sending me there. I also thank Harriet, as well as Chris Elliott, the *Guardian*'s Managing Editor, for giving me a few months off from my work at the paper in order to write it.

I benefited enormously from the views of many Iraqis, without whom this book would not have been worth writing. Some of them, including Salam Ali, Nour al-Khal, Mina al-Oraibi, Sami Ramadani, and Yahia Said, read chapters and made valuable comments. Paul Anderson provided great assistance in researching material for Chapter II, entitled 'Arab Anguish'.

Rory McCarthy, my *Guardian* colleague who was based in Baghdad for much of 2003 and 2004, was always welcoming and knowledgeable. Our team of Iraqi drivers and translators took many risks and gave constant support. The wisdom shared with me by Alissa Rubin of the *Los Angeles Times* and John Burns of the *New York Times* was also a great asset.

The staff of the *Guardian*'s research department in London, including Isabelle Chevallot, Katy Heslop, Linda MacDonald, Richard Nelsson, Jason Rodrigues, and Luc Torres, were always ready to dig out references to newspaper articles and web-based reports.

Several British diplomats and senior military officers who were closely involved in the planning and implementation of the invasion gave me their views on a non-attributable basis, and I am grateful to them for their candour.

Iradj Bagherzade accepted the concept of this book with alacrity, and Abigail Fielding-Smith was always enthusiastic and efficient as an editor.

My special thanks go to Ruth for unflagging love and support and for calmly accepting the anxieties which inevitably went with my many trips to Baghdad, particularly from mid-2004 onwards when security in Iraq took a nosedive. It was not an easy time.

Jonathan Steele

CONTENTS

INTRODUCTION

We had to build a success story here that, like Germany and Japan, still looked good after 50 years.

L. Paul Bremer III, *My Year in Iraq*

They marched away enduring a belief
Whose logic brought them, somewhere else, to grief

W.H. Auden, *The Shield of Achilles*

This book is not a narrative or chronology of the American and British occupation of Iraq. It is an explanation of why George W. Bush and Tony Blair lost their war, and were bound to do so.

Many writers have catalogued the bad decisions made by the Americans and the British in relation to Iraq after April 2003. Some, like myself, are reporters who spent long periods on the ground during the occupation. Others are former officials who worked for the occupying authorities and became disillusioned. On returning home they turned their notes and diaries into illuminating accounts of incompetence, stupidity, arrogance, and corruption. Their common argument is that Bush and Blair failed to plan for the post-war period and to send enough troops, and that they then compounded these blunders with a series of mistakes such as their failure to control mass looting and the dissolution of the Iraqi army. The assumption is that with better pre-war preparation and post-war management the USA could have won the peace as impressively as it won the war.

My thesis is more fundamental. The occupation was doomed from the start. No matter how efficient, sensitive, generous, and intelligent the so-called

Coalition Provisional Authority (CPA) had been, it could not have succeeded. Occupations are inherently humiliating. People prefer to run their own affairs; they resent foreigners taking over their country. A foreign army that topples a regime needs to leave within weeks or at most months. Otherwise, suspicion will grow quickly that the foreigners' real aims are imperial – to run the country directly or through the locals they put in charge, and to exploit its resources. Nowhere is this truer than in the Middle East where feelings of dignity, honour, sovereignty, and humiliation are the currency of daily life.

Opposition to invaders starts with mistrust, grows into anger, and moves on to a refusal to collaborate with the foreign authorities, and the application of pressure on friends, family, and neighbours to do likewise. At any point it may lead to armed insurgency. Different groups in society will go through these stages at their own pace, but none will be immune. In trying to deal with this gathering opposition occupiers are drawn into a cycle of action and reaction that undermines their initial goals.

Improvisation and short-term crisis control replace strategic thinking. Insurgency is met with repression. Those who thought they came as liberators are perceived as murderous outsiders and those who work with them are seen as traitors. Sooner or later occupiers are forced to come to two painful conclusions: their project is unattainable, and the price of any course of action other than retreat has become too high. The main issue becomes how much damage is done, to themselves and the people they occupy, before they leave.

The only exceptions to this rule in modern times have been the Western occupations of Germany and Japan after 1945. In Germany's case the Western occupiers were not imposing alien institutions. They were trying to restore a political and economic system that had been disrupted by an aberrational period of Nazi dictatorship lasting 13 years – in historical terms a short interval. It also helped that the occupiers had a similar background, upbringing, and values to the people they had liberated. There was no major clash of cultures.

In Japan the Americans were dealing with a society and civilisation different from theirs. However, in 1945 Japan was a country whose troops had suffered hugely from four years of expansionist war, while the civilian population endured severe economic deprivation, months of carpet bombing, and two nuclear blasts. Japan's cities lay in ruins, millions of people were dead, and the survivors were in no mood to resist a foreign occupation, especially one that kept the key symbol of state authority and dignity, the Emperor, in office. His powers were cut back but he remained as a guarantee of continuity and a rallying point for national dignity and pride. When he called on his people to submit to the occupying authorities and accept defeat, they loyally obeyed.

For Western powers to invade a Muslim country in the heart of the Middle East in the twenty-first century was a very different story. The region has a strong collective memory of imperial intrusion and a deep sense of anti-Western nationalism based on patriotic resentment against powerful alien outsiders who lord it over local peoples and in the process challenge their Muslim identity. Historically, a mixture of anger, humiliation, and shame informs almost every Arab encounter with Westerners. The Middle East has been repeatedly invaded and occupied by foreigners for the last eight centuries, with its dominant religion despised and belittled.

Today's Western intervention is mainly one of ideas, values, and products. Nevertheless when it takes a military form, as in Iraq, the enormity of having foreign tanks on Arab streets revives memories of an era of imperialism that was supposed to be over and brings back every Arab's latent sense of shame. In the starkest terms it hammers home the myriad onslaughts that the Arab world faces from the West – political, economic, technological, and – by no means least – cultural. Military invasion is the sharp end of the West's penetration of the region. It produces anger and resistance from secular Arabs as much as Islamists.

In Iraq in 2003, endemic suspicion of US and British motives was compounded by the fact that British colonisers had invaded the country, defeated the Ottoman army, and assumed total control in 1918. The Ottomans were Muslims and ran their empire in relatively benign style. With the arrival of the British, Iraqis found themselves truly under foreign rule. The British abolished the elected municipal councils, and dealt with resistance by means of massive military repression. They then occupied the country for two generations. So Bush and Blair were launching their attacks on a nation that was unlikely to welcome another takeover.

Add to that two other facts. Shias remembered the US failure to help their uprising against Saddam Hussein after the first Gulf War in 1991, and Iraqis of all groups hated the following decade of US-sponsored sanctions that threw hundreds of thousands into poverty and joblessness and left hospitals, universities, and other institutions starved of equipment. At best the

USA appeared an unreliable ally; more often it was seen as a hostile outside power with its own agenda.

Iraqis assumed that agenda was about gaining control over the region's oil and protecting Israel. The USA has acquiesced in Israel's occupation of the West Bank for the last 40 years and remains hopelessly one-sided in its approach to the Palestinian issue. The invasion of Iraq would be the second occupation of Arab lands by a Western army in recent times. It ought to be no surprise that it provoked an Iraqi intifada in which both Sunnis and Shias took part.

Nearly every mistake the Americans made after toppling Saddam Hussein – from the use of heavy-handed and abrasive military tactics at checkpoints and during house searches, the failure to spend reconstruction money intelligently, the under-estimation of the armed resistance as nothing more than a few former Baathists and foreign jihadis, the killing of hundreds of civilians in air strikes described as counter-insurgency, the reluctance to transfer genuine sovereignty to Iraqis, and the refusal to name a date for withdrawal – strengthened Iraqis' feelings of outrage at the humiliation they were casually expected to digest. The occupation was a daily affront to their dignity, as well as an increasing source of violence and death.

Bush and Blair seemed unaware of Iraqi history, the broader context of Arab nationalism, or the depth of Arab and Iraqi frustration over Western support for Israel's policies. Blair, if not Bush, paid lip service to the need for a Palestinian–Israeli settlement, but Blair never used the minimal leverage he had over Washington to insist on a radical change in US policy over Israel as the condition for British support for the US invasion of Iraq. He told a meeting of British diplomats, summoned back to London on 7 January 2003:

> The reason there is opposition over our stance on Iraq has less to do with love for Saddam but [is] over a sense of double standards. The Middle East peace process remains essential to any understanding with the Muslim and Arab world.[1]

Blair's description of the problem was correct, but he did nothing to resolve it.

Neither Bush nor Blair made any obvious attempt to understand the complexity of Iraqi society, or the vibrancy of its politics in the 1960s before Saddam's dictatorship and the economic hardships of its last two decades hollowed out Iraq's professional class and the country's pool of activists. Many were executed, forced to flee, or silenced by repression. Even in the 1960s before the Baathist coup, newspapers and political parties were frequently banned, forcing activists underground. But that did not mean the Iraq that emerged after Saddam's fall had no experience or memory of political debate and organisation. There were tens of thousands of Iraqis, still only in their fifties and sixties, who had devoted youthful courage, energy, and idealism to women's groups, political parties, trade union militancy, and the theatre and the arts during the renaissance that followed the toppling of the monarchy in 1958, and in clandestinity in later years. Yet the Bush administration and most US and British officials who moved to Baghdad and Basra operated from the same patronising template that was put on post-Cold War Eastern Europe, the Balkans, Afghanistan, and East Timor. Iraq was perceived as just another 'transition' country with no civil society or history of democratic struggle.

Perhaps the biggest error that resulted from the lack of interest in Iraqi society from the White House and Downing Street was the failure to see the strength of Islamism. Bush and Blair did not seem to know that Islamists were already on the rise in Iraq in the final decade of Saddam's secular regime and were bound to become stronger if he was toppled. Islamism, of course, opposes the West's dominant presence in the Middle East. It is one response – perhaps the most powerful one over the last two decades – to the shame and humiliation caused by the remorseless onrush of Western influence. There should have been a warning here, had Bush and Blair factored it into their pre-war planning. But no. The two leaders' view of Iraq seemed to focus exclusively on the atrocities of the Iraqi dictator's regime.

Saddam was indeed widely hated in Iraq by 2003. Yet it was laughable to think this meant Iraqis would automatically welcome an invasion, treat occupiers as liberators, and be glad that Westerners with their own strategic agendas and long records of Middle Eastern interventionism would stick around to tell them how to govern their country.

Much has been made of the faulty intelligence claim that Saddam had a secret arsenal of weapons of mass destruction, which was used to justify the US invasion. In my view, the failures of political intelligence were equally serious. Why were Bush and Blair not told of the depth of Iraqi nationalism or given a warning that hatred of Saddam did not produce automatic support for an invasion? Why did they not ask for impartial advice on who would inherit Iraq once Saddam was toppled? Why did they not realise that their invasion would lead to a combination of nationalist resistance and the rapid emergence of Shia Islamists, many of them linked to Iran, as the country's dominant political force? Where were the political analysts in the US and British governments who should have told them what would happen in the vacuum after Saddam's departure?

Washington's mistake was not a lack of planning, as is commonly argued, leading to the so-called triple failure (not sending enough troops, not providing security from looting, and not restoring electricity and other basic services quickly). In the run-up to the 2008 presidential election that line of argument has become a useful alibi for Democratic hopefuls: 'I would not have supported the war if I had realised there was no post-war plan.' The more significant US and British mistake was the lack of analysis, and the failure to understand the political and cultural forces in Iraq that would determine the country's future after Saddam.

On behalf of my newspaper, the *Guardian*, I served nine assignments in Iraq between April 2003 and 2008, each lasting around a month or more. My abiding impression from this series of snapshots was of a constantly widening gulf between Iraqis and their occupiers. What little acceptance there was in the early days progressively evaporated, yet this was barely acknowledged by US or British officials. Opinion polls that showed the occupation's lack of popular support received minimal attention from policy makers or coverage in the media. TV news channels occasionally showed Iraqi crowds cheering and dancing over burning Humvees after insurgent attacks but it was not until December 2006 that a high-level public document, the report of the Iraq Study Group (sometimes referred to as the Baker-Hamilton Report) headed by former Secretary of State James Baker and former congressman Lee Hamilton, mentioned the uncomfortable fact that 61 per cent of Iraqis approved of attacks on US forces.[2] Attacks on the so-called coalition were not coming primarily from Al-Qaeda or foreign jihadis. They came from Iraqis, outraged by the fact of the occupation as well as the actions of the occupiers.

Yet indicators of the occupation's unpopularity were brushed aside, when they should have been the starting point for policy makers to analyse what was going wrong and whether corrections could be found to salvage the US position. This book attempts to answer those questions. I accept as a given that the war was illegal, since it had no United Nations support. No other

Security Council members shared the US and British governments' line that UN resolutions going back to 1990 provided sufficient authorisation for an invasion in 2003. I also accept that the war was unnecessary. If the aim was to deal with Iraq's alleged weapons of mass destruction, the UN inspectors had barely begun their work and Washington should have allowed them more time. This book concentrates on the occupation, however, not the invasion.

To emphasise the point that this is not another narrative, the book does not run chronologically. It is divided thematically. Chapter I discusses the origins and extent of Iraqi Arabs' suspicions of the USA and Britain, and the mutual distrust of Iraqis by the new occupiers. It explains how American and British decision-makers failed to take account of Iraqis' complex views about the desirability of having a foreign army topple Saddam. This meant that, for most Iraqis, satisfaction with his downfall did not translate into satisfaction with being occupied. Chapter II looks at the wider context of Arab attitudes to Western intervention in the Middle East from the Crusades to the present day. Iraqis and other Arabs do not view the invasion of Iraq in isolation, as do so many Western policy makers; it was only the latest in a long history of assaults on Arab and Muslim dignity.

Chapters III and IV explain how US civilian administrators and troop commanders created resistance among Sunnis and Shias by raising justified suspicions about American intentions, as well as through a series of political and military blunders. Chapter V poses the question of whether the USA could have withdrawn from Iraq with relatively little loss of life if, after toppling Saddam, Washington had left quickly and allowed Iraqis to run their country on their own. Was there a viable option to 'leave in time' rather than the one that was adopted and by 2005 had already become 'get bogged down'?

Chapter VI discusses the scandal of Abu Ghraib and explains why it was just the tip of an iceberg of mass detention of innocent civilians in a brutal counter-insurgency campaign that shocked and alienated millions of Iraqis while further undermining the US image in the Muslim world. Events at Abu Ghraib prison were not just a disaster of bad management, poor training, and indiscipline. They are important because they demonstrate how culturally unattuned and essentially racist most of the occupiers were. At one level, nothing better could have been expected from ordinary young soldiers with no experience of the cultural nuances of a very different world.

Ignorance is no sin. It becomes vitally important, however, when ignorance is factored into decision-making.

Chapter VII describes how the British went to war with as little analysis as the Americans of the likely political shape of post-Saddam Iraq. Based on interviews with officials who worked for the Blair government in 2003, it reveals for the first time that Britain's Arabists failed to predict the rise of Iraq's Islamists or to realise that the occupation would provoke an insurgency. It also shows why the British army never accepted the US neoconservatives' goals. Officers based their policy on pragmatism rather than ideology and quietly ceded power in Basra and the rest of south-eastern Iraq to Islamic militias, many of which had ties to Iran.

Chapter VIII analyses the sectarian violence between Sunnis and Shias, which has caused the worst ethnic cleansing in the Middle East for a generation, forcing close to 4 million Iraqis to flee their homes for refuge elsewhere in Iraq or abroad. It answers the questions: who is to blame, and what role, if any, did the USA play in provoking the catastrophe?

Finally, Chapter IX looks at the farce of sovereignty. It describes how Iraq's successive governments, whether they were directly nominated by the Americans or picked from members of parliament elected by Iraqis, never had genuine freedom of action. Washington always held the purse strings or had the military clout to enforce the policies it wanted.

The first year of the occupation was decisive in setting the agenda and sealing Iraq's fate. Had the Americans followed their easy military victory over Saddam with an announcement of plans to withdraw completely within a year or less, they could have left Iraq without shedding much of their own or Iraqis' blood. Iraq's political class – not just the exiles who came in with the invaders – would have come forward readily to work out a new social compact and form a government once they knew Americans were not trying to control it. Tension and struggles for power would certainly have taken place, but there would have been no basis for armed insurgency. Had violence by Saddamists, Al-Qaeda in Iraq (sometimes called Al-Qaeda in Mesopotamia) or other outside groups emerged, the UN and the Arab League would have been more open to Iraqi government requests for peacekeeping, if the new Iraqi authorities felt their own police and security forces needed help.

Of course, the option of early withdrawal was not chosen, or even considered in Washington. The neoconservatives always wanted a prolonged occupation as a way to put new pressure on Iran and Syria, develop US military bases on Iraqi soil, and send a message of US dominance across the Middle East. As a result, Iraq's post-invasion landscape rapidly moved from light to shade to black despair. The chaos, the crime, the terrorism, the sectarian violence, and the slide towards civil war, all flowed from the disastrous US decision to control Iraq's government and keep an open-ended presence in Iraq.

The exact trajectory of what happened and the scale of the human tragedy that now engulfs Iraq could not have been predicted. What is certain is that none of the goals that Bush and Blair originally set for themselves in Iraq – democracy, security, and a stable pro-Western regime – have been met nor will be. The day on which Bush decided to have an occupation was the day he ensured its defeat.

I

IRAQ WITHOUT IRAQIS

All donne, go home
Graffiti in Baghdad, June 2003

A rare joke circulated among Iraqis shortly before Prime Minister Nouri al-Maliki met President George W. Bush in Amman in November 2006 to discuss the latest plan to end the country's pervasive insecurity. What would the US president be demanding? Answer: a timetable for Iraqis to withdraw from Iraq.

Every day 3,000 Iraqis were leaving the country to escape the threat of kidnapping, suicide bombers, and sectarian murder. In Baghdad around a hundred civilians were being abducted and killed every 24 hours, their recovered bodies often showing marks of torture and mutilation.

The joke was not just a bitter reference to the accelerating Iraqi exodus from Iraq, however. It reflected a widespread Iraqi feeling that Americans harboured a secret wish: an Iraq without Iraqis. The country's failure to organise a competent government, end the inter-communal violence, create a professional national army to replace the sectarian militias, and knuckle down to building a modern democratic state had drained the last ounce of American patience, it seemed. Blame for the disaster was increasingly being put on Iraqis themselves. The Americans had sacrificed thousands of their troops' lives and billions of US taxpayers' dollars. If things were not working, it must be the Iraqis' fault.

Judging by their behaviour, many US officials certainly seemed to prefer as little contact with Iraqis as possible. Even in the early days of the occupation in 2003, when travel outside Baghdad's Green Zone was perfectly safe, they confined themselves to a narrow set of contacts. When Barbara Bodine, a tough former US diplomat who was appointed by Washington to be Baghdad's first post-invasion mayor, suggested she would open her office in the city centre, 'there were cries of horror – "There are Iraqis there,"' an occupation official told me.

American advisers and other political staff in Iraq made little attempt to read up on Iraqi history or Arab culture. The State Department and other US agencies sent few of their Arabic-speakers. The available pool was not large before the invasion, and many US Arabists avoided applying for posts in Iraq, either because they knew enough about the Middle East to realise the invasion was a blunder, or because they feared a Baghdad posting would be a career-killer.

'The number of Americans who spoke Arabic in the Coalition Provisional Authority was shamefully, shockingly low,' commented Noah Feldman, who was senior constitutional adviser to the CPA, as the US occupation's civilian administration was called.[1] He described how 'a chill went over me' when he peeped at what his fellow passengers were reading in the US military transport plane that flew him and other US officials to Baghdad in May 2003. 'Not one seemed to need a refresher on Iraq or the Gulf region. Without exception, they were reading new books on the American occupation and reconstruction of Germany and Japan,' he recalled.[2]

Three and a half years later, when the USA was mired in massive difficulties in Iraq, the Bush administration's use of expertise was still feeble. The Baker-Hamilton Report revealed that in a staff of 1,000 at the US embassy in Baghdad there were only six Americans with fluent Arabic.[3] It also revealed that the Defense Intelligence Agency in Washington, which was supposed to give advice on the aims and attitudes of America's enemies, had fewer than ten staffers with more than two years' experience of analysing the Iraqi insurgency. Officials were constantly rotated to new assignments.

Was this incompetence or wilful ignorance, a feeling that there was no need to try to understand what the majority of Iraqis were saying or thinking? Iraqis were going to be given a Western-style secular liberal democracy, whether they wanted it or not. Or perhaps the Americans and British subconsciously sensed they might be told things they did not want to hear – it was better to stay in the Green Zone and the coalition's provincial HQs, and talk only to those Iraqis who had clear benefits to gain from the occupation, such as jobs on its payroll or project grants.

Some Iraqis sought to make their views known. Sometimes they tried their hand at English. Spelling was not his strong point, but the person who wrote the graffiti on the pedestal where Saddam Hussein's statue once stood in Baghdad's Firdous Square had a clear message: 'All donne, go home'.

It was less than three months since US Marines had put steel hawsers round the statue's metal neck and brought it crashing to the ground. Shown live on television, the scene was the iconic proof of a great American victory, regularly replayed in countless documentaries. The Marines briefly hoisted the Stars and Stripes above Saddam's head, a humiliating image of conquest that Iraqis and millions of other Arab TV-watchers remember, even if most Americans forget. Weeks later, American troops were still posted outside the nearby Palestine Hotel and US officials frequently visited the building, which housed several American TV networks. They could not avoid seeing that at least one Iraqi graffiti-writer had already lost patience with the occupation.

Prominent Iraqis were more polite, although even they were reluctant to thank the Americans for the invasion. There was a telling moment when the 25 Iraqis whom the USA had just appointed to the so-called Interim Governing Council (IGC) were paraded before the media in Saddam's old convention centre on 13 July 2003. Halfway through the proceedings Ahmad Chalabi, the long-time exile who became the Pentagon's favourite Iraqi, strode to the microphone to say he wished 'to express the gratitude of the Iraqi people to President Bush and Prime Minister Blair for liberating Iraq'.[4] We waited for applause. The other 24 appointees looked stunned and embarrassed. No one clapped Chalabi's remarks, even though comments by earlier speakers had been applauded.

Insensitive to his colleagues' views but with an eye on L. Paul Bremer, the CPA boss who was sitting in the front row below the stage, Chalabi ploughed on. He proposed that 9 April, the day the Saddam statue was toppled, should become a national holiday with the title Liberation Day. Again, there was silence. At its first working session shortly afterwards the IGC did take up the idea of a national holiday but they pointedly rejected Chalabi's title. They decided to call 9 April The Day the Regime Fell.

The council's avoidance of the L-word (in his memoirs Bremer always spelt it with a capital 'L') reflected its members' understanding that few Iraqis were as jubilant about the invasion as Chalabi. This fact had become clear in the very first days when US troops came across armed resistance on the edge of Basra and in the largely Shia city of Nassiriya. It did not conform to the pre-war briefings they had received. 'I imagined Iraqi women would be greeting us with flowers in our gun tubes, and holding up babies to be kissed,' one American soldier who almost lost his life in Nassiriya commented later.[5]

Within hours of Saddam's downfall reporters repeatedly met Iraqis who felt shame and anger at finding their country under occupation. Many were deeply suspicious of American intentions. My translator, Abbas Ali Hussein, took me to his family home in Baghdad on 15 April, just less than a week after the Saddam statue was toppled. His brother Hassan was sitting in the sparsely furnished front room looking depressed. Was he some unhappy Saddam supporter, I wondered? Far from it. Now in his early thirties, Hassan explained he had studied at Baghdad's prestigious oil institute a decade earlier but on graduation decided not to take a job as a geologist or engineer. The state had a monopoly of oil extraction and refining, and Hassan felt he hated Saddam Hussein too much to want to work for the Iraqi regime. Instead, he found a job in the private sector as a taxi driver.

Well educated, a man of principle, and a Shia, here was the kind of man who, the Americans expected, would surely be thrilled by the arrival of US troops. Washington saw Iraq in sectarian terms and viewed the Shias, along with the Kurds, as the biggest victims of Saddam's regime. What did Hassan think of the dictator's removal from power? 'Saddam betrayed us,' he told me.

Startled, I asked him what he meant. 'He didn't organise any resistance in Baghdad,' Hassan replied. He went on to hint that there might have been a secret deal between Bush and Saddam under which Saddam would refrain from ordering his forces to defend the capital. Abbas nodded in agreement. 'The United States must leave Iraq to the Iraqi people. We must rule ourselves,' he said. 'We have many educated people. We can do this. We want the Americans to leave today.'

The next day, at Baghdad's main hospital for children, I found the same sense of shame that foreign troops were in the heart of the Iraqi capital. Dr Abdul Hamid al-Saddoun, a heart specialist, was presiding over a scene of monumental scarcity. Sick children lay on cheap vinyl mattresses under tattered blankets. There were no sheets. Guards at the front gate had done an outstanding job in keeping looters out of the building, but the hospital was chronically short of basic equipment, from oxygen canisters to bandages, gauze, and surgical gloves. Dr Saddoun said he was appealing to the Americans for supplies, but he also wanted them out. 'Everything is settling down now. Iraq will be Iraq. We will not accept an American or British occupation,' he insisted.

On the second Friday after US troops entered Baghdad, nationalist pride and Islamist fervour were in full view on the streets. Thousands poured out of mosques in the mainly Sunni district of Adhamiya, chanting both anti-Saddam and anti-American slogans. The organisers called themselves the Iraqi National United Movement and said they represented both Muslim communities, Sunni and Shia. One of the biggest columns emerged from the Abu Hanifa mosque, whose dome was damaged during the invasion. 'No to America. No to Saddam. Our revolution is Islamic,' some chanted. One protester I interviewed prefigured the insurgency: 'We will give the Americans a few months to leave Iraq. If they do not, we will fight them with knives,' he said. I watched as a dozen US marines appeared in front of the marchers. A few protesters waved their fists and shouted 'America is God's enemy'. The troops turned into an alley and there was no confrontation.

The following week, hundreds of thousands of Shias turned out for the annual pilgrimage to Kerbala to the shrine of Imam Hussein, the grandson of Prophet Muhammad. Hussein was executed or 'martyred', as Shias say, after being taken prisoner. Under Saddam pilgrims were banned from walking along the main roads; they had to make their way to Kerbala in small groups in vehicles or through villages. Now they celebrated their freedom, marching in long columns down the main highway south from Baghdad, or north from Nassiriya and other cities in the Shia heartland. The atmosphere was good humoured, even though the festival of Ashoura is essentially a collective mourning, during which many carry palm fronds and flagellate themselves symbolically.

The mass march was not designed to be explicitly political. However, the huge outpouring of Shias onto one of Iraq's key highways for the first time for a generation could not help but send a political message. Here was a community coming alive at last. The image of Saddam's statue being toppled was what Americans saw as the defining moment of their invasion, even though fewer than 200 Iraqis were on hand and most watched in silence. For Iraqis the televised tides of devout Shias presented a more powerful picture of a new Iraq. It was an exclusively Iraqi event, and there was little in the mood of the marchers to comfort Bush or Washington's neoconservatives.

I heard many points of view firsthand during the march. On 21 April, in Kerbala's outskirts, Umm Zahra, in the long, black cloak known as an

15

abbaya, was standing by her front gate with other women similarly clad. 'I want an Islamic president. Only an educated clergyman can give us peace and security. We want the US troops to go,' she told me.

Halfway along the 50-mile stretch from Baghdad to Kerbala scores of men were resting on the banks of the Euphrates in the spring sunshine. 'If the US prevents us having a religious leader as president, we will reject it,' one said. Referring to the Shia religious and educational establishment in Najaf known as Al-Hawza, he went on: 'If Al-Hawza orders us to turn ourselves into bombs, we can make the US leave Iraq. We say, "Thank you for getting rid of Saddam. Now goodbye."'

I heard a few expressions of unconditional gratitude. 'Please tell Mr Blair "God bless him,"' said Abdullah Ganin, an English teacher from Najaf. 'If Bush wants to become a Muslim, he will enter paradise for sure,' a middle-aged man told me. But comments as warm as these were rare. These were not the cheering crowds, as predicted by Washington's neoconservatives before the invasion. The hundreds of thousands of marchers were Islamists. They did not support secular liberal values; they were not pro-Western.

Without being as starry-eyed as the neoconservatives, most other Western politicians also convinced themselves that Iraqis were so eager to see Saddam removed they would applaud a foreign invasion. In the weeks before Bush gave the go-ahead a stream of Iraqi exiles had passed through the White House and Downing Street, giving this message. Exiles who were against an invasion, including generals and diplomats who had defected from Saddam and strongly opposed him, tended not to be invited. On their way out of their meetings Bush's and Blair's specially selected guests hastened to tell the media they supported the looming invasion. Saddam's three decades of tyranny and war-mongering had brought untold suffering to Iraqis and his support was paper-thin. His army would not fight another war, and certainly not this one. All this was true, but their third point, that the invaders would be greeted as liberators, was highly dubious. Proper political intelligence plus some historical understanding of Iraq would have shown it to be wrong.

Meanwhile, the US and British governments' spin-machines pilloried the swelling crowds of anti-war marchers in New York City and London as appeasers. They gave prominence to anti-war politicians like Tony Benn and George Galloway, who had campaigned against US and British sanctions on Iraq and made trips to Baghdad to see Saddam. Their presence at the head of demonstrations was falsely trumpeted as evidence that the protesters understood little of Saddam's atrocities and that anti-Americanism was blinding the marchers to the side that was the biggest violator of human rights.

Bush and Blair wanted to believe the pro-war exiles' encouraging words. They took the line that if you were against Saddam you would be for the invasion. They also latched on to the supposed corollary – if you opposed the invasion you must be a Saddam supporter. It was easy to fall for such a set of arguments.

What did Iraqis really believe, however? Would there be gratitude and cooperation or sullen acquiescence, which might develop into active resistance? Getting the right answer was surely as important as verifying whether Saddam possessed weapons of mass destruction. It should have been a crucial factor in the war-planning in Washington and London, at least if serious options were to be considered for how to govern the country after the fall of Saddam.

Yet almost nothing was done to assess the true state of Iraqi opinion. The USA had no embassy in Iraq, and nor did Britain, unlike every other major European country. So the two countries most anxious to launch a war were the ones with least information about Iraqi society and an invasion's likely consequences. Western intelligence services were equally hamstrung; they had few human assets in Iraq to provide an accurate picture. As a result, the views of pro-war Iraqi exiles rose to prominence by default. Conveniently, they agreed with what Bush and Blair already wanted to do.

The US National Intelligence Council, which coordinates and summarises the analysis of the various US intelligence agencies, produced two reports on the regional consequences of regime change in Iraq and the principal challenges in post-Saddam Iraq. A heavily redacted version of these reports was released by the Senate Intelligence Committee on 25 May 2007.[6] The agencies were right in some predictions but spectacularly wrong in others. Among their correct assessments was their view that 'the building of an Iraqi democracy would be a long, difficult, and turbulent process, with potential for backsliding into Iraq's tradition of authoritarianism'.[7] They also noted that Iraq's political culture did 'not foster liberalism or democracy'[8] and that 'the practical implementation of democratic rule would be difficult in a country with no concept of loyal opposition and no history of alternation of power'.[9]

The intelligence agencies were less well informed about the crucial issue of Islam. They expected the 'US-led occupation of Arab Iraq probably would boost proponents of political Islam',[10] but thought this would happen throughout the Middle East rather than in Iraq itself. They completely underestimated the strength of Iraq's Islamists, saying efforts at democratisation after an invasion would benefit from 'the current relative weakness of political Islam in Iraq'.[11] They couched their analysis of Iraq in sectarian terms and thought the risk of violent conflict between Sunnis and Shias was high. With hindsight this may seem prescient, but it was a conclusion that the intelligence analysts based on faulty assumptions. They felt Sunni–Shia tensions were endemic in Iraq and the occupying force would act to prevent them becoming violent.

In fact Sunni–Shia tension was not a significant feature of modern Iraq, as the thousands of mixed marriages and mixed neighbourhoods testify. It was the occupation's policies that played a role, though not the only one, in increasing Sunni–Shia tensions, thereby contributing to the appalling sectarian violence of the last two years (as I explain in Chapter VIII).

Four months before the invasion Blair made a brief stab at getting expert views from outside the circle of his official advisers. On 19 November 2002 he invited six academics to Downing Street, three specialists on Iraq, and three on international security issues. George Joffe, a distinguished Arabist from Cambridge University, and his two fellow Iraq experts – Charles Tripp and Toby Dodge, who had both authored books on Iraq's history – took it in turns to make opening statements of about five minutes each. They were not asked to produce written memos. Before the meeting they decided not to risk antagonising Blair by saying an invasion was unwise, they thought they would have more impact by concentrating on the nature of its consequences.

Joffe recalled that 'We all pretty much said the same thing: Iraq is a very complicated country, there are tremendous intercommunal resentments, and don't imagine you'll be welcomed.' He spoke last of the three. He still remembers exactly how Blair reacted: 'He looked at me and said, "But the man's uniquely evil, isn't he?" I was a bit nonplussed. It didn't seem to be very relevant.' Recovering, Joffe went on to argue that Saddam was constrained by various factors, to which Blair merely repeated his first point: 'He can make choices, can't he?' As Joffe puts it, 'He meant he can choose to be good or evil, I suppose.'[12]

The six men left Downing Street after an hour and a half. There had been no meeting of minds. Joffe got the impression of 'someone with a very shallow mind, who's not interested in issues other than the personalities of the top people, no interest in social forces, political trends, etc.'[13] Dodge had a similar recollection that he and his fellow academics had tried to give a flavour of the difficulties ahead in Iraq:

> Much of the rhetoric from Washington appeared to depict Saddam's regime as something separate from Iraqi society ... All you had to do was remove him and the 60 bad men around him. What we wanted to get across was that over 35 years the regime had embedded itself into Iraqi society, broken it down and totally transformed it. We would be going into a vacuum, where there were no allies to be found, except possibly for the Kurds.[14]

Tripp recalls telling Blair, 'There's a force in Iraq called Islamic nationalism. When you look at the effects of the West's sanctions, you must be aware of something cooking there.'[15]

One potential source of information on Iraqi attitudes was the foreign press corps. Discovering Iraqi views became one of the main challenges for the few Western reporters who were able to get visas to work in Baghdad in the final weeks before Bush launched his 'shock and awe' campaign. It was a tough assignment since independent interviewing of Baghdadis in Saddam's Iraq was almost impossible. Reporters had to be accompanied by official minders, and even if a correspondent managed to slip away on the excuse he or she was going out of the hotel to buy cigarettes or get a haircut, Iraqis were usually cautious about revealing their true thoughts. Finding an Iraqi ready to offer even a veiled hint of opposition to Saddam was something of a triumph, and these nods and winks of anti-Saddam sentiments were often reported in Western despatches as a sign that people wanted the Americans to remove him.

The Western press corps that was poised outside central Iraq on the eve of the invasion in March 2003 was split into three groups, none knowing who would reach the capital first. The front-runners were based in Kurdish-controlled northern Iraq. They expected that Kurdish forces, the *peshmergas*, would quickly smash through the Iraqi army's thin defence lines once the war started, allowing reporters to rush to Baghdad's outskirts, if not to the heart of the capital itself.

The second group was in Kuwait, embedded with US and British forces or planning to follow the advancing Western armies independently. Ironically for an administration that prided itself on its unilateralism in foreign affairs, the Pentagon dubbed these determined risk-takers 'unilaterals' and did its best not to help them.

I was in the third group, based in the Jordanian capital, Amman. Our hope was that the isolated guards on Iraq's remote south-western border with Jordan would disappear into the desert on Day One of the war, either in fear of US attack or under actual attack. US special forces had been using Jordanian bases for several months and we knew they were already operating on the ground inside Iraq before the invasion. One of their missions was to reconnoitre two Iraqi air force bases where Saddam held Scud missiles that might be ready to strike Israel, and to prepare for US troops to seize them as soon as the war began (or even pre-emptively a day or two earlier). The desolate terrain between the Jordanian border and Baghdad was inhabited largely by Arab nomads, and we expected to storm to the capital fairly rapidly once the border guards fled.

While we spent much of our time impatiently preparing camping gear for the nights we might have to sleep in the sand on the way, a fantastic reporting source was available on our doorsteps. Jordan was home to at least 350,000 Iraqis. Many were refugees from Saddam's terror; others were students and businessmen who travelled to and fro to Baghdad. Almost all kept close contact with their families, but unlike their relatives in Iraq they could talk to Western reporters freely. They might prefer not to have their names published, but at least their views did not have to be couched in the misleading ambiguities that our colleagues in Baghdad ran into. You could spend time with them, sitting in their homes or in cafés and hotel rooms, rather than grabbing quotes in brief 'vox pop' encounters on the pavement.

Over the course of a week I made contact with a cross-section of Iraqis, of different age-ranges, income groups, and sectarian backgrounds. The first finding, which was hardly surprising, was that the vast majority – over three-quarters – opposed Saddam, variously describing him as a dictator, thug, and megalomaniac.

Did that mean they were looking to the invasion with optimism? Wathiq Abadi, a professor of marketing at Amman's Applied Science University, was firmly in the pro-war camp. A Shia from Basra with a Sunni wife from Baghdad, he had lived in Jordan for two years. They decided to emigrate after the failed uprising against Saddam in 1991 but hoped to do it legally. However, until 2001 couples had to split if one wanted to leave. They were not ready to do that but then Iraqi law changed, making it possible for spouses to emigrate a month after their partner had taken a job abroad.

Professor Abadi admitted to some anxiety for their relatives in Basra and Baghdad in case the planned US bombing campaign caused civilian casualties, but he expected the regime to collapse within 72 hours. 'My main fear is that the USA and the UK will not go to war. Their target is the regime. They must go through with it,' he told me.

His concern was that if the US and Britain backed down at this late stage, Saddam would have felt he had won a great victory in his showdown with the West. Confidence in his apparent immortality would lead to even greater repression.

In the coffee shop in the Hyatt hotel I spoke to an Iraqi comedy actor, whose speciality was an extraordinary ability to make his eyes pop, looking as though they might jump out of their sockets and chase you. He would only give his name as Abdullah, although his unusual gift would surely identify him to any Saddam agent who read my report. He said he did not mind.

In 1999 he paid smugglers to get him out of Iraq after refusing to take part in a film called *The Victories of Iraq's Armies*. He had already spent a month in prison after declining to act in a play glorifying Saddam. Abdullah was anxious to see Saddam toppled, though he expected substantial resistance to US forces as they advanced towards Baghdad. He was also worried about what would happen in Iraq after Saddam fell. He had little faith in the Iraqi exile opposition and hankered after a powerful but democratic leader. 'I don't see any strong leader who can unite Iraqis. It's in our dreams,' he said.

Other Shias I spoke to were opposed to a US invasion. A 31-year-old art teacher and writer from Babylon who had also paid smugglers to get him to Jordan was pessimistic to the point of total bleakness about his country's future. He believed the USA was only making war on Iraq for its own purposes and that the post-war situation would be chaotic since Iraqis were not ready for freedom. He had no faith in the rest of the Arab world and was hoping to emigrate to the USA.

An enthusiastic talker, he seemed to get carried away by his own eloquence, making every sentence and idea gloomier than the previous one, telling me:

> This war will happen but the Iraqi people cannot benefit from it. The main beneficiaries will be the United States, Britain and other European countries. Iraq's opposition parties are financed by foreigners ... We've never tasted freedom. We won't know what to do with it. That's the big catastrophe.

He went on bleakly:

> I'll be very sad. I have very strong feelings of patriotism. We don't differenti-
> ate between Shia, Sunni, and Kurds. I don't know why this is happening. I
> feel this is a kind of genocide … Saddam has helped the Americans and the
> British. Through his invasion of Kuwait he allowed the US to install armies
> in various Arab countries. But they're right. They deserve it. They're smart
> … I respect Bush. He's working for his country. I even respect [then Israeli
> prime minister] Sharon. He's a nationalist. He's working for his country. I
> wish Saddam was like Sharon. I respect Sharon because he pushes all for-
> eigners out and runs his own show. Saddam can't because he's an Arab.

One evening an older Shia came round to my hotel. Wearing a red and
white traditional headscarf, the *kuffiya*, he turned out to be a firm secularist
who distrusted religious leaders. A one-time supervisor of art in secondary schools in Najaf, the site of one of Iraq's holiest shrines, he produced a
quotation from Imam Ali, the cousin of Prophet Muhammad whom Shias
revere as his true successor: 'It's better to have a ruler who is an atheist and
fair than one who is a Muslim and cruel.'

This man, who only wanted to give his first name (Wathiq), was a communist who desperately wanted Iraq to enjoy intellectual and political freedom. 'I dream of going to a country where I can learn about freedom and
all its meanings and then go back to Iraq and implement it,' he explained.
He wanted Saddam to resign and leave Iraq before the American bombing
started. But if the dictator refused, then the Americans would have to attack. 'The scorpion has to be stamped on. If it's not an Iraqi shoe, let it be an
American one,' he declared.

The trouble Wathiq foresaw was that the Americans might not leave
quickly. If that happened, there would be resistance and he would support
it. He concluded:

> The Iraqi people will rebuild their house the day after Saddam goes. If the US
> tries to meddle, we will fight them to the last breath. Iraqis hate Saddam, but
> they love their country more. That's why Iraqis are torn about the invasion.

Among the Sunnis I spoke to, all but one were united in opposing the
war. At the headquarters of the United Nations High Commission for Refugees (UNHCR) I ran into a distinguished-looking man who had come to
volunteer his services as a translator or adviser. It turned out he had recently

been Iraq's ambassador in a leading Asian country but was jumping ship. 'Everyone's against Saddam, including the Sunnis. The demonstrations Saddam is organising are not representative. People will not fight,' he said.

In spite of his opposition to the regime, however, he feared chaos after the war and a Shia backlash against the Sunnis. 'The United States is with the Shias. They've helped to create the idea that all Sunnis support Saddam. The Iranians also want the Shias to run the country – that's why they support the Shias,' he argued.

Muna, a young student from Baghdad doing a masters degree in English literature, also worried about the Shias, though in her case the object of her anxiety was the huge Shia underclass living in eastern Baghdad in the overcrowded district known as Saddam City (which was renamed Sadr city after Saddam fell). The daughter of a wealthy surgeon who had trained in Britain, she feared there could be massive looting:

> Abdul Karim Qassim [president from 1958 to 1963] brought Shia villagers to Baghdad to settle there. People are afraid of them. They are beggars and thieves. None of my family would have the guts to drive a BMW into Saddam city. We're afraid of a revolution. They always say that if the police lose control, people from Saddam city will rush into good areas like ours and steal everything.

Her views underlined a point that many Western analysts failed to understand – that the tensions that were to explode in Iraq after the invasion often had a class dimension. By overthrowing Saddam the Americans and the British would be creating social as well as political instability.

Muna was not against Shias as a sect, she hastened to explain. There were plenty of mixed marriages among her parents' generation and she would have no hesitation in marrying a Shia if she fell in love with one. 'Half my friends are Shia and it never comes into my head to ask someone what they are,' she said. In fact, her family was firmly secular, and she confessed never to have been inside a mosque. Her main complaint against Saddam was the isolation to which he had condemned Iraq – the lack of foreign literature, the controls on the Internet and the ban on email and chat services.

She was in regular telephone contact with her parents and siblings in Baghdad. They were digging an underground shelter in their garden and telling her to stay in Amman. She was in a dilemma. She would like to be with them during the war, and knew they would lose contact as soon as the bombing began. But her main worry was the vacuum that would follow Saddam: 'We're not afraid of war. We're afraid of the consequences. Yes, we're tired from all the previous wars but if we get rid of Saddam, what will happen? We may have civil war between Shias, Sunnis, and Kurds.'

I asked her whether the regime might not be deliberately stirring up anxiety to turn people against an American attack. She responded:

That could be, but I know some of our fears are true. People in the small towns are very poor. When the war started with Kuwait, they piled in and looted everything. I have a friend in Basra who saw these trucks coming back from Kuwait and selling everything from the back of them. What they did in Kuwait, they would do in Baghdad too.

Her final fear was that Iraq would lose its oil:

It feels like an invasion. My family are afraid the Americans will stay for ever or leave some friendly stooge in charge and then pump out our oil for half a century. I want peace but I don't want to be exploited.

Wa'il, a Sunni butcher in his thirties who fled Iraq in 1997, was completely torn over the invasion. He had left for political and economic reasons – the lack of human rights and the dire situation caused by sanctions. Educated people were forced to work as taxi drivers because they could earn more than in their state jobs as teachers or doctors. Shop workers like himself had to live off bribes – 'you had to become a liar or a thief'. But he could not decide whether he wanted to see the Americans topple Saddam. 'I want the war to happen. I don't want it to happen. I want Saddam out but I don't want anyone to invade my country,' he said in helpless confusion.

My sample of 20 Iraqis in Amman was neither large nor scientific, but it conveyed what seemed to be a plausibly accurate sense of a nation's mood. Even those of my interlocutors who wanted the war to happen had serious qualms about what would follow. None used the word liberation. Several suspected Washington's motives. The breakdown of views was marginally against the war. I counted nine who were clearly opposed, seven in favour and four who could not decide. In percentage terms that would be 45 per cent against, 35 for, and 20 on the fence. This was a long way from the notion of massive Iraqi support for the looming attack of which Bush and Blair claimed to be confident.

The interviewees had given various reasons for concern about the war and its aftermath: fear of a power vacuum; distrust of the opposition politicians; anxiety over looting; and concern that Iraq would lose control of its oil. The themes that recurred most often, however, were suspicion of the Americans and national pride. Failure to understand this Iraqi patriotism was the single biggest mistake made by Bush and Blair, both in the months before the war and in the years that followed Saddam's downfall. They ignored it, they minimised it, their policies often provoked it, and they never appreciated its strength and importance. It was this inability to put themselves into the mindset of Iraqis that doomed the occupation to defeat.

The war on Iraq was illegal in the eyes of the UN Security Council since there was no resolution to authorise it. Its stated purpose turned out to be hollow since Iraq possessed none of the weapons of mass destruction claimed by Washington and London. But however important these flaws in undermining the legal and political basis for the invasion, they were not bound to cripple the occupation. The larger factor which undermined it was American and British blindness to Iraqis' pride as nationalists and Arabs, and the degree to which an occupation would help Iraq's Islamists.

Invasion was bound to create resentment, even if US and British troops behaved impeccably both during and afterwards. In fact, almost every policy adopted by the occupiers and every tactic they used served only to increase that resentment. Success for the occupation was always a mirage. Failure could be delayed but was inevitable.

Outright racism, the bane of all colonial rule, added to the gulf between the occupiers and the local population. George Packer, a writer for the *New Yorker*, recounted how even the few Iraqi 'Americanophiles' were treated with suspicion and contempt. Working as translators, he described the group of 'mostly young men and women who embraced America's project so enthusiastically that they were prepared to risk their lives for it' as Iraq's smallest minority.[16] They had learnt English secretly by listening to the BBC or watching American movies. However, in spite of working for the USA, they had trouble getting passes to use the priority lane and avoid the dangerous queues into the Green Zone. When they reported to their American bosses that resistance groups or militias had threatened them, they were either sacked or left without protection. Their desperate applications for visas to the USA were almost invariably turned down. To escape the problem and avoid responsibility the US embassy gradually replaced its Iraqi translators with Jordanians.[17]

The first opinion poll conducted after the invasion produced an almost exact match with the breakdown of attitudes that I had found among Iraqis in Jordan before the war. More people saw it as an occupation than a liberation. The survey was made by the Iraq Center for Research and Strategic Studies, a polling organisation set up by Saadoun al-Dulaimi. He was an enterprising former army officer who had fled Iraq for Saudi Arabia in 1986 and returned soon after Saddam's downfall. He set up shop in a pleasant single-storey villa in an upper-middle-class suburb. In the months when travel round Baghdad was still safe and easy, it was always a pleasure to drop round to his offices for a sneak preview of the results of his monthly temperature-taking a day before he would hand them to his paying clients. They included the US embassy, who felt his survey methods were reliable and comprehensive.

Indeed they trusted his low-key professionalism so much that they approved his selection as Iraq's defence minister in the government elected in 2005. Unusually thin and with sunken cheeks, al-Dulaimi looked and talked more like a professor but his former life as an officer and a Baathist, and his membership of one of the largest Sunni families in Anbar province, made him a valuable asset to a government trying to win Sunni confidence.

Six months into the occupation, al-Dulaimi's researchers interviewed a sample of 1,620 Iraqis in seven cities. They were asked how they perceived coalition forces at the time of the survey and how they had felt when the troops arrived – whether they saw them as occupiers, liberators, or peace-keepers. In Baghdad, 45.9 per cent said they saw the Americans in April 2003 as occupiers while 38.4 per cent saw them as liberators. (Some 4.6 per cent saw them as peacekeepers and the rest had no opinion.) By October 2003 the numbers had moved firmly against the Americans. The view that they were occupiers was up to 66.6 per cent, while only 14.8 per cent still saw them as liberators.

In the mainly Sunni cities of Ramadi and Fallujah negative views of the Americans were overwhelming. In April 2003 over 85 per cent saw them as occupiers, a figure that had barely changed six months later. In the Kurdish areas, by contrast, people were sympathetic. At least two-thirds saw the Americans as liberators. The joker was the city of Basra. Because it was predominantly Shia, it was assumed to be strongly anti-Saddam and therefore pro-invasion. The city had risen up against Saddam after his defeat in Kuwait in 1991. However, al-Dulaimi's survey found that 52.3 per cent in Basra took the view in April 2003 that the foreign troops were occupiers, a higher figure than in Baghdad. By October 2003 this figure was up to 75.7 per cent.

These findings ought to have sounded alarm bells in coalition headquarters, but in practice they had little impact. Only rarely did US and British officials acknowledge that Iraqis were unhappy with the occupation. The coalition authorities accepted that 'sovereignty' would have to be transferred back to Iraqis at some point; how they tried to delay and dilute that transfer is discussed more fully in Chapter IX. However, few policy makers appreciated the depth of Iraqi suspicions, or understood the continuing impact on Arab minds of the long legacy of Western intervention in the Middle East, which made any attempt at occupation in the twenty-first century a non-starter.

I remember one comment that L. Paul 'Jerry' Bremer, the head of the Coalition Provisional Authority and Washington's pro-consul in the country, made to me and some other reporters. He came across as an arrogant, high-handed, and peculiarly unself-critical man who rarely took advice that contradicted his intentions. Like other US officials, Bremer was fixated on the analogy of Germany and Japan after 1945. He was confident that it would be as easy to run an occupation of Iraq as it had been in those countries. There was no need to give any timetable or name a target date for withdrawal. As in Germany and Japan, the occupation could be open-ended. There would be no pressure to get out. Besides, Bremer rather liked the image of being an imperial ruler, bringing democracy to the natives. He fancied himself as a latter-day version of General Douglas Macarthur, the US post-war overlord in Japan, as one leading Washington politician observed.[18]

Bremer sometimes followed his formal press conferences by offering to meet a few reporters afterwards in a smaller room at what was known as a 'gaggle'. His line did not depart from his publicly announced position but his language was more chatty. In March 2004, exactly a year after the invasion, Bremer was asked about the resistance to the occupation at one of these gaggles. The Iraqis had a 'perverse resentment that we liberated them,' he told us. 'There's an underlying feeling of guilt that they weren't able to liberate themselves.' Then he recalled that he had been a student in France in the 1960s: 'The French have also never forgiven us for liberating them,' he smiled flippantly. His smug tone implied that this psychological inability to say 'Thank You' was only a minor irritant. He clearly felt that in both the French and Iraqi cases it did not have to be taken seriously. He saw no need to find a deeper explanation of why the Iraqi resistance was attacking and killing US troops – something which the French, however disgruntled, had never done to the US soldiers based amongst them.

Donald Rumsfeld, the US defense secretary, consistently refused to define the resistance's military activities as either a guerrilla war or an insurgency, on the grounds that most Iraqis did not support it. He said he had looked the terms up in the Pentagon dictionary and preferred to call it an 'unconventional war'. Lawrence Di Rita, the assistant secretary of defense, elaborated: 'It's a low-intensity conflict in our doctrinal terms.' [19]

At other times US spokespeople claimed the resistance was made up exclusively of 'remnants' of Saddam Hussein's regime plus foreign jihadis. They implied foreigners predominated and that Iraqi nationalists and Islamists could not therefore be a main element behind the improvised explosive devices (IEDs) that were already taking a toll on US troops by the summer of 2003.

The British were no different. Rory Stewart, a former British diplomat who was sent to southern Iraq in 2003, reports on the advice he was given by British officials when he took up his job. There was no mention of Iraqi nationalism or Islamism. Blame for the incipient violence was put largely on Iran. He was told simply, 'There is a potential for Shia opposition here, connected to Iran and criminal gangs.' [20]

At a June 2004 Baghdad briefing led by Lt Gen John McColl, the deputy commander of the multinational forces and the most senior British officer in the occupation, British journalists were startled by what they heard. A PowerPoint presentation referred to problem people known as AIF. Queried about the acronym, the officer conducting that part of the slide show spelt it out as 'Anti-Iraqi Forces'. There was a collective intake of breath among the reporters, and one of us asked whether 'anti-coalition forces' or perhaps 'anti-government forces' might not be more accurate. The resistance was, after all, Iraqi. Lieutenant Gen McColl jumped in and tried to smooth over the embarrassment by telling us the acronym was not a British invention or exclusive to today's briefing. It was standard usage in the US-led coalition.

We wondered whether this did not make it worse. If the coalition did not even start by accepting that many Iraqis saw legitimate reasons for resistance, how could the Americans and British ever win people's hearts and minds?

II

ARAB ANGUISH

Humiliation is continuous: it's felt all the time.
Adnan Abu Odeh, 2003[1]

Do not attempt to do us any more good. Your good has done us too much harm already.
Muhammad Abduh, 1884[2]

I t was the bravest collective action I have ever seen a bunch of journalists take. As US Secretary of State Colin Powell took his place at the podium in Baghdad's convention centre for a press conference on 19 March 2004, an Iraqi correspondent rose to his feet. With Bremer at his side, Powell looked on in astonishment as Najim al-Rubaie from the newspaper *Al-Dustour* began to read a statement: 'We declare our boycott of this press conference because of the martyrs. We declare our condemnation of the incident which led to two journalists being killed by American forces.'

Around 30 other Iraqi and Arab journalists then stood up and followed al-Rubaie out of the hall. We watched them leave, as stunned as Powell and Bremer. Our Arab colleagues had not warned us, let alone asked for solidarity. They probably guessed that few Western reporters, if any, would share their boldness or their anger. I have attended press conferences in several dozen countries where journalists compete with each other in the usual macho way to ask foreign officials the toughest question. A collective protest, and taking a stand on an issue? It never happens.

Two Arab journalists stayed behind in the hall. 'I didn't walk out because I wanted to cover the press conference. Everyone is responsible for themselves,' said Muthir al-Zubayet from *Al-Sabah* newspaper. Zeinab al-Bakri from the daily paper *Al-Furat* said she sympathised with the walkout but wanted to hear how Powell would respond. 'We're under occupation. Iraqi journalists have a right to be respected and protected,' she said.

The incident that sparked the protest had happened the previous day. Ali Abdelaziz, a cameramen from the popular satellite TV channel Al-Arabiya, and Ali al-Khatib, his reporter, were shot by US forces near a checkpoint in central Baghdad as they investigated a suicide car-bombing. In those days such bombings were still rare. Ahmed Abdul Amiya, the Al-Arabiya driver, later explained:

> I stopped in front of the checkpoint and then I saw another car coming fast towards it and I thought it was going to explode … I tried to race away … then the Americans started firing at random. They hit the first car and then started shooting at ours.[3]

The cameraman was killed instantly. The reporter died a few hours later. Describing the shooting as a crime, Al-Arabiya demanded an inquiry.

After the Arab reporters' dramatic walkout Powell tried to regain the initiative by making a political point. 'I respect people's right to express their feelings in a way that never happened in recent Iraqi history,' he said, before adding perfunctorily: 'I regret the loss of life of a journalist just as I respect the loss of any life.' It was a clumsy reaction and neither of the two Arab journalists who stayed in the hall to hear him found his attitude satisfying. They were upset by his tone as well as his failure to promise an inquiry.

The two Al-Arabiya journalists were not the first Arab reporters to die in the year since the invasion, so their colleagues' indignation was not a sudden flare-up – it was more like a slow burn. As press casualties mount-ed, they felt their identity as Arabs put them at greater risk than Western reporters. Evidence suggested US soldiers were using racial profiling and would take less care with people who looked Middle Eastern than those who were white.

Our Arab colleagues' anger went far beyond the human instinct for self-preservation, however. It was a protest against the visceral sense of impo-tence and lack of dignity that an occupation imposes and demands. It was also a sharp reminder to us non-Arabs that everything the Americans and the British were doing in Iraq looked and felt different if you were an Arab. No one could seriously pretend to report on Iraq, work as a coalition official, or patrol Iraqi streets in military uniform, without always keeping that in mind. We were uninvited foreigners in another people's country.

The gulf between Western intentions and Arab perceptions of them goes back to the first encounters between the two cultures at the time of the Crusades. To a greater or lesser degree every Arab inherits the legacy of resentment and suspicion that flows from the subsequent centuries of Western involvement in the Middle East. Their land, their natural resources, their culture, their religion, and they themselves were always being targeted. They were never treated as equals.

When Bush described the war on terror as a 'crusade' in a speech five days after the 9/11 attacks, his remark struck at the core of Arab feelings. Once again, foreigners were intervening to change Muslim beliefs and the Arab way of life. Although his advisers took care that Bush never repeated the word, it did not matter. Even before the US president made his verbal blunder, Arabs already sensed his actions since 9/11 amounted to the launching of a crusade, and they reacted accordingly. To most Westerners the Crusades are known as a brief moment in European history, easily eclipsed by more recent conflicts, not least the two World Wars. To Arabs they were the opening shot in a struggle that continues to this day.

The Syrian émigré poet Ali Ahmad Sa'id, who is usually known by his pseudonym 'Adonis', put it in a 1998 essay:

> No-one would deny that the problems of Muslim Arabs with the foreign 'other' are urgent and immediate. Especially since there is an old war that is still going on between the two, which is sometimes hidden but never ends.[4]

The Lebanese writer Amin Maalouf has pointed out that the Crusades had very different effects in the West and in the Orient. In Western Europe they were a dynamic force, igniting an economic and social revolution. In the Middle East they led to centuries of decadence and obscurantism while progress came to be seen, humiliatingly, as something only outsiders could bring:

> Assaulted from all quarters, the Muslim world turned in on itself. It became over-sensitive, defensive, intolerant, sterile – attitudes that grew steadily worse as world-wide evolution, a process from which the Muslim world felt excluded, continued. Henceforth progress was the embodiment of 'the other'.[5]

31

Although the Arabs eventually succeeded in driving the Crusaders out, European armies returned to the Middle East a few centuries later as part of the great wave of worldwide imperial expansion. Arabs saw them as an awesome threat. According to Maalouf:

> The Arab world – simultaneously fascinated and terrified by these Franj (Crusaders), whom they encountered as barbarians and defeated, but who subsequently managed to dominate the earth – cannot bring itself to consider the Crusades a mere episode in the bygone past … The Arab East still sees the West as a natural enemy. Against that enemy, any hostile action – be it political, military, or based on oil – is considered no more than legitimate vengeance. And there can be no doubt that the schism between these two worlds dates from the Crusades, deeply felt by the Arabs, even today, as an act of rape.[6]

In Arab eyes the abiding features of Western behaviour have always been the use of double standards and the masking of self-interest behind the claim of bringing civilisation. To the Arab mind, the American neoconservatives' purported goal of installing democracy in Iraq in 2003 was only the latest episode in a long history of duplicity.

In 1952 Charles Malik, a Lebanese philosopher and diplomat, argued that Napoleon's foray into Egypt, the first military penetration of the Middle East in modern times, was a re-run of the Crusades with their mixture of territorial conquest, economic greed, and missionary arrogance:

> There has from the beginning been an element of hypocrisy in Western policy: Napoleon's claim to be the protector of Islam, the use of Christian missions for political ends, the use of minorities by all Powers, a facade of morality given to the mandate system – moral principles to justify their own actions and the ignoring of them when they were inconvenient.[7]

This resonates with the quotation from Muhammad Abduh (often described as the father of modern Islamism) at the beginning of this chapter, who made similar observations back in 1884.

Along with hypocrisy goes treachery. One of the greatest betrayals Arabs are taught about in their schoolbooks is the Anglo-French Sykes–Picot agreement of 1916. It tore up the promises of independence that the British had made to Hussein, the sharif of Mecca and the head of the Hashemite family, in order to encourage him to revolt against the Ottomans. The

Sykes–Picot agreement divided the region into spheres of influence, with the French taking Syria and Lebanon and the British Iraq and Palestine. Hussein's supporters rebelled against the deal, realising too late that the Ottoman empire they had helped to bring down might have been the lesser evil compared with European rule. In response, the French reneged on a second promise: Hussein's son, Faisal, would not be allowed to become the King of Syria. Instead, he was fobbed off with the Iraqi throne under British patronage, an option he clearly considered second best.

Only two parts of the Arabian peninsula, Yemen and Saudi Arabia, escaped direct or indirect European rule, but even their sovereignty was limited by British naval and military power. In North Africa Egypt came under British control, while further to the west France took the ultimate step in colonial penetration by sending hundreds of thousands of French settlers to seize or buy land.

It was hardly surprising that this region-wide system of foreign control by non-Muslims would spark resistance. It came from two quarters, the nationalists and the Islamists. They directed their hostility not only at the European colonisers; local Arab elites who collaborated with the new foreign rulers were also criticised. To many Iraqis the exiles who rode back to Baghdad with the Americans and British in 2003 were following a long tradition of puppets in the hands of foreign masters.

Military intervention is aggression at its most naked, but many Arab clerics and intellectuals found the West's all-pervading cultural expansion across the region more dangerous. It was harder to expose and confront because it was insidious. Edward Said, brought up largely in Cairo in a Palestinian Christian family, eloquently described how he was favoured in later life because he had been to an English school: 'They liked me because I spoke English well. As if that's it. If you don't speak English well, you're really not in the same world with their exalted highnesses.'[8] Said was from a wealthy family but his experience was not unique. In the 1920s and 1930s most secondary and higher education in Egypt, Lebanon, Palestine, and Syria was provided by European or American cultural and religious missions. The historian Albert Hourani has argued that for any Arab boy or girl to attend one of these schools was a form of social and psychological displacement. They were lifted out of their native culture and made to feel it was inferior.

Said became famous for his dissection of 'Orientalism', the way many Western scholars constructed a false and patronising image of the Arab world. His analysis had a morale-boosting effect on other Arab intellectuals, and at times he let his pride in Arab culture lead him into exaggeration, claiming in one interview that the very idea of the West 'comes largely from opposition to the Islamic and Arab world' and that 'Islam is the only non-European culture that has never been completely vanquished'.[9]

Said was essentially a secular nationalist but his criticisms of the West were shared by the Islamist movement that developed in the 1930s. In his 'Five Tracts' Hasan al-Banna, who created the Muslim Brotherhood in Egypt, made a fierce attack on Western education:

> They founded schools and scientific and cultural institutes in the very heart of the Islamic domain, which cast doubt and heresy into the souls of its sons, and taught them how to demean themselves, disparage their religion and their fatherland, divest themselves of their traditions and beliefs, and regard anything Western as sacred, in the belief that only that which had a European source could serve as a model to be emulated in this life.[10]

Secular nationalism and Islamism revived strongly after the Second World War. The founding of the state of Israel in 1948 was seen as a massive Arab defeat that had to be corrected. Hundreds of thousands of Palestinians lost their homes, and many were murdered. Independence movements in Asia and Africa, which forced Britain and France to abandon the territories they had occupied for decades, also helped to push Arabs into a more assertive anti-Western stance. A new wave of resistance leaders argued that it was not good enough for the people of individual Arab states to revolt; there had to be a pan-Arab uprising. After all, the borders of the various states were artificial, and had been imposed by European powers which cynically fragmented the region in order to make it easier to capture or control the Middle East's oil.

Michel Aflaq, the Syrian co-founder of the Baath party, was one of the first Arabs to argue that the USA was inheriting the Anglo-French colonial mantle and emerging as the new outside power in the Middle East. The threat he perceived from the USA was not based on military muscle alone. Eisenhower had used diplomatic and economic means to force British and French forces to withdraw from Egypt after the treacherous invasion of Suez in 1956, a move which allowed the USA to supplant European dominance in the region. In other countries, the venality of local Arab rulers meant that an outside power could control an Arab state without even having to send a single soldier. This was as humiliating and demeaning as military invasion.

In a text entitled 'Let us unify the leadership of the Arab struggle', which came out just after Suez, Aflaq argued that US power enabled it,

> besides threatening us from without by its aggression and that of the countries under its influence, to plot from within against our independence, liberty, and the integrity of our national structure with the weapons of bribery and corruption as well as the instigation of discord, disunity, and civil war. All this requires from us a new view of the world and a new preparedness commensurate with the danger we are facing.[11]

Aflaq's words were read by thousands of educated Iraqis in the days before Baathism was discredited by Saddam's rule. They found a clear echo in the arguments I heard from many Iraqis after the invasion. They complained that the new leaders appointed by the USA, first to the IGC and then to the government after formal sovereignty was transferred, had been corrupted during their time in exile or once they returned to Baghdad. When sectarian violence erupted, many Iraqis assumed the USA had deliberately promoted it.

The most influential Islamist after the Second World War was Sayyid Qutb. His book *Social Justice in Islam* argued that the difference between Christians and Muslims is that Muslims recognise no gap between faith and daily life. Declaring that too many Muslims had forgotten this point, Qutb praised the first era of Islam as the great age of Islamic justice, before it was perverted by a string of rulers who were not approved of by the people. He thus argued that Islam needed to go back to its first principles, which had been crushed under a great superstructure of dishonest rulers, ill-informed priests, and rival theological schools.

The current complaint of many Western analysts, particularly the neo-conservatives but also some liberals, is that Islam, unlike Christianity, 'has had no Reformation'. 'Where is the Muslim Martin Luther?' they ask, overlooking the fact that Qutb was the Martin Luther whose absence they lament. His denunciation of corrupt priests and a hypocritical ecclesiastic hierarchy was very similar to the charges Luther brought against the Vatican. 'Go back to the Qur'an,' Qutb argued, just as Luther had said, 'Go back to the Bible'.

Human beings have to show responsibility to one another, Qutb insisted. Rulers have to uphold the law and promote social justice. The right to property has to be protected but it must be used to benefit the community. There should be community ownership of basic necessities. Rulers should only be obeyed so long as they act fairly and justly. While the ideologues of the new Islamism in Egypt came mainly from prominent and well-educated families, the message that Qutb and his followers promoted clearly had more resonance among the poor. Qutb was a Sunni and the Muslim Brotherhood that developed in Syria and Iraq also consisted mainly of Sunnis, but his arguments were similar to those used later by some Shia clerics in Iraq who appealed to the poorest sections of Iraq's majority Shia community by calling for social justice and a pure Islam. This form of Islamism had a social as well as a religious component.

The other rallying-point against the West's cultural, economic, and political interventions was secular nationalism. Egypt's President Gamal Abdel Nasser personified this for Arabs well beyond Egypt's borders. Using arguments echoed by the Baathists, he tried to revive Arab pride through internal modernisation and social reform, coupled with a dynamic foreign policy that confronted the West. The army coup that toppled the Hashemite monarchy in Iraq in 1958 had strong Nasserist overtones. Its leaders aimed not just to change Iraq's political system. Theirs was a revolt against the British-inspired Baghdad pact that linked Iraq with Iran, Turkey, and Pakistan in an alliance against communism and the Soviet Union.

Qutb, the Islamist, shared the analysis, arguing that, 'the crusader spirit runs in the blood of all Occidentals'.[12] He warned his fellow Arabs against Western efforts to split the Arab world by enlisting some Arabs in an alliance against the atheist Soviet Union. He maintained that:

> the Islam which the Americans and their allies want in the Middle East is not the sort of Islam that resists colonialism or tyranny but only communism. They don't want Islam to rule. They could not bear Islam in power, because Islam, when it rules, will raise peoples up again, and will teach them that preparation of power is a duty, that the sweeping away of colonialism is a duty, that communism like colonialism is a plague. Both are an enemy, both an aggression. The Americans and their allies want an American Islam in the Middle East.[13]

Like Frantz Fanon, the great Francophone analyst of the colonised mind, Qutb wanted to warn his fellow Muslims against the dangers of cultural penetration:

Spiritual and intellectual colonialism is truly treacherous. The colonialism of fire and iron naturally provokes resistance and nationalist resentment ... whereas spiritual and intellectual colonialism is soft and gentle and intoxicating – it lulls people and quietens their sacred resentments which should be aflame with anger.[14]

The decade from the mid-1950s to mid-1960s was a time of euphoria, especially in Egypt, Iraq, and Syria, the most developed Arab states. Pan-Arabism was at its height, and there was a strong sense that oil would bring prosperity as well as a chance for political dignity and economic independence from the West. Israel's existence was opposed and resented but the West, Israel's protector and patron, was seen as the main threat to Arab aspirations.

Defeat in the Six-Day War of 1967, between Israel on one side and Egypt, Jordan and Syria on the other, changed everything. Nasser was discredited. Arabs felt humiliated. A sense of shame and impotence fell across the region again. As the USA had aided Israel unequivocally during the war, Israel's occupation of the West Bank and Gaza intensified the feeling that yet another violent step had been taken in the region's century-long penetration by an ever-expanding and hostile West. If the success which Anwar Sadat, Nasser's successor as Egyptian president, had in breaching Israeli lines on the east bank of the Suez canal six years later revived Arab pride, it was short-lived. Israeli forces counter-attacked within days, regained the briefly lost ground, and advanced to within 70 miles of Cairo. Only among certain circles in Egypt was there any feeling that the war had achieved anything positive. Sadat's trip to Jerusalem in 1977 and the peace deal he made with Israel at Camp David a year later in order to secure an Israeli withdrawal from the Sinai was greeted across the region as a surrender and an unforgivable breach in the pan-Arab united front.

Meanwhile, the 'oil shock' that the Arab oil-exporting states had administered by cutting supplies to the West during the 1973 Arab–Israeli War and the price rises that followed it failed to win a significant shift in the regional balance of power. Saudi Arabia and the Gulf states invested their windfall profits in Western banks and their foreign policies became even more pro-Western. At the same time, the secular regimes of Egypt, Iraq, and Syria abandoned their populist domestic policies and became increasingly autocratic. The new Arab frustration was directed not only at Israel and the

West, but once again at Arab rulers – hence the invention of the concept, the Arab 'street'. It was meant to highlight the psychological gap between pro-Western elites and anti-Western people, who saw their rulers as failures and traitors, allowing the West to re-intrude everywhere with its products, values, and ideas.

Arab views of the West were neither monolithic nor universally negative. There was chronic ambivalence. As Khaled Hroub, director of the Cambridge Arab Media Project, put it, 'The West is seen as the source of aggression and war but also of knowledge and enlightenment. Arabs have felt this for the last 200 years. It makes it hard to react. Arabs feel a lack of confidence.'[15] Yet even this recognition of the West's richness of ideas and the freedom of debate within Western societies could be a spur to further resentment and new feelings of Arab inadequacy.

Many Arabs were stunned by the findings of the UN's first Arab Human Development Report, which was written by an independent team of Arab experts in 2002. The report described the Middle East as 'richer than it is developed'.[16] It asserted that although income poverty was low compared with other parts of the world, the Arab region was hampered by a different kind of poverty – poverty of capabilities and poverty of opportunities. There was a deficit in freedom, knowledge, and women's empowerment. The report's researchers polled young Arabs and found 51 per cent of older adolescents and 45 per cent of younger ones wanted to emigrate.

Israel's military occupation of the West Bank and Gaza in 1967 was only the most visible feature of a new and deeper cultural, economic, and political occupation across the Middle East. It was not just the 'street' which felt this had to be challenged and reversed. Many Arab intellectuals took the same view.

Ghassan Salame, a Lebanese minister (who was later to become an adviser to the UN in Iraq in 2003), put it sharply in 1982:

Can Arabs still doubt the need to confront American policies and interests in the region after everything that has happened to them at the hands of the USA since before the beginning of the Second World War? No, there is no question. Whoever wants to shut their eyes to the scale and seriousness of American threats to the independence of the Arabs and their wealth, liberation, and future – and these threats are fast entering the stage of implementation – must pretend to forget. He cannot sincerely deny these threats.

The US, as an essential part of a totally hostile world system, played a central role in stealing the Arabs' oil at rock bottom prices for years. The US played with Arab destinies on a daily basis, sometimes imposing rulers who do not enjoy the confidence of their people, and defending others who had lost that confidence. Washington considered the whole region as an arena for its soldiers and its gluttonous corporations. It continuously plundered the region's resources, threatened to interfere, broke wills and brandished sanctions. Over the last four decades, Washington has played a key role – and regrettably an effective one – in smashing the unity of Arab opinion and positions whenever Arab unity was on the point of establishing itself. This happened with Eisenhower's plan for the Arabs, with Kissinger, and the two Camp David agreements.[17]

Many Westerners, particularly in the West's foreign policy establishments, reacted to views like these by claiming Arabs were suffering from paranoia and conspiracy theories. In a new wave of 'Orientalism', Western analysts described Arabs as self-hating and hysterical. Mohammed Heikal, the great Egyptian journalist/historian and long-time editor of the most famous Cairo newspaper *Al-Ahram*, tried to counteract the trend. In a book about the Gulf after the successful US-led war to drive Saddam out of Kuwait in 1991, he wrote:

When Westerners accuse Arabs of being over-suspicious, they tend to forget that the West has never shown even-handedness on issues which affect the survival of the Arab nation. History's influence in creating what the West says is an over-suspicious Arab attitude to Western involvement was much stronger than most people in the West realised ... the crusader, the colonist, the mercenary, and the spy have all made their mark on Arab attitudes.[18]

While Saddam's invasion of Kuwait angered most Arabs because it was a clear violation of an Arab nation's sovereignty – this time by another Arab ruler – the US-led war to recover Kuwait divided Arab opinion. Washington's motives were, as always, suspect. Heikal reported that most Arabs hoped the USA would leave the region once victory had been achieved – the issue that returned to haunt Washington in 2003 after the fall of Saddam:

With the exception of a few tribal sheikhs, most Arabs wanted foreign forces to depart ... Americans assumed that Arabs were glad of protection against Iraq's ambitions to dominate the region and against its vast chemical weapons capabilities, without realising that the whole affair was wounding to Arab self-respect.[19]

Some anti-Saddam Iraqis claimed Heikal was over-emphasising Saddam's role as a rallying-point for Arab pride. They argued that the Palestinian leader Yasser Arafat, who denounced the US-led Gulf War, was exaggerating Saddam's relevance in the struggle against Israel. He had fired a few Scud missiles at Israel but most of his claims to be the leader of the Arab world were empty rhetoric. What was more important, they stated, was the fact that he was a dictator and an adventurist who launched foolish and costly wars against Iran and Kuwait.

While Arabs disagreed over the Gulf War, there was universal acceptance that the sanctions against Iraq that the Americans persuaded the UN to impose after the Iraqi attack on Kuwait (and to maintain after the war was over) were a disaster for the Iraqi people. Their stated purpose was to force Saddam to comply with UN demands that he dismantle his weapons of mass destruction, but their effect was to push millions of Iraqis into poverty and ruin the country's basic services. In an excellent study of the Arab media, *Voices of the New Arab Public*, Marc Lynch writes:

> Iraq became central to Arab identity as a result of the intense arguments in the new Arab media. The 'suffering Iraqi people' became a vital touchstone for all Arab debate. Indeed, concern for the Iraqi people became in a very real sense part of what it meant to be Arab in the late 1990s.[20]

The iniquity of sanctions became a central theme of the cassettes and videos of Friday sermons put out by Islamists. With its unveiled women announcers, Al-Jazeera was hardly the traditional face or voice of Islam. For devout Muslims the Islamist cassettes were preferable, and this new medium also became increasingly political and international in its choice of subjects, perhaps in competition with TV. Iraq, Palestine, and Chechnya were regularly discussed in the sermons. As Lynch puts it, 'the ongoing sanctions on Iraq provided a crucial unifying theme as Islamists and Arabists could agree on condemnation of the unjustified misery of the Iraqi people.'[21]

Lynch's phrase 'the new Arab public' describes the way the explosion of satellite TV in the 1990s created a completely new impetus for public discussion about politics and a new sphere in which to conduct it. The Qatar-based TV station Al-Jazeera, which started broadcasting in 1997, was not the first satellite channel to appear but it was the first to make a priority of covering politics instead of the previous diet of soap operas and belly-dancing. It also pioneered the talk show on Arab TV, with people taking stands and debating. Al-Jazeera's reviews of the daily press gave mass prominence to opposing columns in Arab newspapers. Viewers were invited to phone in, live on air. The previous decades of censorship and self-censorship in the Arab media were suddenly over, and Al-Jazeera's audiences soared.

The station's news coverage was also refreshingly different, with live broadcasts from scenes of crisis giving an immediacy and emotional impact to stories of suffering and tragedy that were bound to have a political effect on audiences. Its coverage of the American and British air strikes on Iraq in 1998, the so-called Desert Fox campaign, which killed scores of civilians, mobilised a wave of anger. So did its images and reporting of the second Palestinian intifada in September 2000.

As Saad Eddin Ibrahim, an Egyptian sociologist and human rights activist, put it, 'Arab satellites have probably done more for the Arab world than any organised critical movement could have done in opening up the public space and giving Arab citizens a newly found opportunity to assert themselves.'[22] Because it was the one station that everyone watched and also knew their friends had seen, Lynch says Al-Jazeera created 'a real sense of a single common Arab "conversation" about political issues'.[23]

After detailed analysis of the transcripts of almost a thousand Al-Jazeera talk shows as well as hundreds of opinion pieces in Arab newspapers from the 1990s, Lynch found no accuracy in the conventional Western wisdom that Arab media ignored or downplayed the nature of Saddam's regime. That line was pushed by the prominent Iraqi exile Kanan Makiya, in *Cruelty and Silence*,[24] and the Lebanese–American pundit, Fouad Ajami, with his negative picture of Arab political culture *The Dream Palace of the Arabs*.[25] Their books, published in the mid-1990s, had a strong influence on Washington liberals as well as neoconservatives.

Long before Al-Jazeera's emergence in 1997, the Arab print media had already been discussing the pros and cons of Saddam's regime. From its inception, Al-Jazeera continued this trend. Viewers regularly heard Saddam's regime being described as a 'tyranny'. Iraq's suffering was blamed on him as well as on the USA and Britain, the states most associated with the imposition of sanctions. This helped to provide more material for a negative view of the West, making Washington's claim in 2003 that it wanted to liberate Iraqis seem suspect.

Hundreds of articles appeared in *Al-Hayat*, *ASharq Al-Awsat*, and other major Arab dailies, written by Iraqi opposition figures as well as regime sympathisers, discussing the possibilities for change in Iraq and offering proposals for how a post-Saddam era should look. While the dominant view was that Saddam was a corrupt dictator, only a minority supported a US invasion. On this point Iraqis and other Arabs agreed. The Bush–Blair view, that opposition to Saddam would translate into support for an invasion, was no more valid in the Middle East as a whole than it was inside Iraq.

An April 2002 Zogby poll found only 3 per cent of Egyptians favoured an American attack on Iraq while 84 per cent were against. Among Lebanese 7 per cent supported an invasion, among Saudis 11 per cent. Even in Kuwait, Iraq's arch-enemy and Saddam's most recent victim, only 17 per cent favoured a US attack on Iraq.[26] The message was largely lost on Washington and London.

Bush and Blair preferred to rely on what their diplomats were hearing from Arab governments. Jordan and Saudi Arabia, as well as Kuwait and the other Gulf states, indicated that they backed the invasion, even though they could not say so directly. Jordan denied it was allowing US special forces to use its territory to penetrate Iraq, even though I and other reporters saw their helicopters at Jordanian airfields. Jordan's King Abdullah presumably knew what his subjects felt. A BBC poll of Jordanians in February 2003 found 64 per cent believed removing Saddam would not make Iraqis better off. Some 68 per cent thought Bush's real motive was to secure US oil supplies.[27] A Zogby poll in Saudi Arabia around the same time found 95 per cent felt the invasion would create less democracy rather than more, and 97 per cent thought it would create more terrorism.[28]

This strong hostility to US policy tended to make it hard for Iraqi exile politicians to get support from Arabs. Those who argued in favour of sanctions and US and UK military action against Saddam were seen not just as wrong but also as 'non-Arab' – hence their image as puppets of Washington and London. This view was reinforced once the exiles returned to Baghdad and got government jobs in the new US-installed regime.

By regularly questioning the sincerity of Arab regimes and exposing their acquiescence to US policy in the Middle East, Al-Jazeera had become the best-known voice of the 'Arab street' in opposition to Arab regimes. It was a phenomenal achievement, especially as the station's owner was the government of Qatar, which hosted a US naval base. Arab governments were routinely portrayed in Al-Jazeera talk shows as incompetent and corrupt, a view which in some eyes applied equally to Qatar's rulers. Al-Jazeera and the other Arab TV stations had managed to form a new pan-Arabism and sense of solidarity for the first time since the 1960s.

With classic imperial arrogance Washington refused to take them seriously. Instead, it demonised the messenger, claiming Al-Jazeera and Al-Arabiya (formed with Saudi money in February 2003) were created as a safety valve by authoritarian regimes to deflect audiences' attention from the faults of Arabs themselves. Benjamin Gilman, a leading Republican in Congress, described the Arab media in 2002 as offering nothing but 'non-stop incitement'.[29] Martin Indyk, a senior State Department official under Clinton, said there was no point in trying to win Arab hearts and minds because, although Al-Jazeera aired a wide range of views, 'most of them were extreme in their anti-American and anti-Semitic sentiments'.[30]

The British understood the issue better but did not change any minds in Washington. A diplomat who worked in the Foreign Office's Iraq policy unit before the invasion recalls, 'I was jumping up and down, saying "People in the West don't understand how unpopular the Americans are in the Middle East." It goes back to the June 1967 war and the October 1973 war.'[31] Blair accepted the importance of resolving the Palestinian issue, at least as a way of deflecting Arab anger in advance of the invasion of Iraq. He raised it with Bush, but Arabs saw how he failed to get any response. His efforts won him little praise in the Arab street.

Jordanians I spoke to as the invasion went forward thought Blair was just trying to give cover to Britain's support for it. It was less than a year since Israel's prime minister Ariel Sharon re-occupied the West Bank with massive military incursions into Jenin and Nablus. Bush had made one verbal protest but did nothing to stop it.

Bush's one-sidedness confirmed a widespread Arab view that the USA was a hostile state that would never support Palestinian calls for justice and would always oppose Arab interests. Taher al-Masri was a Palestinian with family in Nablus, who served as Jordan's ambassador to London before becoming foreign minister in the 1980s and, for a few months, prime minister. I spent some time in discussion with him at his home in Amman in late March 2003. He admired Western values but despaired of Blair, telling me: 'He has no influence with Bush. His influence only goes as far as Bush wants it to. He cannot push Bush into something he wasn't already going to do.'

As an Arab nationalist who had 'worshipped' Nasser, al-Masri admitted he cried himself to distraction after the June 1967 war: 'In six days we lost everything. We lost Jerusalem. I lost my family in Nablus.' Watching the American and British attack on Iraq on TV, he said he felt the pervasive pessimism with which Arab intellectuals – not only the Arab 'street' – viewed it. He lamented:

> In Jordan we've been frustrated and angry for a long time, far longer than this war. Bitterness is with us across the board – rich, poor, young, old, even among the US-educated. It's an accumulation. It didn't come out suddenly.

He predicted the invasion of Iraq would produce a rise in 'extremism, introversion, and suspicion of the West':

> You won't be able to say anything positive about the US. People won't believe you. It'll make it harder for governments to have good relations with the United States. The consequences of the war will be far-reaching, especially in a region like this with a lot of historical and cultural depth. You won't see tangible effects immediately but there will be an increase in fundamentalism, radicalism, extremism, and terrorism.

Masri's house was in the pleasant hill-top suburb of Abdoun, where tree-lined streets lead to avenues with chic restaurants and discos. His road had a wide pavement where it was easy to walk, a rarity in Amman where the car is pre-eminent. As we talked, Masri's mood became ever gloomier. He had just turned 60.

> I am a ruin psychologically. I go to bed exhausted, and sleep like a dead man. If you're under all this stress, perhaps you start losing your stability and rationality. I'm comfortable. I live well. I have no complaints. I don't work hard. But what about ordinary people? Their feelings will turn inwards, like those of the Arabs who went to fight in Afghanistan. After defeating the Soviets, they turned inwards. Osama bin Laden may not benefit directly, but his concept will.

Conservative Islam had been on the rise long before the Iraq war, but he was sure it would accelerate. His wife used to wear a mini-skirt, but now almost every young woman in Amman was veiled. 'Don't judge Jordan by Abdoun,' he warned. 'We're an enclave. In five years' time you won't find people like me who're ready to accept and admire Western civilisation and Western standards. We're becoming isolated. Many are emigrating.' With prescience, he concluded: 'It's not difficult to defeat Saddam, but that is not victory.'

In Jordan Islamists operate legally, unlike in Syria, or indeed in Egypt where they have to run for parliament as independents (albeit with considerable success). Laith Shubailat was a former member of parliament and one of the leading Islamists, but an independent who kept apart from official Islamist clubs or organisations. When I went to see him, in Amman in late March, he was still excited by the success of an initiative he had launched. Ninety-nine prominent Jordanians of all political views had written a letter of protest to the King, asking him to condemn the invasion or at least express some sympathy for Iraq's civilians as the American 'shock and awe' campaign of bombing went on. The King complied obliquely with a careful statement, saying he was against the war – but without directly criticising Washington.

To Shubailat, the invasion was not only wrong but stupid, since Bush was forfeiting the strong position the USA already had in the Middle East:

> This war was lost politically before it started. Bush is a fool. He had actually occupied most of the Arab world without firing a shot. Wasn't that enough for the emperor? If I were him, I would have said: 'Look, this chap Saddam's contained. I'll leave it at that.'

The only people who would benefit from the war, in Shubailat's view, would be 'fundamentalists, Zionists, and big business'. As he put it, 'The Israelis will get a political victory, a few businessmen will take the oil, and Americans will pay for it by becoming ugly Americans.'

If members of Jordan's political class were gloomy over the war on Iraq, their mood was shared by Amman's intellectuals. Dr Mustafa Hamarneh founded the country's leading think-tank, the Centre for Strategic Studies. Like al-Masri, he was a Palestinian who still remembered the catastrophic defeat of 1967 as a formative moment. But his fury was directed at the self-deception of so many Arabs at the time. 'I was at boarding school in Beit Jala on the West Bank. We were told Nasser was shooting down Israeli planes like flies. Then we saw tanks advancing. A boy shouted: "The Jews", he recalled when I spoke to him in Amman in late March. Jubilation had turned to occupation in the twinkling of an eye.

He found himself on the same see-saw on two further occasions, first in October 1973 when Egyptian troops crossed the Suez canal but were then driven back by the Israelis, and then in February 1991 again. Hamarneh was teaching at Amman university at the time. 'I remember kids crying when Saddam told people he was pulling out of Kuwait. My room was full of young men and women saying, "Please tell us it's not true", he said. At that time Jordan was one of the few countries that supported Saddam, so the controlled media suppressed coverage of the US military advance into Kuwait to drive Iraqi forces out. TV viewers and newspaper readers were not prepared for the truth until it could no longer be denied.

In the freer climate of 2003 the same one-sidedness was back in action. Although Jordan's King supported the Americans, even the state media were quoting without reservation the bombastic wartime lies of Moham-med Saeed al-Sahhaf, Iraq's information minister, the so-called Comical Ali, about Iraq's great victories over US forces. Hamarneh produced copies of Jordan's two main papers, one state-owned, the other private, and laid them out on the desk. Both had front-page headlines claiming Iraqi forces had counter-attacked and re-taken Baghdad airport, killing hundreds of Ameri-can troops. Every word was nonsense. 'The danger lies in the psychological and moral collapse which we will go through, and it's happened with every war in my lifetime,' Hamarneh said.

He took issue with Shubailat's 'Letter of the Ninety Nine'. Most of its signatories were self-promoters and has-beens who had failed to take any serious steps towards reform when they were in parliament or government, he claimed. He saw no chance of an Islamist resurgence in Jordan as a result of the Iraq war. The Islamists had had their chance over the last decade. They lost ground after failing to produce any vision of economic progress. Now and then they could pull a crowd into the street, but that was all. They showed no self-criticism and could not mobilise the forces of change in Jor-dan's culture.

The only people who would benefit from the war would be Islam's funda-mentalists, the Al-Qaeda jihadis who were far more extreme than the Islamists of the Muslim Brotherhood. Hamarneh reflected that, 'The losers from this war will be the modernisers, the progressives, the democrats. They won't be able to side with the Americans any more because the Americans are seen as aggressors.' He agreed with al-Masri that many would try to leave the Middle East and emigrate. A few would emigrate within the region, perhaps to Qatar. With a smile, he pointed out that Al-Jazeera's radicalism and pluralism came about because 'most of Al-Jazeera's staff are Jordanians and Palestinians'.

Meanwhile, the invasion of Iraq was well under way, but the Iraqi guards on Jordan's border remained stubbornly in place, blocking access for journalists. The mood among the foreign media was getting increasingly frantic. We were convinced the Americans had done a deal with the Iraqi guards, promising not to attack as long as they stayed on duty. The Pentagon, we muttered, was trying to stop 'unilaterals' rushing around on the battlefield, filing news stories by satellite and generally getting in the way – unlike 'embedded' journalists who were under control.

I decided to use the time to go to Damascus to see if the mood of alternating excitement and depression was the same as in Jordan. Laith Shubailat had primed me: 'Syria's less democratic but more nationalist than Jordan. The Syrians haven't sold out yet. Syria is a dictatorship but at least the leadership abides by the country's raison d'etre. They're Arabs.'

His assessment was correct. Damascus was in turmoil. Almost every day demonstrators marched through the streets, denouncing the USA and Britain, and carrying effigies of Bush and Blair. In Syria no protests take place unless they are approved by the government, but the people on the march seemed genuinely committed. Some carried portraits of Nasser as a symbol of the new sense of pan-Arab solidarity. During the Iran–Iraq war Syria had taken Tehran's side, and relations between the Baath party in Iraq and its counterpart in Syria had been tense for decades. In 1991 Syria had backed the US-led military campaign to force Saddam out of Kuwait.

The 2003 war changed everything. Syria was firmly against it, partly for fear that if the Americans were successful their next target would be Damascus. Syria's president, Bashar al-Assad, even gave an interview in the main government-owned newspaper, saying he hoped the USA would be defeated. No other Arab leader dared to go that far.

Damascus became the staging-point for hundreds of Arab volunteers – Palestinians, Algerians, Yemenis, Saudis, and Syrians themselves – who wanted to cross into Iraq to defend Arab soil. These were not suicide bombers, but untrained and undisciplined enthusiasts who rushed into Iraq in the heat of the moment, expecting to pick up a gun and shoot Americans.

Iraq's embassy in Damascus is less than a hundred yards from the US embassy. The contrast between the two was dramatic. One building was a half-deserted fortress with bullet-proof metal screens and concrete bollards on the pavement to prevent cars ramming through. The other was a hive of excited young people who wanted to help their Iraqi Arab brothers and were impatiently milling around as they waited for papers authorising them to cross the border. It was an Arab version of the International Brigade, made up of young European and American radicals, who had rushed to support the republican side during the Spanish civil war in the 1930s.

Many left Damascus without telling their families, as I discovered at a funeral in the Yarmuk refugee camp for Palestinians on the edge of the Syrian capital. Two cousins had rung their parents from the border to say they were about to go over. Within hours one was dead and the other lay wounded in a strike on their bus by US warplanes a few miles inside Iraq.

Saddam's defeat would leave the survivors of this Arab nationalist venture in despair. They saw it as a defeat for Iraq and all Arabs. Back in Amman in early April, I went to see Adnan Abu Odeh, a Palestinian-Jordanian who had been Jordan's ambassador to the UN in the mid-1990s but fell out with King Hussein over a book he wrote on Jerusalem. The Americans were about to enter Baghdad, and Odeh foresaw a mood of humiliation taking hold across the Arab world. 'An Arab sadness will reign everywhere, except in Kuwait. It's like a family which loses one of its members,' he said. 'In 1991 Iraq was the aggressor. But for the last 12 years it's been a victim, and the underdog which was able to challenge the United States.'

Abu Odeh's first job was in Jordan's intelligence service, where he was trained in 'psy-ops' by the British, he told me with an ironic smile. Arab feelings were multi-layered. 'Humiliation is continuous. It's felt all the time,' he said. There was a massive sense of frustration that had been building for three decades since the October war, and accelerated to full throttle with the Palestinian intifada. Arabs saw themselves as colonised, and there was no obvious way out. According to Abu Odeh:

> What's going on in Iraq now recalls 1258 when the Mongols entered Baghdad. It's also like Britain's arrival in Baghdad in 1918. Iraq had the first civilisation in history which domesticated animals and sowed plants for agriculture. Now it's being re-colonised for the second time. We see a new type of colonisation with a transformed mission. In the past it was guns, ships, and priests. Now it's guns and the gift of democracy.

Faced with constant foreign intervention and defeat, Arabs were falling back on every kind of psychological defence mechanism. He added:

> At the moment these mechanisms are working flat-out. The fall of Baghdad will create an extra level of suppression. There will be more frustration, anger, uncertainty about the future, and hopelessness ... Humiliation is being fuelled not just by the external impact of defeat but by an internal sense of impotence.

His analysis of what would happen inside Iraq sounded especially acute. 'Iraq is the hardest place in the Arab world to imagine building prototypes of democracy. It's only possible in a cohesive society, not a highly diversified one,' he claimed. Saddam's defeat would trigger resistance within six months, he predicted: 'There will be national or patriotic resistance, and we may see Islamic resistance from the Shias.' The problem was that only in Algeria, Palestine, and south Lebanon had Arabs had a tradition of national resistance with a folklore and skills passed down through the generations. 'In Iraq we are entering a very messy era,' he warned.

Abu Odeh assumed Saddam would soon be killed – 'he will pass into history as a man who defied the Americans. He will die a hero, like Zapata' – but he thought the main issue was how Iraqis would feel about US actions after the regime fell. Their judgement would be coloured by what happened to Iraq, not to Saddam:

> The Americans are masters at making other people hate them. People used to be ambivalent about America. They admired American education, technology, freedom of expression. Until this war they only hated one thing about America, its Middle East policy. This war will take the scales of hatred, and add new degrees to them.

The following day I set off with colleagues for the border. The Americans were in Baghdad and we felt sure the Iraqi guards would have vanished. Just to be sure, we went down to the Iraqi embassy the night before, where consular officials were doing a roaring trade in selling Iraqi visas for four-figure sums in dollars. Greed had overcome the regime's orders to refuse visas. It was clear the regime had collapsed, and officials were rushing to finance their lives in exile. I had never paid so much for a visa since the day before Yugoslavia's Slobodan Milosevic was toppled.

In Iraq the mood was more varied than in Jordan or Syria, as was to be expected. Getting rid of Saddam was a relief to almost everyone, but the sense of humiliation and suspicion felt by many Iraqis about having a foreign army in their midst was similar to that of Arabs elsewhere. There were conflicting emotions about the Americans. Many Iraqis felt aggrieved and patronised to hear Bush proclaim his mission was to give Iraq democracy. They regularly told foreign reporters that Mesopotamia was the birthplace of human civilisation and the site of the world's oldest cities. At the same time they expected the superpower that had toppled Saddam to be able to get electricity and public services going again quickly. They noted that the Americans and British stood by while public buildings were looted, with the exception of the oil ministry, which was put under US guard as soon as US troops reached Baghdad.

One of the quickest and most visible changes in Iraq after Saddam fell was the sprouting of satellite TV dishes on hundreds of thousands of roofs. Under the dictatorship satellite TV was banned. This did not stop people putting up illicit dishes, which they tried to hide from the street or neighbouring roofs. The punishment was usually a fine, which created new opportunities for corruption as people paid the inspectors rather than the fine. When the ban was lifted in April 2003, satellite dishes were the first electrical goods that most people bought, ahead of fans and air-conditioners. The world of Al-Jazeera, Al-Arabiya, Abu Dhabi TV, and Al-Manar, the station run by Hizbullah in Lebanon, suddenly opened for Iraqis. Iraq rejoined the Arab mainstream.

Many Iraqis were quick to take advantage of their new freedom and join in phone-ins to the talk shows. Some described life in Saddam's dictatorship, and ex-prisoners talked of torture and cruelty. Some thanked the Americans for liberation. In the first call to an Al-Jazeera programme on 21 April that was devoted to Saddam's fate, an Iraqi from London expressed a mixture of anti-Saddam and anti-American emotion: 'We must all hope that Saddam is gone, that the tyranny has ended, and everyone in the Arab world would know that he was a tyrant, and he is to blame for the Americans ending up in our country.'[32]

His delight over Saddam's departure, muted hope for the future, and concern about what the occupation would bring were a perfect reflection of the emotions that ran through Iraq's Arab communities in those early post-invasion days. We ran into them in almost every encounter we had with Iraqis. Liberation and occupation were intertwined.

These complex and sometimes contradictory attitudes meant the Americans were on trial. Would they retain the gratitude which a few, but only a few, Iraqis were willing to express? Would they earn it among the rest of the population? Or would the jury come back and call for the mass resistance to the American and British presence, which Saddam had failed to mobilise while the invasion was under way?

At the least, it was already clear that comparisons with the occupations of Germany and Japan were absurd. The long history of humiliating Western interventions and Arab resentment throughout the Middle East, as well as US and British support for sanctions on Iraq in the decade before the war, meant the invaders were running into a very different set of cultural, political, and religious attitudes from those experienced by the occupiers of Berlin or Tokyo in 1945.

III

CREATING RESISTANCE: THE SUNNIS

We had no idea we weren't wanted.

Lieutenant Col Eric Nantz, battalion commander,

82nd Airborne Division[1]

ngry residents crowded round as I approached the al-Qa'id prima-ry school in Nazal with my interpreter. It was a relatively well-to-do suburb of Fallujah. Two- and three-storey villas lined the road opposite the school, with the ornate columns and pompous balustraded balconies that Iraqi families love. Men stood in the street, wives were in the front yards.

Fourteen people had died the previous evening, apparently shot by troops of the Second Brigade of the 82nd Airborne division, the US army's elite paratroopers, after several hundred protesters converged on the school. It was 28 April, just under three weeks since the fall of Baghdad, and around a hundred US soldiers had been billeted in the school for four days.

'We came to tell them to leave,' Abed Jumaili, an electrician, explained to me. The community wanted to get their children back into class as schools across Iraq started to re-open after the war. The other complaint was more sensitive. 'The Americans are looking at the women inside our houses with their special goggles,' Jumaili said. It was a suspicion we were to hear regu-larly in other parts of Iraq. People were convinced the Americans' infra-red night-vision equipment allowed soldiers to see into bedrooms – perhaps they could even see through clothes.

We showed our press credentials and a soldier pulled a piece of razor wire aside to let us into the school yard. Inside the building Lt Col Eric

Nantz, the battalion commander, said the protesters had been anything but peaceful. Some threw stones, others fired into the air. A soldier was struck and burned by a lighted flare that was hurled over the wall. Then came heavy firing towards the school and across its roof, which the troops returned. 'We later found eight AK-47 Kalashnikov rifles on the ground and nearby rooftops and more than 50 expended rounds. I don't know if it was planned,' he said.

A soldier who was standing by the stairs of the two-storey school told me:

> We've been sitting here taking fire for three days. It was enough to get your nerves wracked. When they marched down the road and started shooting at the compound, there was nothing left to do but defend ourselves. They were firing from alleyways and buildings where we couldn't see. Guys were in line with hot chow. When bullets fell into the compound, people in that chow line ran for cover. From that moment it was all business. We started putting on body armour and went up on that roof.

I asked if I could go upstairs and he led the way. From the roof we had a commanding view of the dusty street. Cradling his M-4 rifle, he conceded the soldiers had not just fired single shots. Many put their weapons on automatic; some had fired M-60 machine guns.

To the Iraqis it was murder, to the Americans it was justified self-defence. Who was right? The evidence seemed to tip towards the Iraqi side. In addition to the lack of American casualties (with the exception of the soldier burnt by a flare) there was the fact that the school's walls showed no sign of any bullet holes while several houses opposite had gashes in their concrete walls and multiple perforations from heavy-calibre weapons. When they heard the Iraqis fire into the air, had the Americans panicked, thinking they were being directly targeted?

In Fallujah's hospital relatives were waiting at the morgue to identify bodies. Others huddled beside the beds of wounded loved ones. Osama, a 35-year-old, who would not give his last name, explained how he had been shot in the leg but managed to crawl into the yard of a house two streets away, from where friends took him to hospital. The Americans had blocked ambulances from coming in, he claimed. Muthanna Saleh Abdul Latif, a taxi driver, lived opposite the school. He was hit in the foot by a bullet and bled for 90 minutes before a car could get him to hospital. Asked about the weapons found by the Americans after the shooting ended, Muthanna said, 'All Iraqis have weapons for self-defence. There are lots of armed robberies.'

By one of the main intersections in Falluja's town centre we found the mayor's office. It was alongside a former Baathist social club and office that the Americans had taken over, planting razor wire and a sandbagged observation post on the roof. Omar Minar Esawi, a young policeman guarding the mayor's office, gave us a short history of life in Fallujah in the three weeks since Saddam was toppled. There was some looting but nothing on the scale of the mayhem in the capital, and the imams and sheikhs had managed to stop it. Local people had also put up neighbourhood checkpoints to block strangers. The city is around 30 miles west of Baghdad and American troops arrived more than a week after the fall of Baghdad. One of their first acts was to go to a central mosque and arrest Sheikh Kamal and Sheikh Mohammed al-Karem. 'We already controlled the town. People from local villages and the town were in charge,' the policeman said with obvious pride. He saw no reason for the Americans to behave as though they should decide who would run Fallujah.

His account of a town that had liberated itself seemed to ring true. The mayor had abandoned his offices; the Baathists were staying at home; and a new mayor had been chosen by the imams of the Fallujah mosques and tribal leaders in several villages around the city who had formed a governing council. The policeman told us:

> Fallujans don't like the Americans coming into the market area. They don't like the checkpoints they put up everywhere. The Americans said they would only stay for two or three days, but everyday the number of soldiers is increasing. We can control Fallujah without the Americans. I want them to leave now.

Inside the town hall Taha Badawi Hamid al-Alwani, the new mayor, took up the story. He used to be the manager of a private supermarket in the neighbouring town of Ramadi, and was not a Baath party member, he said. He came from the Obeidi tribe, which had had constant problems with Saddam, and he was glad the Americans toppled him. He was not asking the Americans to leave Iraq, but they should withdraw from the school and move out of the city, he told me. Their presence was unnecessary and provocative. He had held a conference with the *ulema* (the religious leaders) and they all agreed.

Fallujah was later to become known in US circles as a pro-Saddam stronghold. In Iraq, however, it had a reputation as an independent city with a strong religious flavour and conservative social customs. It was sometimes called the 'city of mosques', with over a hundred for a population of around 350,000. Seven large branches of the al-Dulaim tribe, the biggest tribe in Anbar province, dominated the town and surrounding villages. Set beside the Euphrates on the main route to Jordan and Syria, it was well situated for both agriculture and trade. This gave it relative prosperity, along with the general boom in the Iraqi economy in the 1960s and 1970s after the nationalisation of the country's foreign-owned oil company, before living standards collapsed again with the war with Iran and the following decade of sanctions. Saddam directed oil revenues to Iraq's mainly Sunni areas rather than the largely Shia south-east, but Fallujah was not particularly favoured over other Sunni cities. In 1998 Fallujans angered Saddam when local imams refused to praise him in their Friday prayers. Many were imprisoned. Saddam tried to punish the city by cutting food supplies but was forced to back down because he needed the imams' support.

Fallujah also had a history of nationalist resistance to foreign occupation. There were several clashes with Fallujans in the early years of British rule. During the uprising of 1920, Sheikh Dhari (grandfather of Dr Harith al-Dhari, who became a thorn in the US side as chairman of the Association of Muslim Scholars) helped to kill Lt Col G.E. Leachman, a famous British commander. Later the British built a large airbase on the shores of Lake Habbaniya outside Fallujah, which they kept until 1958. It was one of the main staging posts for seaplanes flying from Britain to India.

Many Iraqis were angered by the Anglo–Iraqi treaty which authorised British possession of these bases and gave British troops the right to move freely round the country. By the start of the Second World War anti-British feeling was so strong that the British-installed monarchy had to cede to nationalist pressure and refuse British requests for Iraq to declare war on Germany. After an anti-British prime minister took power in a coup in 1941, Britain flew extra troops into Habbaniya to help to remove him. They defeated the Iraqi army in a major battle at Fallujah and moved on to Baghdad, where they replaced the prime minister with one who was more pliant. British troops remained in Iraq throughout the Second World War and it was not until 1947 that they withdrew. However, the Royal Air Force remained at Habbaniya outside Fallujah until 1958, when the nationalist government that toppled the monarchy asked it to leave.

A generation later, during the Gulf War in 1991, Fallujah's two bridges over the Euphrates were destroyed from the air, cutting off the town and causing major disruption. On 13 February the town suffered a severe atrocity, when British planes dropped several bombs on the main market, killing 276 civilians. So, although the bombing Fallujah suffered in the 2003 war was less heavy, memories of earlier encounters with the British and Americans were not likely to make the city greet the 82nd Airborne Division with delight. US troops, and their neoconservative masters in Washington, would have benefited from knowing a little of the city's nationalist history and Islamist tradition before they invaded Fallujah.

Saddam had supporters in Fallujah, of course. In the Saddam era many young men from Fallujah joined the army and the regime's security services. In the crowd outside the school we came across people who said they still admired their deposed leader. The day of the shooting had been Saddam's birthday and some boasted that they fired into the air to celebrate that. 'Saddam Hussein is a thousand times better than the Americans. He's a Muslim. We hope he will come back. He will protect us. He knows us,' said Ahmed Mohammed, a 22-year-old student.

American officers claimed there were pro-Saddam provocateurs in the crowd. The new mayor also alleged that Saddam Hussein loyalists were paying young people to make trouble, but he was sure most Fallujans were happy the dictator was gone. The dominant mood of the protests had not been in favour of the old regime, he said. Many shouted, 'No to the US. No to Saddam.' Others chanted, 'God is great. America is God's enemy.'

I asked Lt Col Nantz whether he had ever considered keeping his troops on the edge of Fallujah rather than occupying a school in a suburb. He replied:

> No, I never considered that at all. This is the place where you need to be engaged. We want the Iraqis to build themselves up and you can't help them do that if you're sitting outside. Our way is to be inside and help them build a police force and so on. We had no idea we weren't wanted.

The colonel's revealing phrase – 'We had no idea we weren't wanted' – could be the epitaph for the whole occupation. The Americans and British never took on board how mistrusted and unpopular they were. As happens with colonial rulers everywhere, the people they talked to were mainly their own employees or others who stood to benefit from the occupation financially – civil society activists seeking grants for projects, or ministers and officials who wanted salaries and funds for public service budgets. These were not the sort of Iraqis who would tell the Americans and British to go home. As time went on, these were also the people who would suffer threats and assassination because of their identification with the occupation and would beg to be given asylum in the USA and Britain.

This did not mean the occupiers were doomed never to discover Iraqis' true feelings. They only needed more subtlety and a little imagination to understand how occupations are usually perceived. The default mode was that Iraqis, like any other people, would not want US troops in their country. If there was strong evidence to the contrary, fine. Otherwise, the Americans ought to have checked and double-checked, and not assumed blithely that goodwill existed.

Two days after the incident at the al-Qa'id primary school there was a second clash in Fallujah, this time along the main street. A small convoy of US vehicles happened to drive past while a new protest was being held outside the US command post. Stones were thrown and a soldier in one of the vehicles fired, killing three people. It took several more anti-occupation demonstrations before US tactics in Fallujah changed and the paratroopers withdrew from the school and their city centre command post.

The damage was done, however. The brief but bloody incursion into Fallujah contained all the ingredients for the tensions that subsequently led to full-scale armed resistance. With hindsight, it was the spark that lit the insurgency. Twenty people lay dead (three more succumbed to their wounds some days after the shootings) because of clashes between Iraqi nationalism and what was at best American insensitivity and at worst an American drive to impose foreign control over a proud Islamic city.

There were no foreign jihadis or Al-Qaeda operatives in Fallujah in April 2003. If a few Saddam-era intelligence agents or other Baathist sympathisers tried to orchestrate the trouble, they were only successful because their anti-Americanism was in line with the mainstream Fallujan view. A town that had felt itself freed woke up a week later under an unnecessary occupation by foreigners from a different culture. Heavily armed strangers put up roadblocks, checked identity cards, arrested community leaders, took over schools, and peered into houses. No wonder they were unwelcome.

No wonder, too, that word of the incident quickly spread throughout Anbar province. Fallujah and Ramadi are the province's main cities, the centre of a closely knit network of loyalties where humiliation and injury to any one member is felt by the whole tribe.

There were other significant lessons from the Fallujah incident. It undermined the notion that widespread looting and the disappearance of the police had left Iraq with a huge security vacuum and a 'collapsed state'. This, many US officials argued, justified a long-term American presence in the country, in order to restore law and order and rebuild the institutions of government. In Baghdad the looting of public buildings was indeed massive, but in Fallujah and the provinces it was on a much smaller scale. Hospitals in Fallujah were undamaged and the schools quickly resumed work. The police returned to their duties, even if many senior officers laid low for a time.

The tragedy at the al-Qa'id school also showed how unprepared the US army was for peacekeeping or any of the other duties an occupation force has to perform. After the event US officers failed to order an inquiry or make an apology to the victims' families. Either action might have reduced some of the antagonism towards the occupation. A report by Human Rights Watch two months after the incident commented:

> US military and political authorities who placed combat-ready soldiers in the highly volatile environment of Fallujah without adequate law-enforcement training, translators, and crowd control devices followed a recipe for disaster ... They had no tear-gas or other forms of non-lethal crowd control ... They lacked enough translators, and thus the ability to communicate effectively with the community they were now policing.[2]

The US military digested a few lessons from Fallujah and, at least for a time, adjusted their tactics. The main concession was that the occupation had to have a much lighter footprint. Throughout May and June American troops largely stayed in their base two miles east of the town, coming in only for occasional patrols. US officers established links with the town's governing council, and made plans for spending money on improving infrastructure and other services.

The Americans came under sporadic attack but it was small-scale and amateurish. On 21 May and 28 May men with machine guns and rocket-propelled grenades attacked US vehicles. The second incident left two US troops dead. The US retaliated each time, killing four Iraqis in all. In early June an attack on a US checkpoint killed one American.

When I visited the US base outside Fallujah on 15 July, the atmosphere was relatively relaxed. There were no blast walls at the front. Cars could park close to the entrance to allow visitors to walk the short distance to the gate house. Suicide bombs by pedestrians or vehicles had not yet started, and journalists could walk into US bases and get interviews without prior notification or having to be 'embedded'. I was told by Staff Sgt Antony Joseph, the spokesman for the 3rd Infantry Division, which had replaced the paratroopers:

> We stopped daytime patrols in the city last week. We've had no night-time patrols since early June. The mayor asked us to stop them because of the noise which disturbed people's sleep. After the police graduated a new class, they asked us to give them responsibility for the city, which we did.

His commander, Lt Col Eric Wesley, sat in a room full of computers and a map, screened from outside eyes by a black curtain. He too gave a picture of a fragmented and amateur enemy:

> There's no evidence of activity by the Special Republican Guard [the most professional armed force in Saddam's regime] in Fallujah. The indications are that the majority are not well trained. Their tactics are relatively crude and elementary. Their marksmanship is poor.

He described the insurgents as a 'cocktail' of different groups: 'disaffected people, the poor, former members of the Saddam regime, maybe third-country nationals and fundamentalists'. But he accepted that the opposition was largely fuelled by local imams, anti-Western nationalism, and revenge for actions taken by the occupation rather than by Baathists:

> I hear the language of incitement coming from the mosques, and we've seen printed messages on the street … there are people who've been taught their whole life to hate the West … there's revenge killing by someone who lost a family member in the war.

Senior US officers in the field sometimes seemed to have a better grasp of Iraqi realities than the men in the Pentagon and the White House. At least, they were better at talking the talk. Lieutenant Col Wesley was a good example. The way to keep the peace was for Iraqis to take more control, he argued:

> The best thing is to have the people and leadership of Fallujah take ownership of the town. The police want more autonomy now they've been trained. They want to step out from under the umbrella of the coalition. For seven weeks there hasn't been a major incident between US forces and anti-coalition forces. The relationship with the town has significantly improved. I see it as a success story. We meet the mayor almost every day and see the imams and sheikhs on a weekly basis and resolve any concerns they may have. We want to jump-start their markets and rebuild a lot of infrastructure by giving contracts.

Behind the colonel's optimistic talk, two storm clouds lurked. The police had held a protest a few days earlier against the presence of US troops in their compound since it fuelled charges that the police were 'collaborators'. A week before that a young sheikh, Laith Khalil Dahham, had died when an explosion destroyed his home in the compound of his mosque in Fallujah's working-class al-Askari suburb. Six young men, his students, were also killed.

An investigation by Patrick J. McDonnell and Terry McDermott, two reporters for the *Los Angeles Times*, found friends and family who said the preacher had been entirely devoted to spiritual themes until the invasion radicalised him and made him increasingly political.[3] The Americans were monitoring his sermons, which were fiercely anti-occupation, though it was unclear whether he called for general 'resistance' or actual armed attacks. The Americans consulted the mayor and some religious leaders who summoned the preacher to a meeting. The results were not apparent by the time the explosion occurred.

Angry neighbours claimed the Americans had killed him in an air strike. Some said they witnessed a plane fly overhead followed by a flash. Lieutenant Col Wesley denied the claims:

> The imams, the mayor, the police chief all spoke with one voice. It wasn't a strike from a coalition missile or aircraft, but an explosion from inside the building. It's kind of damning when a building explodes from inside, and it wasn't natural gas.[4]

Two days after the blast, US Central Command in Florida issued a statement that the explosion was 'apparently related to a bomb-making class that was being taught inside the mosque'.[5] The next day Lt Gen Ricardo Sanchez, commander of ground forces in Iraq, said Iraqi police told his investigators that bomb-making was going on in the building. However the *Los Angeles Times* reporters said Fallujah's police chief, Riyadh Abbas, insisted he had given no evidence to the US in support of the bomb-factory theory.[6]

None of Fallujah's secular leaders endorsed it. The mayor and police chief preferred a third theory, that some unknown group had caused the explosion to drive a wedge between the people of Fallujah and the Americans. Their claim seemed to flow from their increasingly precarious position, as they tried to maintain credibility with Iraqis while also working with the occupation.

The men's deaths, and the US accusations against them, upset many Fallujans. They also highlighted the growing gulf of suspicion between local people and the Americans, though not yet in the form of an outright insurgency. 'We are not calling for war. We are always calling for peace,' Khalid Hamed Mahal, another imam, told the *Los Angeles Times*. 'But when war is declared against us, we have an expression: our leadership will be the teachings of Mohammed.'[7]

The mood in Fallujah in those early days of the occupation was mirrored in Tikrit and Ramadi, and other towns in what the Americans came to call the Sunni triangle. It reflected suspicion of US intentions; a feeling of wounded national pride and honour; a determination to show that Iraqis could run their own affairs; and a sense of resentment that the Americans did not accept the right of Iraqis to be in charge.

Crammed with six other journalists into an armoured van hired by the *Los Angeles Times*, I set off for Saddam Hussein's home town of Tikrit a few hours after it was 'liberated' by US marines on 14 April. Our route took us past the giant al-Taji military complex. It was unguarded. Looters were pouring out of the main gates and streaming up the road with booty. A boy who looked about 14 years old carried three Kalashnikovs. A man had six bayonets in his arms. Another was pushing a bicycle onto which he had strapped several rifles.

In Tikrit we discovered that US expectations of a last-ditch stand by Saddam loyalists had come to nothing. The regime had gone out with neither a whimper nor a bang, local residents and the Americans confirmed. The city felt as though it had woken up with a collective hangover: exhausted, groggy, and not sure what to do next. Most shops remained shuttered, but a few people were on the streets comparing their experiences with those of their neighbours. For the US forces who had raced north to seize the town, capturing Tikrit had been billed as the culmination of the three-week-long invasion. It turned out to be an anti-climax. 'We got to the edge of town two days ago, and secured the palace this morning without any resistance. A small group of fedayeen hit our position last night with Kalashnikovs and hand grenades but they were wiped out,' said Capt Ben O'Rourke, an actor and writer from Santa Monica, California, who was called up as a reservist in early 2002. His matter-of-fact tone seemed to disguise some disappointment that it had been so easy.

Abdul Hussein al-Maliki was standing outside his home directly opposite the archway into the Omar al-Farouk palace, where US trucks were parked. The first Iraqi looters were walking past the Americans, but he was biding his time. Between two and three hundred families used to live on the site before Saddam built the palace, he explained. The richer families got compensation for losing their homes, but most did not. He had worked on constructing the palace for a wage of around a dollar a day. 'Look, my friend,' he declared. 'This is my house. Do I look rich? The people of Tikrit are like people all over Iraq. They don't like Saddam. I have no job. I want to kill him.' But he made it clear he was not a fan of the Americans either: 'This is an occupation. There's no two ways about it. The Americans will stay for ever and take our oil. We'll stay quiet for a year but then we will kill them,' he said.

Emad Ahmed Yasser, a 32-year-old taxi driver in a long black *jalabiya*, was just emerging from the palace. He had similar views of Saddam, but was more charitable to the Americans. He explained in a tone of shock and awe:

> Don't think we love Saddam just because we live in Tikrit. We all hate him. We are very poor here. I'm very happy today. This is the first time I've seen the luxury he lived in. It's as though I entered a paradise that was banned for us.

Asked about the US troops, he gave them the benefit of the doubt: 'If the Americans behave like Saddam, we won't respect them. We don't know them. We hope they're better than Saddam.'

Iraqi troops and the police had disappeared from Tikrit ten days into the war, and even before Baghdad fell, he said, adding:

The Iraqi army could only smash Iraqis, not the Americans. The army's main job was to prevent a popular Iraqi uprising … The fedayeen abandoned their weapons and put on civilian clothes. A few Syrian volunteers stayed around a bit longer and were desperately asking people for food before they vanished.

At Tikrit's main hospital Dr Bashar al-Dulaimi, an ophthalmologist, was organising teams of doctors and nurses to prevent looting. But pride would not allow him to seek US help, he indicated. 'If the Americans are ready to offer us protection, they can. But we will not ask them. We will not take that step,' he said. He was glad Saddam had gone, but 'we're sad because our country has been destroyed and many civilians were killed and injured without any proper reason and against the law'.

The city of Ramadi lies 20 miles west of Fallujah. Like Fallujah, it is a trade and agricultural centre on the Euphrates, and both places were later twinned in the minds of US officials as hotbeds of the Sunni insurgency. On my first post-invasion visit there in July 2003 I found one significant difference from Fallujah. There the Americans had a fixed presence in the town centre, a guard post at the governor's office that gave them a commanding view of the main street and all the comings and goings of Iraqi visitors to Ramadi's newly chosen officials.

As a result, the building came under frequent fire and tension was higher than in Fallujah, from which the Americans had withdrawn. 'There are attacks on the governor and all local officials, including the police. It includes verbal threats, drive-by shootings, and RPGs [rocket-propelled grenades]', Capt Michael Calvert, the information officer for the 3rd Armoured Cavalry Regiment, told me. The attacks were not sophisticated and the Americans saw no reason to believe that they were coordinated by a national or regional organisation. The captain described how one day a fortnight previously a man on a motorbike stopped briefly outside the governor's office and threw a grenade. A few minutes later this was followed by mortar fire.

Like a ripple effect, the attacks produced an American response that local people considered excessive, leading to more antagonism. I dropped into a small grocery store that was situated across the road from the US guard post at the governor's office. It had a bullet hole in the plate glass window from the American reaction to one of the drive-by shootings, according to the owner, who preferred not to give his name. Ahmed Rajab, a metalworker who was buying cigarettes, complained that US troops had arrived at his home in a nearby street shortly after midnight on one recent night. They searched it for an hour, asked if there were weapons in the house, but took nothing. This had happened to several people. He admitted he supported Saddam and talked sympathetically of one 'mujahed brother' who had been shot by the Americans. 'We are Iraqis. Our dignity is more important than our lives,' he said.

In his cluttered and book-lined study I met Dr Jihad Abed Hussein al-Alwani, who had a PhD from the Islamic University of Baghdad and was the imam of the al-Saleh mosque in Ramadi. He was proud of the fact that he did not support Saddam, he said, at a time when most other local people did. He was related to an air force general, Mohammad Madhloum al-Dulaimi, who was a hero from the war with Iran in the 1980s and took part in a failed coup attempt against the dictator in 1995. After torture and execution, his mutilated body was given back to his tribe, sparking several days of disturbance in Ramadi. Dr Jihad was gaoled for three years and his son was fired from his job at the Police Academy and imprisoned for a year.

He rejected the American claim that the attacks were organised by former Baathists:

> They come from the Islamic resistance, and the ordinary people of Ramadi, because the Americans don't fulfil their promises. We're short of electricity and security is bad. The Americans and British accuse Muslims of having no civilisation, so Muslims in Iraq see this occupation as a crusade.

Dr Jihad said he was recently interrogated by US military police for eight hours. They asked him whether he considered US troops to be an occupation force. He replied evasively by giving them a short, intense lecture about Iraqi history and culture. When they went on to ask why he was urging people to attack Americans, he said he told them, 'You know my name is Jihad.' He produced a mischievous grin. More seriously, he added, 'If the Germans or French occupied Washington, wouldn't you defend it?' When I suggested the attacks could be counter-productive by delaying an American pull-out, he agreed but said, 'The Americans force Iraqis to do this. I hope the US pulls its troops out of the cities and puts them in desert bases. Then it can negotiate with Iraqis about having an Iraqi government.'

On 16 May 2003, L. Paul Bremer, the head of the CPA, Washington's overlord in Iraq, issued a decree disbanding the Baath party and barring its senior members from government or public service jobs. A week later, he decreed the dissolution of the Iraqi army, the Republican Guard, the Fedayeen Saddam, and all other security and military formations from the time of the old regime. The two decrees were aimed at Iraq's Sunnis, since Sunnis were said to be the bastions of Saddam's rule and had formed the backbone of the Iraqi army since the end of the Ottoman empire. US officials argued that as a minority in Iraq, with an estimated 20 per cent of the population, Sunnis had always wielded disproportionate power. This had to be corrected.

Many of Bremer's critics saw the decrees as the CPA's biggest mistake. They were described as unintended triggers for the insurgency. As time went on and Iraq descended into chaos, this view became the conventional wisdom in Western policy circles. It was a major issue in the blame game, as leading officials in Washington and London attempted to distance themselves from the mounting disaster by claiming they had opposed the plan to dissolve the Iraqi army and ban the Baathists. Without these blunders, they argued, the occupation could have succeeded.

The decrees were foolish, but it is important to get the timing right and recall the mood in Iraq before they were published. This is why I have dealt at length in this chapter with the attitudes I and other reporters discovered in the major Sunni cities in the month before the Bremer decrees, as well as in the first few weeks afterwards. From what I saw, the occupation was already encountering hostility before Bremer took aim at the former Baathists, the Iraqi army, and the Sunnis in general.

Even in the immediate aftermath of the decrees, they were not a major issue in Ramadi and Fallujah. Opposition to the occupation was based on existing national pride and loyalty to Islam, as well as on resentment at heavy-handed US tactics in searching homes or in firing at protesters. It was led from the mosques rather than by disgruntled Baath party members or unemployed army officers.

Compared with Baghdad and the southern cities where some Iraqis expressed the 'Thank You and Goodbye' view, I never heard this kind of comment in Fallujah, Ramadi, or Tikrit. Their view was a crisp, 'Goodbye'. Was it because people in these places saw how Saddam's forces disappeared before the Americans reached them, and therefore felt there was no reason to be grateful for the arrival of foreign troops in their midst? Was it because they had a deeper suspicion of US intentions? The view that the invasion was an occupation was certainly much stronger in Fallujah and Ramadi in April 2003 than anywhere else in Iraq, as the survey cited in Chapter I made clear.

US officials gradually came to recognise that disaffection in Sunni areas was a problem that needed to be addressed. They mistakenly insisted, however, that Sunnis were upset by what the occupation had done (i.e. removed them from power) rather than by what the occupation was (i.e. an insult to Islam and a stain on the nation's honour). It re-inforced Iraqis' sense of humiliation while also challenging them to overcome their impotence and resist. Within days of the decrees, thousands of former army officers started demonstrating outside the gates into the Green Zone, carrying banners with slogans such as 'Dissolving the Iraqi army is a humiliation to the dignity of the nation.'

Bremer's supporters saw the two decrees as intimately linked. The fact that one followed so soon after the other, and marked the CPA's first stamp of authority on the 'new Iraq', was deliberate. One decree took down the regime's political pillar, the other its instruments of force, they said. This also revealed a mistaken understanding of Iraqi reality. Air Force Gen Madhloum's story in Ramadi was a graphic illustration of how senior officers were angered by Saddam and plotted against him. There were dozens of comparable cases. The military were one of the main sources of opposition to Saddam, which is why he constantly reshuffled the high command or stacked it with cronies from his own al-Bu Nasir tribe, the only people he felt he could trust.[8]

It was not just that professional officers resented Saddam's military pretensions and scorned the way he promoted himself to Field Marshal even though he had never spent a day in the army. They despised his strategic blundering. Many senior officers disagreed with the attack on Iran in 1980. Ten years later, the high command was not even told in advance of the plan to invade Kuwait.

Saddam was well aware that army officers were not instinctively loyal to him. So it is an irony that senior Americans should have believed it. If the US aim was to remove the pillars of Saddam's regime, there was no need to disband the Iraqi army in May 2003. Political necessity dictated the opposite. The CPA was more likely to create problems for itself by getting rid of the army than by purging the few officers who might be crypto-Saddamists.

There is historical evidence that some senior US officers opposed the idea of dissolving the army when it was raised several weeks before the invasion. Lieutenant Gen John Abizaid, the deputy head of Central Command, who was of Arab origin and knew the language, commented: 'What we've got to do is provide an opportunity for the Iraqi army to emerge with some honour.'[9] Gen Jay Garner, who preceded Bremer as US overlord, produced a long memo on post-war tasks, which included the point 'Postwar Use of Iraqi Regular Army: We're going to use the army. We need to use them. They have the proper skill sets.'[10]

The disbanding of the Baath party and the army made several hundred thousands of Iraqis unemployed – a significant part of the country's professional middle class. The decrees were compounded by Bremer's decision not to pay their pensions. Unrewarded and humiliated, these men resented the 'guilt by association' which implied that every army officer or party member was implicated in repression, torture, or murder. Their economic plight and their alienation from the Americans was bound to seep, through the networks of the extended family and the tribe, into the attitudes of millions of other Iraqis who were never Baathists or army officers themselves. It did not, of course, follow that they would become insurgents or even take part in funding or organising insurgents. But it might well mean that they supported the insurgent's efforts to end the occupation and would only work with the Americans with extreme reluctance.

I have deliberately concentrated in this chapter on the first few weeks of the occupation. In the welter of bloodshed that engulfed Iraq after 2005 it is easy to forget how calm and non-violent things were at the beginning, before the occupiers out-stayed their brief, initial welcome. The old British embassy in Baghdad is on Haifa Street, an area of high-rise apartments used by former Baath party and government officials. 'I used to run inside the compound in full view of the Haifa Street flats every morning. They could have popped me off at any time,' Christopher Segar, the British diplomat who re-opened the embassy after the invasion, told me. He knew the flats were full of officials from Saddam's regime 'but we were comfortable until August 2003'.[11] That was when bombers struck the Jordanian embassy and the UN headquarters in quick succession. The British then retreated to a new embassy inside the Green Zone.

In Segar's view, it was the occupation's behaviour that provoked Sunni alienation. 'The shooting in Fallujah in April 2003 created a bloodfeud,' he said. The attack figures bear that assessment out. In May 2003, armed incidents against the Americans were still rare and spasmodic. Only six soldiers died from hostile fire or other attacks. Casualties mounted in June and July as a result of a more aggressive American strategy of hunting and detaining suspects. In one six-week campaign along the Tigris valley starting some 50 miles north of Baghdad, the US military detained several thousand Iraqis and admitted killing 300. US officers told a *Washington Post* reporter they thought the war was almost won; a Central Command official said, 'I think we could be over the hump fairly quickly – possibly within a couple of months.'[12]

His optimism came to nothing. The insurgency gradually grew in strength, spreading west and south into the so-called Sunni triangle. A cycle developed of insurgent attacks, a heavy US response, then more attacks.

In March 2004, it was Fallujah's turn. The city hit the headlines for the first time for almost a year when a car carrying four armed Americans working for the security company Blackwater came under attack on the city's main street on 31 March. The men were pulled from the disabled vehicle and killed. Their bodies were then mutilated and dragged through the dust. Two corpses were left hanging from a bridge over the Euphrates.

Apart from the bestiality of the bodies' treatment, the incident shocked Americans because it seemed totally unprovoked. The media described the men as civilians and their murder was written up as though it came like lightning out of a blue sky. In fact, Iraqi anger towards the Americans in and around Fallujah had been growing for weeks, unreported. Home-made roadside bombs, which the Americans called IEDs (improvised explosive devices), were hitting Humvees, oil tankers, and other occupation vehicles with increasing frequency throughout January and February 2004. Survivors who jumped out were often struck by grenades and small-arms fire. Iraqis saw contractors in their conspicuous SUVs as an adjunct of the US army, which indeed they were.

This atmosphere of rising tension coincided with the long-planned transfer of operations in Anbar province on 20 March from the 82nd Airborne Division to the Marines under Lt Gen James Conway. The new commander decided to make his mark early by showing the people of Fallujah there was not going to be any lull while his troops got to know the area. They had barely arrived at their base a mile outside the city when Conway launched a series of heavy raids and house searches over a period of several days.

It was too dangerous for journalists to cover since we did not know where the Americans would strike and how much resistance they would meet.

However, the US military's daily communiqués, listing a handful of US casualties and the killing of 18 suspected insurgents, indicated that something bigger than usual was under way.

On Saturday 27 March I drove to Fallujah with my interpreter. We started in the suburb of Jumhuriya just north of the main road that slices from east to west through the city. The streets here are wide, and many of the houses had palmtrees in their gardens and bougainvillaea trailing over the high, sand-coloured front walls. It was a pleasant, apparently affluent area, but on that morning it seemed uncannily quiet, with only a handful of people and cars moving about. We entered one of the few open shops, a small grocery store on a corner, and asked whether the Americans had been in Jumhuriya. The question unleashed a torrent of anger, and we were promptly taken on a tour of the suburb where residents showed us the results of the four days and nights of US incursions.

Rockets from helicopter gunships had punctured bedroom walls. Patio floors and front gates were pockmarked by shrapnel. Car doors looked like sieves. People pointed to rooftops where they said US snipers had taken position. Residents gave the impression that the Americans had a monopoly of violence but I occasionally heard the word *muqawama* (resistance). My interpreter confided later that he had been advised by our interviewees not to tell me there were any armed Iraqis around during the American incursion. He broke the rule on one occasion when the notion of armed defence was raised in a general context. 'The United States is indirectly supporting the resistance by targeting innocent people. It makes us more sympathetic to the resistance,' he quoted Shaban Rajab, a middle-aged resident as saying while we inspected a huge hole in the wall of his living room, caused by some heavy weaponry.

For Tha'ir Turki and his siblings the Americans piled insult onto injury. A handsome man in his early twenties, he pointed out the blood stains by the front gate where his father had been shot and killed at 2am. While they attended his wake later in the day, more grim news arrived. 'Don't go home,' a group of neighbours warned them. 'The Americans are in there.' The grieving family had to sleep with friends or at their grandfather's house until word came that the Americans had pulled out at dawn the next day.

'Even if there was some resistance from among [us] here, what have we done? Our women and girls are not part of it,' Tha'ir Turki insisted, as he showed the trail of chaos the Marines had left in their home. Its position on the corner of two streets made it a good place for soldiers to keep watch while the rest slept. Cupboards were ransacked, a computer had gone, and empty brown plastic bags that once contained army rations (MREs – Meals Ready To Eat) littered every room. Tha'ir was particularly upset at finding them in his teenage sisters' bedroom. Little jewel boxes were scattered across the dresser, their lids off. Women's clothes had been pulled out of drawers.

Like the residents of Fallujah's Nazal suburb, who were outraged at having their school occupied the previous year, the people of Jumhuriya were ordinary families. The US incursions were bound to wound their sense of pride and honour and create a desire for retaliation after their homes and neighbourhoods were violated and their relatives killed. I was not surprised when I heard of the four contractors' murder, on the edge of Jumhuriya, four days later. Far from coming out of the blue, it looked like Jumhuriya's response to several days and nights of being under US attack. The people of Fallujah make no secret of having a revenge culture.

The US military, by contrast, would never acknowledge revenge as a motivation. However, the assault on Fallujah that the Marines mounted after the contractors' killing had all its hallmarks. Even though community leaders in Fallujah had condemned the mutilation of the contractors' bodies, describing it as un-Islamic and inhuman, a strike force of several hundred Marines surrounded the city in preparation for what was called 'Operation Vigilant Resolve'. Access by journalists and other Western visitors was blocked. Iraqi police were told to distribute US military leaflets at the mosques, imposing a daily 7pm to 6am curfew and ordering people not to congregate in groups or carry weapons, even if licensed. If American troops entered their homes, residents should gather in one room and if they wanted to talk to the troops, keep their hands up.

Officially, the aim was to capture the people who had killed the contractors and bring them to justice. Nevertheless, the size of the force suggested broader goals. The Marines wanted to smash the insurgency in Fallujah once and for all. Instead of adopting police methods to try to locate the contractors' murderers, the aim was to use military force to warn the entire town to abandon resistance to the occupation.

The assault began on 6 April when US warplanes went into action in the first aerial attack on a city since the invasion. Firing rockets, they destroyed four houses. Overall 26 Iraqis, including women and children, were killed, and 30 wounded in this one strike, according to a doctor at the main hospital.[13] The main hospital in Fallujah was hit by US tank and missile fire overnight. Hospital sources said the next day at least 45 Iraqis were killed and 90 injured.[14] On 9 and 10 April fierce confrontations left over 300 dead and 500 wounded.[15] Thousands of people fled the city by car.

As should have been predicted, the carnage failed to end the resistance; it had the opposite effect. In Baghdad, the political reaction was dramatic. Several members of the US-appointed governing council, including the interim president Ghazi al-Yawer, denounced the US attack. Adnan Pachachi, a distinguished former foreign minister from pre-Saddam days who was known for his normally moderate views, described it as 'collective punishment' of the people of Fallujah. The US assault also produced an outpouring of solidarity from Baghdad's Shia community. Scores of Sunni refugees were taken in by Shias in the western Baghdad suburb of Shula, one of the first suburbs reached on the road from Fallujah. The simplistic Western notion that Sunnis and Shias were natural enemies was not borne out.

On Friday 9 April, the anniversary of the fall of Baghdad, and while the Marines' assault was still under way, a huge rally was held in the grounds of the vast Sunni mosque, Umm al-Qura. With its extensive colonnades and side offices the mosque compound had been taken over after the invasion by the Association of Muslim Scholars, a radical group of Sunni Islamists who were to act as intermediaries with the insurgency as it grew stronger. That Friday the grounds were packed. Scores of young men had climbed on to some rickety scaffolding near the front steps. One held a picture of Moqtada al-Sadr, the Shia cleric who had become a hero in Baghdad's Shia suburb. The largely Sunni crowd chanted anti-occupation slogans, as well as support for Fallujah, but the pro-Shia chant 'Long live Moqtada' also rang out, as well as 'No to sectarianism, no to ethnicity, yes to Islamic unity'. One man carried a banner saying, 'The palm trees of Iraq will turn into swords in the attackers' faces just as the olive branches of Palestine do in the faces of the Zionists.'

When the prayers started, my translator Wail advised me to be discreet. We had seen no other foreign journalists around. I would look odd if I was not going down on my knees, so I took cover in a small outhouse in the mosque grounds while Wail made notes of the speeches. Dr Harith al-Dhari, the chairman of the Association of Muslim Scholars, was in fiery mood. He thundered:

The Americans invaded the land of Iraq a year ago, but not the people or their souls. With his ally, the British devil Tony Blair, the Americans launched their attacks. A year has passed but where is the democracy they promised? Instead, we have terror and censorship and rivers of blood. We want the coalition to leave this country.

Many Iraqis had started to suspect the Americans of trying to stir up sectarian tensions as a policy of 'divide and rule'. Dr al-Dhari warned the crowd against it, shouting, 'The Americans describe themselves as a barrier against sectarian war, but all Iraqi factions are showing their solidarity.' At the end of the impassioned rally many were weeping. Others punched the air with their fists. As people started to move off, I emerged nervously from my hiding place. I need not have worried. An elderly man broke from the crowd and politely asked me what country I was from. On hearing I was British, he produced a piece of A4 paper and thrust it into my hands. On it were the neatly printed words: 'No dignity with occupation'.

The pressure from within Iraq's governing council as well as the adverse media coverage forced the Americans to announce a ceasefire so that a delegation from the governing council could enter Fallujah to talk to community and religious leaders. The Marines had tried to give their operation a partial Iraqi face. Five battalions of the newly formed Iraqi Civil Defence Corps had been sent to Fallujah, but two refused to fight against fellow Iraqis. This also undermined the US position. On 29 April, the USA agreed to withdraw to the city's outskirts and lift the siege.[16]

The occupation was just one year old, and it ought to have become clear to the US and British governments that keeping troops in Iraq was the problem, not the solution. The longer they remained, the more the insurgency would grow. In April 2004 US sources estimated the size of the insurgency as 5,000. By April 2005 they estimated it as 16,000. The US presence in Iraq had become a magnet for Al-Qaeda and other foreign jihadis with an anti-Western agenda. They welcomed the chance to kill Americans, and they were successful. Between May 2003 and March 2004 the monthly average of US troop deaths from hostile action was 23. A year later it was almost three times as high.

US officials should have foreseen this. They should also have expected that, regardless of Al-Qaeda's involvement, Iraqis themselves would increasingly support armed resistance, even if they did not take a direct part in it.

Insurgents who are part of a local civilian population first have to be isolated before they can be eliminated. As long as they can rely on cover, protection, and help from non-combatants, they will always be able to avoid being hunted down by outsiders. A poll carried out by the Iraq Centre for Research and Strategic Studies in May 2004 found that 66 per cent opposed the presence of coalition forces in Iraq, while 41 per cent said they would feel safer if they withdrew. Only 32 per cent said they would feel less safe.[17]

The deputy director of the Central Intelligence Agency (CIA), John McLaughlin, wrote a classified briefing note in November 2003 entitled 'Who is the Enemy?'. It identified four groups behind the insurgency: former Baathists who wanted to restore Saddam to power; foreign fighters; Iraqi nationalists who hated the occupation; and tribal members angry over the death of family and the insensitive kicking down of doors and heavy-handed house searching by US troops.[18] Other US officials conceded that the number of foreign fighters never constituted more than 10 per cent of the insurgency. I attended several of Bremer's press conferences where he was asked about the insurgency and who was behind it. McLaughlin's last two categories were never mentioned in his answer. Was this deliberate spin or, as a neoconservative, could Bremer not bring himself to accept that many Iraqis had legitimate reasons for taking up arms against the Americans, and that they outnumbered the foreigners in the insurgents' ranks?

With their invasion and the refusal to name a date for withdrawal, the Americans had dug a well of anger and unhappiness in Iraq's Sunni areas that they were never able to drain. The occupation had created the resistance and there was no way to end it without ending the occupation itself.

IV

CREATING RESISTANCE: THE SHIAS

Iraq is one of the most invaded and violated territories in the history of the world, and over a long period of time the people developed survival and accommodation skills that would confound the most determined of occupiers. None of this should have come as a surprise.

Ali Allawi, *The Occupation of Iraq*[1]

A s preparations for the Iraq invasion accelerated throughout 2002, the Bush administration assumed the country's Arab Shias would be its most important allies.

For Iraq's entire history Shias had been dominated by Sunni rulers, of whom the worst was undoubtedly Saddam. Many had risen up against him at the end of the first Gulf War and been brutally repressed. Thousands of Shias were gunned down by Saddam's helicopters. The leaders of the uprising were arrested and executed. The Shia revolt was not confined to south-eastern Iraq. Violence also erupted in Saddam City, Baghdad's poor, overcrowded, and largely Shia suburb where crowds overwhelmed police stations and the offices of the intelligence service, the *mukhabarat*, before being beaten back.

Shias would surely welcome being liberated now that a new opportunity for removing Saddam was emerging 12 years later, Bush's officials believed. US troops moving north-west from Kuwait along the river Euphrates towards Baghdad would pass through friendly territory. Resistance would be minimal and it was highly probable that US forces' first real fight, the battle for Baghdad, would also be their last. The Iraqi capital was the only place where Saddam's forces were expected to make a stand.

Washington also expected no problem with the Kurds. They too were bound be delighted to see US and British troops topple Saddam Hussein. They had suffered massive atrocities at his orders in the 1980s, and since 1991 were living with precarious autonomy enforced by a US-imposed no-fly zone. Having the dictator removed would strengthen that autonomy and bring them a stage closer to eventual independence for Kurdistan.

However enthusiastically the Kurds endorsed and assisted the US invasion, the Arab Shias mattered more. They were Iraq's majority community, living in the country's southern heartland as well as having a substantial presence in and around Baghdad. Their support for the invasion would ensure that the subsequent occupation also ran smoothly.

US officials saw no reason why the Shias would not back the US project for a modern, secular, and pro-Western system for Iraq. It was predicted that they would participate eagerly in the transition to Iraq's first free administration once Saddam was toppled, since their demographic majority would guarantee Shia control over parliament and the committees to draw up a constitution as well as an eventual national government. The neoconservatives even had their Shia candidate for Iraq's new president waiting in the wings. He was Ahmad Chalabi, a secular Westernised millionaire businessman who ran the exiles' Iraqi National Congress and had had close contacts with the Pentagon for many years.

However, the decision-makers in Washington and London failed to appreciate three crucial factors. First, feelings of Iraqi nationalism were just as strong among Arab Shias as among Arab Sunnis, with the result that Shia support for liberation would not guarantee support for occupation. Support would have to be earned, it could not be taken for granted.

Second, they did not see that while there was a coincidence of view between them and the Shia leaders over the value of electoral democracy, this did not translate into majority Shia backing for secular politics or power-sharing with other religious, ethnic, and sectarian groups. The dominant forces in the Shia community were Islamists and they saw elections as a simple device for introducing their own sect's permanent rule. They were not well disposed towards political compromises, let alone a system in which individual rights rather than sectarian solidarity had the upper hand. On social issues they were conservative. To them political power was a way of enforcing rigid standards of dress and behaviour that were very different from those of the secular exiles whom the Americans favoured.

The third point is that the Shia Islamists were not united. There were three powerful trends among them, and as these trends competed with each other for recognition and authority within the Shia community, one major terrain for rivalry would be the degree to which any group or leader was seen to be pro- or anti-American. It would be hard for any Islamist leader to endorse a Western occupation and retain his credentials as a good Muslim. Not just in Iraq but throughout the Middle East, many Arabs turned to Islamist parties precisely because of their frustration with the long history of Western intervention and what they saw as its disrespect for their culture and traditions. Iraqi Shia cooperation with the occupying authorities would be grudging and short-lived at best. It was more likely that Shias would choose to confront them, especially if Washington and London refused to give any signal that they would soon be withdrawing their forces and leaving Iraqis to run Iraq themselves.

How could Bush's pre-invasion assumptions about the Shias have been so dramatically wrong? Were these errors which anyone might have made and which only appear as mistakes with the benefit of hindsight? Regrettably, no. A little reading of Iraqi history and some awareness of the nature of Shia Islamism in Iraq could and should have prevented them.

In relation to recent history, the Bush administration failed to understand that Shia memories of the uprising of 1991 and Saddam's response to it were not as clear-cut as thought by Washington and London. Many Shias considered George Bush senior to have deceived them after Saddam's defeat in Kuwait by calling for a rebellion against the dictator but doing nothing to help. US forces had soundly beaten Iraqi ground troops in Kuwait by obliterating them in their barracks and trenches, but chose not to destroy Saddam's helicopters as they mowed down the Shia rebels inside Iraq. To Shias it looked like a failure of nerve in the White House at best, and a cynical betrayal at worst. In either case, it was yet another humiliation and affront to dignity in a centuries-long narrative in which foreigners called the shots. Once again, Arabs were being treated as playthings, expected to perform or be punished at the whim of an outsider.

Bush junior and his advisers had equally little awareness of the effect that the sanctions imposed in 1990 had on Iraqis. The sanctions amounted to a full trade embargo with some exceptions for food and medicine. The initial purpose was to press Saddam to withdraw from Kuwait, but they remained in force under a revised mandate once the war was over. The new purpose, ostensibly, was to press Saddam to dismantle his programmes for weapons of mass destruction, to block exports to Iraq that might help him develop such weapons, and to get him to cooperate with the UN weapons inspectors.

Sanctions were part of the US policy of 'containment', designed to keep Saddam's regime weak and gradually open up possibilities for it to change. Under Clinton in the 1990s Washington's main hope was remove Saddam, while effectively maintaining his regime intact. There were attempts at encouraging a palace coup, the so-called 'silver bullet solution'.

Containment strengthened Iraqis' widely held conviction that the USA was actually conniving to keep Saddam in power, while making the Iraqi people suffer the catastrophic consequences of sanctions. Sanctions left the country on its knees. Iraq's infrastructure crumbled because spare parts could not be imported for power stations, hospital equipment, water treatment plants and a host of other facilities, on the grounds they might be diverted for military purposes. This prohibition of 'dual-use' items was so strict that even lead pencils could not be imported. A UN committee sat in New York to oversee every category of product intended for Iraq. The US and UK representatives on the sanctions committee always took the hardest line, so the impression went back to Iraqis that these two countries were in charge. 'Fathers had to sell their daughters to get money. It was the worst time in our lives,' a woman in her thirties told me in Basra.[2] Coping with daily hardships to feed their families meant Iraqis had little time or scope for political activities to overthrow the regime – even if they wanted to take the risk after all the repression that had already happened.

Sanctions served mainly to strengthen Saddam. They created an economy of need in which every family's key to survival was to have good connections with people in the regime who could provide favours, jobs, or direct forms of help, including food. By handing power to selected tribal chiefs and religious leaders to act as his agents, Saddam set up a shadow state based on these survival networks, as the British historian Charles Tripp has pointed out:

> Secular Iraqi professionals, several generations removed from their rural forebears, found themselves swearing allegiance to the sheikh of their 'tribe' or submitting to the local imam in an attempt to find protection. Both winners and losers were systematically brutalised and humiliated in the process.[3]

Iraqis saw that sanctions did nothing to curtail the life of luxury led by Saddam and other senior members of his regime. For Iraq's people, however, they were collective punishment. Politically and psychologically, the sanctions strategy reminded Iraqis that to get rid of a bad Iraqi leader it was foreigners, and specifically non-Arabs and Westerners, who were setting the agenda. The humiliation of being regarded by the world as a pariah state was compounded by the message that Iraqis were not in a position to provide their own remedies. Some Western critics of sanctions opposed them precisely on these grounds. Only if Iraqis were able to live normal economic lives would they have the energy to find solutions to the Saddam problem via political resistance or organising to remove him. The task would not be easy, but at least Iraqis would be taking their own decisions instead of having regime change engineered from abroad.

This line of thinking was not acceptable in Washington or London. Every time a few UN member states even hinted at lifting sanctions, the USA fiercely opposed it. An Oil-for-Food programme was set up under UN control, which allowed Iraq to export a certain quantity of oil per year in return for food and humanitarian items. Although the amount was tripled in 1996 to allow more items to be imported, it was too little to avoid a severe humanitarian crisis inside Iraq. Between 400,000 and 800,000 children are estimated to have died because of poor diet, disease, and hospital shortages of drugs and other medical equipment during the sanctions decade. Denis Halliday, the UN Humanitarian Coordinator in Baghdad, resigned in 1998 saying sanctions were killing up to 7,000 children under the age of five every month and the programme undermined 'the moral leadership and credibility of the United Nations itself'.[4] Madeleine Albright, Clinton's secretary of state, rejected this, commenting at one moment that the death of half a million Iraqi children during the sanctions period was 'worth it' because sanctions were containing Saddam.[5] Her remarks confirmed many Iraqis in their view that US policy towards their country was cynical.

Other UN officials were also unhappy. Sergio Vieira de Mello, the UN special representative sent to Iraq after the invasion, made a practice of referring to sanctions in his speeches. He realised how hard they had been for Iraqis. A consummate diplomat, he never publicly accused Washington or London but his mere mention of sanctions showed he understood Iraqi thinking, in contrast to Bremer who never mentioned them. When Bremer referred to Saddam's period he talked only of the repression, torture, murder, and unnecessary wars. Sanctions were air-brushed out of the picture in a clear sign that US officials had no inkling of the misery they had caused or the fact that Iraqis blamed the USA and Britain for sanctions as much as Saddam. In Iraqi eyes Bremer's myopia was not just insensitive; it demonstrated that foreigners could never be relied on to behave other than in the ways they always had.

If Bush and Blair were weak on recent Iraqi history and its negative impact on their nations' reputation, they seemed totally unaware of more distant events, in particular Britain's colonial role in Iraq. The parallels were uncanny. Almost every issue that confronted the new occupiers had arisen generations before under the British. Almost every Iraqi reaction echoed that of their great-grandparents.

Britain's invasion had started with the capture of Basra in 1915, followed by the fall of Baghdad two years later. Some Iraqis were willing to accept British rule in preference to rule by the Turks. Others, like the young Arab nationalists who formed al-'Ahd al-Iraqi (the Iraqi Covenant), called for Iraq's independence. British officials hesitated, torn between an outright takeover of Iraq and the argument put forward by Gertrude Bell, a maverick traveller and archaeologist, who had joined the British administration with the title of Oriental Secretary. She favoured a system of indirect rule in which Iraqis took political decisions under British supervision. This looked better than full colonial rule. The similarity to what the Americans would try to do in Baghdad in 2003 is striking.

Of course the historical circumstances were not identical, and Gertrude Bell's version of partial democracy gave prominence to Iraq's secular Sunnis rather than the Shia majority. She thought 'the British should work with the largely urban and Sunni nationalists to modernise the country and end what she regarded as the reactionary and obscurantist influence of the Shia clerics and their tribal followings,' as Tripp puts it.[6]

While the British argued among themselves about the best way to run Iraq, rebellion stirred among Iraqis. In Baghdad in the spring of 1920 huge protest meetings were held alternately in Sunni and Shia mosques, bringing both sectarian communities together to denounce the mandate over Iraq that the League of Nations had awarded Britain. Armed revolt broke out in June, led by Shia clerics and tribal leaders, after Ayatollah Mohammed Taqi al-Shirazi, the senior Shia cleric, issued a fatwa calling for it. The revolt was put down with enormous brutality as the Royal Air Force bombed towns and villages that supported the rebels. On the ground the British brought in Indian troops as reinforcements. At least 6,000, perhaps as many as 9,000, Iraqis were killed, compared with 500 British and Indian deaths.[7]

The revolt was crushed but the turbulence convinced London to go for Bell's scheme for indirect rule. Sir Arnold Wilson, the newly appointed British high commissioner, was the forerunner of Washington's L. Paul Bremer – a foreign overlord whose total power over a subject people was concealed, but not reduced, by the fact that a council of hand-picked Iraqi ministers implemented his decisions. The council was chosen, like Bremer's, on sectarian lines. It had a majority of Sunnis, a few Shias and Christians, and one Jew. British 'advisers' were attached to every ministry, just as were US ones in 2003.

Wilson was a very different personality from Bremer, a soldier as well as an administrator, and a scholar on the languages and culture of Iraq, as William Polk, the veteran Arabic-speaking American historian and diplomat, has pointed out. Yet, for all his academic expertise on Iraq, Wilson was contemptuous of Iraqis' abilities, even more so than Bremer. According to Polk, 'He did not expect advice and he would not tolerate opposition from the natives.'[8]

On one issue, Wilson and Bremer were similar: they were both blind to the true state of majority opinion in Iraq. Wilson once reported to London: 'The Iraqi Arab, as opposed to the handful of amateur politicians of Baghdad, sees the future as one of fair dealing and material and moral progress under the aegis of Britain ... The Arabs are content with our occupation.'[9]

Arrogance and amateurism were deeply embedded in the British colonial system at all levels (again, not unlike Bremer's CPA where volunteers from Washington were given huge responsibilities in Iraq with minimal qualifications or experience). One young British civil servant described how he was given control over Kirkuk in March 1918: 'Wilson flew up in an RAF aircraft, had a bit of lunch and a talk, said, "You have full powers, judicial and financial", and flew off again.'[10] At a conference in Lausanne that was asked to agree on the borders between Iraq and Turkey, the British Foreign Office lost the report of a plebiscite of local leaders' wishes that had been conducted by British colonial officers. So a junior official who had read the original was permitted to summarise it from memory for the delegates. It later turned out he got the border line wrong.[11]

Winston Churchill, Britain's colonial secretary at the time, called a conference in Cairo in March 1921 to modify the system of indirect rule. Although described as an international conference, it did not involve Arabs from across the Middle East. Cairo just happened to be a convenient midpoint in the British empire and the site of Britain's headquarters in the region. British military and civilian officials converged on the Egyptian capital from London, India, Jerusalem, Basra, and Baghdad. The only foreigners invited were two Iraqi ministers.

The conference decided to impose a monarchy on Iraq. The throne would be offered to Faisal, a non-Iraqi Sunni from the Hashemite family who had worked with T.E. Lawrence (Lawrence of Arabia) in the Arab revolt against the Ottomans. In Tripp's words, 'he was well aware that most of the inhabitants of Iraq either knew nothing of his existence or saw little reason why he should be installed as ruler of the country'.[12] For Iraqis it was yet another insult and humiliation, as well as a reminder of their impotence. Throwing off the Ottomans had been a victory for the Arab cause, but what followed? Another group of foreigners – this time not even Muslims – took over and decided who should rule Iraq.

Faisal and the new elite in Iraq's council of ministers found themselves in the classic quandary of puppet rulers everywhere. To satisfy the nationalist sentiments of the Iraqi population as well as their own ambitions, they wanted greater powers leading ultimately to full independence. On the other hand, they also realised they would need the colonial overseers' support for some time to come. They could not afford to challenge them directly. Once again, the echoes of what was to happen in Iraq in the summer of 2004 are obvious. The Americans appointed a prime minister and his key Cabinet ministers and promised the new government sovereignty, even as they continued to hold the country under military occupation. The new Iraqi government continually sought greater powers but never dared to demand a US troop withdrawal.

As Iraqis' dissatisfaction with their subordinate status increased throughout the 1920s, the British came to see they would have to make further concessions, or at least find a constitutional arrangement that looked more democratic. This time the device they picked was to put their relations with Iraq into treaty form, as if Iraq and Britain were two sovereign states making a normal bilateral agreement. In fact, the treaty was unequal. It gave Britain final authority on all defence, financial, and international matters.

The new council of ministers gradually started to flex its growing muscles. In an effort to satisfy Iraq's nationalists, it told the British the treaty would have to be ratified by elected representatives. They suggested there should be an elected constituent assembly. Their demand was a response to rising impatience, particularly among the Shias. As Iraq's largest community, they wanted their weight to be acknowledged through the ballot box.

With the electoral genie out of the bottle, a new stage in the anti-British struggle was reached. How genuine would the election system be? The British insisted on an indirect poll with a restricted franchise, whereupon several of the '*mujtahids*', the Shia religious leaders in the holy cities of Kerbala and Najaf, issued fatwas calling on Shias not to take part.

Trapped in the middle, King Faisal decided to take the British side. He had the most prominent *mujtahid*, Ayatollah Mahdi al-Khalisi, arrested and deported. The ayatollah took up residence in Iran (then still known in the West as Persia), and was joined by several other leading clerics who preferred exile to the repression of Iraq. However, the Shias were not united. Faisal and the British had wooed many tribal sheikhs with offers of cash, positions, and local backing from the state. Among the secular politicians some felt it was worth participating in the elections in the hope of gradually squeezing the system open. Others saw no chance. Many Shia clerics found the dilemma overwhelming. They chose to retreat from politics altogether in favour of a return to the tradition of scholarship and jurisprudence. From now on they would confine their public utterances to issues of social and individual morality. Thanks to the splits among the Shias, the indirectly elected constituent assembly managed to approve the pro-British treaty – though by a very narrow majority.

Below the surface resentments continued to grow. Nevertheless it still took almost another decade of struggle and protest before Iraqis persuaded the League of Nations to remove Britain's mandate over Iraq. The League recognised Iraq's independence in 1932.

Those Iraqis who hoped British influence over their country was at last at an end, 15 years after the British occupation began, were soon disappointed. Thanks to its treaty rights as well as the links it had with the Iraqi elite, Britain still held enormous sway, expressed through control of the economy as much as via direct pressure on politicians. When oil was discovered in 1927, Britain had ensured the new Iraq Petroleum Company (IPC) was registered in London. Every share was foreign-owned and one of the largest stakes was in the hands of the Anglo-Persian oil company, which the British government controlled. As a result Iraq's official relations with Britain remained closely intertwined for the next quarter of a century.

For most Shias the key event in modern Iraqi history was the overthrow of the monarchy on 14 July 1958 by an army coup. General Abdul Karim Qassim, the new leader, had a Kurdish Shia mother and a Sunni Arab father. This made him the first Iraqi leader with a strong personal commitment to a united Iraq. He and his fellow officers had a popular nationalist agenda of social reform, much influenced by the Free Officers' Movement under Nasser that had removed the Egyptian monarchy in 1953 and sought to end British influence in Egypt. Qassim and his brother officers were determined to ensure that after centuries of foreign occupation Iraq's fate should finally rest in Iraqi hands.

They ended the treaty with Britain, ordered British forces to leave Iraq, and pulled out of an agreement the monarchy had signed with the USA for the supply of weaponry and military equipment. They lifted the ban on the Communist party, passed a radical land redistribution law, supported workers' rights, and invested heavily in health care, education, and public housing. They brought in Law 80, which took back all the oil concessions the foreign-owned IPC had been granted but were not yet using, effectively shutting the company out of future exploration and development.

Because Shias formed the bulk of Iraq's underclass, they benefited most from the new regime's reforms. Thousands of landless Shias moved from the countryside to Baghdad where they received subsidised housing in what was known as Revolution City, later renamed Saddam City (and now Sadr City). Emigration to the cities had started during the 1940s and 1950s as a result of the dire conditions for the peasantry in the south and mid-Euphrates, but it accelerated after 1958.

Ideas of social reform were not the monopoly of the new regime. They were also promoted by the Communist party and the Baath party, an Arab nationalist movement that favoured pan-Arab unification over Qassim's 'Iraq-first' agenda. Iraq's next decade and a half were marked by constant rivalry and occasional collaboration between the Communists and the Baathists. The Baathists always came out best. Qassim and his nationalist officers had thousands of Communists imprisoned or executed. Others were assassinated by extremist nationalists and Baathists between 1959 and 1961.

The Baathists finally ousted Qassim in a coup in 1963 with help from the US CIA, which disliked his anti-Western nationalism.

In toppling the monarchy, Qassim and his brother officers had brought the army into play as a political force for the third time in Iraq's recent history. Earlier army coups had taken place in 1936 and 1941. The Qassim coup was different, however, in that its leaders tried to engineer a major social revolution, a precedent the Baathists were to develop massively as they turned the state's security apparatus into a formidable machine for internal repression and external adventure after they seized power.

Qassim's period was marked by see-sawing attitudes to civil liberties, as political parties and public demonstrations were permitted one day and banned the next at the ruler's whim – another trend the Baathists were to magnify, particularly after Saddam became their leader. Nevertheless, it was no surprise when posters of Qassim suddenly re-emerged on the streets of Baghdad after the American invasion The 45th anniversary of the toppling of the monarchy happened to fall a few weeks after US troops reached Baghdad, and on 14 July 2003 scores of people carried Qassim's pictures in demonstrations marking the occasion. Qassim was still revered by many older Iraqis as a social reformer and nationalist who had stood up to dominant foreign powers.

Yet the abiding lesson of Qassim's brief years as Iraq's leader, and the much longer and bloodier Baathist rule that followed under Saddam Hussein, was yet another humiliation for Iraqis. Here at last were rulers who were Iraqi nationalists and who paid lip service to pan-Arabism. The problem was that while they tried or appeared to try to realise their people's aspirations for unity and development they became dictators. Having rid themselves of self-serving foreigners, Iraqis now found themselves ruled by self-serving cliques. It was bound to fuel a new sense of shame, frustration, and anger.

If Qassim was a nationalist with some respect for principles, Saddam's nationalism was opportunistic. He had no qualms about taking help from any convenient source, not excluding the USA, which had joined in toppling Qassim and bringing the Baathists to power. In 1975 Washington helped Saddam and the Shah of Iran to crush the Kurdish nationalist movement. Donald Rumsfeld visited Saddam in 1983 to launch close US–Iraqi collaboration in the war with Ayatollah Khomeini's Iran. It led to Baghdad being supplied with invaluable US satellite pictures of Iran's troop deployment, as well as poison gas technology from German and other Western companies. At the time of the 2003 invasion many Iraqis remembered these facts. Perhaps it relieved their sense of shame to feel (and it was not far from the truth) that Saddam was not a nationalist at all. He was a creation and plaything of the West. This meant that, like Arabs in virtually every other Middle Eastern state, Iraqis too were ruled by a puppet.

This was a point many Iraqis made in the months that followed Saddam's fall. Some used the phrase '*Rah al sani', ija al ussta*' – 'gone is the apprentice, in comes the master'. Many Western reporters and coalition officials had difficulty in taking the point seriously. They tended to write it off as crazy anti-Americanism or proof of 'the Arab love of conspiracy theories'. Brought up with the view that Saddam was the most anti-Western leader in the Arab world and that the US neoconservatives wanted to remove him in large part because he was too independent, many Westerners failed to see how Saddam appeared to Iraqi eyes. To them he was a Frankenstein's monster, a Western artefact that had gone out of its master's control.

Some Iraqis rather admired him for that. Although they were the ones who suffered from his vicious dictatorship, they liked it when he fired SCUD missiles at Israel in 1991 and refused to give in to US and British threats in 2002 and 2003. Millions of people in the 'Arab street' shared these feelings.

For most Iraqis, whether they admired Saddam's anti-Western defiance or, more frequently, loathed and feared his brutality and paranoia, the crucial point was that he fitted into the country's long tradition of bad rulers. Whether they were led by foreigners, Iraqi puppets, or self-styled patriots, the people of Iraq and in particular its poorest community, the Shias, had never enjoyed freedom or fairness. Over centuries this could not help but fill a deep well of anger.

In Iraq and the rest of the Arab world, nationalism was not the same as nationalism in Europe. In nineteenth- and twentieth-century Europe nations built identities around language, a shared culture, and memories of generations of resistance to foreign occupiers. In the Arab world economic issues added an extra emotional component. Opposition to unjust systems of land tenure, landlessness, laws that favoured foreigners, and restrictions on local business development played a key part in creating a shared sense of identity. Nationalist movements in Europe rarely had the same ingredients of anger and revenge for past discrimination as those felt by Arabs.

The culture of the times also matters. Seeking independence in a world that was not yet globalised was different from doing it at the turn of the twenty-first century, when satellite television and the Internet magnify the sense of oppression and shrink the opportunities for real change. Those who come late always feel at a special disadvantage. Having been so long under outside rule, can they really break free – and stay free – at last?

With their gloomy history and this backlog of frustration and disappointment it was hardly surprising that when Saddam finally fell from power Iraqis would want to ensure their hopes of independence would not be thwarted again. Washington and London should have understood that a new occupation was the last thing Iraqis wanted.

While breathing new life into Iraq's secular parties, the atmosphere of radical change following the overthrow of the monarchy in 1958 also gave a boost to Islamism. Here was a whole new strand in Iraq's politics that was to grow over subsequent decades, which Bush and his war planners underestimated. They did not realise that one of the main consequences of Saddam's removal would be the resurgence of Islamist parties, giving them a chance to dominate Iraq's new political spectrum. This was seriously to undermine US neoconservatives' hopes of implanting Western liberal democratic institutions.

It would also create a powerful pole of opposition to the occupation, since most Islamists would not accept a non-Muslim army of soldiers and political missionaries in their midst. The Arab brand of Islamism was an expression, in different language, of the same demand for dignity and self-determination that secular nationalists were also raising. Those nationalists and Islamists who did work with the occupation always had to justify it as a temporary expedient or a necessary evil.

Sunnis and Shias had come together to form the Islamic party in Iraq in 1960. Its leader was a Sunni but the main sponsor was Ayatollah Mohsin al-Hakim, the patriarch of one of the best-known Shia clerical families. Other Sunnis founded the Muslim Brotherhood based on the model of similar organisations in Egypt and Syria. (After Saddam's fall the Islamic party re-emerged, this time as a largely Sunni party, incorporating many members from the Brotherhood.) Among the Shias in the 1960s the main religious party was Dawa (the Call), led by a member of another prominent Shia family, Mohammed Baqir al-Sadr. Rivalry between these two powerful families, the Sadrs and the Hakims, would continue until the present day.

None of the new religious parties wanted to confront General Qassim and his military regime, but they were concerned to challenge the atheism of the then relatively powerful Communist party as well as the secular tone that was dominating public discourse. Radical in attempting to enlist a mass following, they were conservative in their views. They opposed land reform on the grounds that expropriation went against Sharia law. The Hakim family was particularly anti-communist. Grand Ayatollah Muhsin Hakim issued a fatwa in 1960 ordering people not to join the Communist party and three years later put out another, which authorised the killing of communists.

When Saddam took power he clamped down on all religious parties. Islamic schools were closed and clergy were executed, prompting large protest demonstrations in Najaf, Kerbala, and Basra. Saddam focused his attention on the Shias, partly because of the size of their community but also because their clerics were more practised in mobilising their followers than the Sunni clergy. In July 1979, fearing Iraq's Shias would take a lead from the newly triumphant Shia revolution in neighbouring Iran, Saddam arrested Ayatollah Mohammed Baqir al-Sadr. He and his sister were executed the following year. Another top Shia cleric, Ayatollah Abu al-Qasim al-Khoei, was put under house arrest and tens of thousands of Shias were deported to Iran, on the spurious grounds that they were not Iraqis. Several senior members of the Hakim family fled to Iran; others were killed.

In spite of this repression the religious movements were still the major force in Shia opposition to Saddam two decades later. Inside Iraq it was the Sadrs, outside Iraq it was the Hakims.

In exile in Tehran Mohammed Baqir al-Hakim, the son of Grand Ayatollah Muhsin Hakim, was given strong support by the new Iranian regime. Baqir created the Supreme Council for the Islamic Revolution in Iraq (SCIRI) in the early 1980s. The aim was to unite all the various anti-Saddam exile forces under a single umbrella but SCIRI gradually developed into a political party under the exclusive control of the Hakims. They formed an armed wing, the Badr brigade, which was made up partly of Iraqi Shia soldiers captured by the Iranians after Saddam's attack in 1980. By 2002, Western diplomats in Tehran assessed its strength at between 7,000 and 15,000 men.[13]

US plans to invade Iraq put SCIRI in a quandary. Its nationalist credentials could not allow it to endorse a Western intervention, although it wanted to see Saddam fall and it had good contacts with British and other

Western embassies in Tehran. By the late 1990s, SCIRI had established direct high-level contacts with US agencies and was one of the Iraqi groups listed under the 1998 Iraq Liberation Act as entitled to receive US support. Its Iranian sponsors were fully aware of these contacts. They too had mixed views: however keen it was to have Saddam removed from power the Iranian government did not want the USA to set up bases on Iran's western border with Iraq. The fall of the Taliban in Afghanistan had already put US bases to Iran's east.

The strength of the nationalist aspirations, which underlay the attitudes of Iraqi Islamists, struck me forcefully when I went to see Ayatollah Hakim in his heavily guarded office in central Tehran in March 2002. Here was a man whose desire for independence was as fierce as his hopes for building an Islamic society. He had opposed the use of sanctions against Iraq and could not publicly endorse a foreign invasion of his country.

The ayatollah's visitors were asked to wait in a mournful room with closed curtains. Looking down from the walls were close-up photographs of around two dozen men whom my escort explained were martyrs, all members of the Hakim family who were murdered in Saddam's prisons. There was no other feature in the darkened room, so one's eye could not help roaming over these blank faces. That was presumably the intention. Suitably humbled, I was ushered into a long meeting room with armchairs and sofas along all four walls in classic Middle Eastern style, along with ugly wooden coffee tables with a box of Kleenex tissues on each one.

The ayatollah was already in place in an armchair. I was shown to an adjacent sofa while a man who had filmed my entry now set up his camera opposite us. I was told I need not take notes because I would be given a CD at the end. Hakim had a wispy greying beard and rather moist-looking lips. He was soft-spoken and almost shy but gave plentiful eye-contact as he fiddled with a set of black worry-beads. 'We don't agree with an American attack on Iraq. It will cause great damage and suffering to ordinary people,' he told me.

It was a year before Bush would launch his invasion but the media were already reporting that the White House had started planning. The ayatollah wanted to add his voice to the debate. There should be no unilateral action against Iraq without UN approval, he insisted. The UN had the authority under Resolution 688, passed after the Gulf War, he argued, to bomb Iraq's heavy weaponry anywhere in the country if it had been used to kill civilians.

The UN should implement the resolution. This, he went on, would be the signal for the Badr brigade and other elements of the Iraqi opposition to use ground attacks to topple the regime.

What the ayatollah was proposing was a replay of the campaign that had successfully brought down the Taliban three months earlier. The so-called Northern Alliance of Afghan opposition groups provided the infantry while the USA and UK used bombs and missiles under cover of a UN resolution but sent no combat troops of their own (at least, not until after the Taliban defeat).

Several months later SCIRI took part in the conference of exiles held in London in December 2002, by which time US plans for a military intervention were clear. SCIRI still refused to endorse the imminent invasion publicly. On the eve of the invasion, at the next conference of Iraqi exiles in Salaheddin in Kurdistan, the ayatollah's brother Abdel Aziz al-Hakim went so far as to warn Zalmay Khalilzad, the special US envoy (who later became the US ambassador in Iraq), that an occupation would spark Iraqi resistance.

SCIRI's reticence towards a foreign invasion and its warnings about the dangers should have been something to which Washington and London paid attention and from which they could learn. If a group that was strongly committed to the goal of toppling Saddam and had suffered so personally from his oppression was reluctant to come out in favour of the invasion, how much greater would the reluctance of other Iraqis be?

Shia ambivalence about the invasion grew stronger once US and British troops appeared on Iraq's streets. The three main Shia currents, the Hakims, the Sadrs, and the leading Shia cleric, Grand Ayatollah Ali al-Sistani, all had reservations about the occupation or were totally opposed. The Hakim family refused to take part in the meeting of prominent Iraqis organised by the USA in Nassiriya just after Saddam's regime fell. They hesitated for several days before Abdel Aziz al-Hakim accepted Bremer's invitation to take part in the Interim Governing Council, which he set up in July 2003. After hours of discussion Sergio Vieira de Mello, the UN special representative, had persuaded him it was not just an American front. The council would have an executive role with the right to appoint ministers and oversee the budget. Meanwhile, the Dawa party split after some of its leaders decided to authorise one of their number to join the council.

Ayatollah Sistani was the leading authority in the Shia community. His words carried great weight. He gave no speeches or Friday sermons but his views were made known through statements and fatwas. On principle, he refused to meet US or British officials because they were occupiers, a position he maintained throughout the occupation. No doubt he remembered how an earlier generation of Shia leaders refused to meet the British after a Sunni monarch was imposed on them. They did not wish to be thought to be stooges and sell-outs. Some Americans liked to believe Sistani was boycotting them on religious rather than political grounds. They claimed he would not talk to any non-Muslim. This was false. Sistani regularly received de Mello, a Brazilian Christian, since he represented the UN (which had not authorised the invasion).

Moqtada al-Sadr, the young cleric who took up the mantle of his much-revered father after the invasion, came out strongly against the occupation from its first day. He knew this represented the feelings of many of the urban poor, his main constituency. Just six weeks after Saddam's statue was toppled, he brought 10,000 people into Baghdad's streets on 19 May, shouting, 'No, no to foreign rule. Yes, yes to Islam.'

The three Shia leaders' positions were not, of course, identical, and Shia politics during the occupation were heavily affected by competition for influence between them. Hakim represented a conservative, middle-class, and older constituency than Sadr. Sistani's differences with Sadr centred on the role of the clergy, the wisdom of mass mobilisation, and the issue of how radical the opposition to the occupation should be, and in particular whether armed resistance was legitimate. Another significant Shia player was the Dawa party, which had also conducted armed actions against Saddam during its 20 years of exile. The first prime ministers after the 2005 elections, Ibrahim al-Jaafari and Nouri al-Maliki, were from Dawa. They relied on support from the Sadrists.

The Americans seemed totally unprepared for the complexity of intra-Shia politics when they reached Iraq. Gen Jay Garner, the first US overlord in Iraq, was urged by his officials to make overtures to Sistani. 'Why?', he asked. 'Who is this person?'[14]

The Americans also misunderstood the way Shias saw themselves, or at least they understood only part of what the Shias stood for. To the war planners in Washington and London, the Shias were seen only as victims. From this it followed they were the West's natural allies. Ali Allawi, a secular Shia academic and businessman who served briefly as defence minister and finance minister in Iraq in 2004 and 2005, has argued that some Western war advocates, like the academic Bernard Lewis, went so far as to see the Shias as the best promoters of modernism in the Middle East because they were, in his view, outsiders who were not wedded to traditional Islamic orthodoxy.[15] This was nonsense, however, since Shias do not regard themselves as heterodox. Rather, they feel they are 'the repositories of true Islam'. In Allawi's words

> Shias were victims – of despotic rulers, of Wahhabi bigotry, of indifference and contempt by their Sunni co-religionists – but they were still identifiably and defiantly Muslim … Hostility to Zionism, to imperial designs on Muslim territory and resources, and to the infiltration into their societies of Western mores and culture were built into their identity as custodians of true Islam.[16]

The first shock to the American and British stereotype of a Shia population eager for the USA to invade came within hours of the commencement of the invasion. US and British forces met resistance on the outskirts of Basra and Nassiriya after entering Iraq from Kuwait. Much of it came from black-uniformed members of the Fedayeen Saddam, his specially organised militia. Although they were part of the Baathist regime, they were local Shias. The lesson the Americans and British should have drawn was that Saddam's regime was not an entirely Sunni affair. It had many Shia members, including at high levels in the government and the *mukhabarat* (the intelligence apparatus). The simple view that Saddam's regime was an instrument for Sunni domination was wrong. Saddam knew he needed control in Shia areas. He became adept at manipulating sectarian and tribal differences and coopting many leading Shias to his side.

I got a taste of the extent of Shia representation in the army in Basra in July 2003. Bremer had just begun to realise the depth of feelings aroused by his disbandment of the Iraqi army two months earlier, as well as the outrage among the Iraqi military caused when US troops shot two officers dead during a protest at the gates of the Green Zone. To try to soften their anger Bremer announced that retired military officers would be given a $40 one-off 'emergency payment'.

Outside a branch of the Rasheed Bank in central Basra I came across around four hundred men queuing for their payments in ferocious heat. In Saddam's time money went directly into officers' accounts but in the chaos of the new regime everything was done with cash, on production of an ID card. Hence the queues. It was a disorderly scene as small groups were allowed at periodic intervals through a gap in the razor wire. Young British soldiers were shouting in English at people who tried to force their way in. In sign language the soldiers asked the Iraqis to form two queues to reduce the pressure. They had no interpreters. In frustration a soldier occasionally grabbed a man and held him back, or pushed others into line. Middle-aged and elderly army officers found themselves being herded about by foreign soldiers half their age – and for what? To receive a humiliating handout from an occupation army.

'I've been here four hours. Our treatment by British soldiers is very bad. You can't push officers around. This is an insult,' said a colonel who would not give his name but said he had retired in 1992. His long white robe, known as a *dishdasha*, was dirty, and blood was oozing from a small cut in his hand where he had been forced onto the razor wire. Abdullah Ibrahim, 47, who retired from a teaching job at the Naval Academy four years before told me:

> We have no respect now. What we are getting is what you call welfare …
> What about jobs, security, and elections? This is a big problem which will
> drive people in the wrong direction. I told the British yesterday that I would
> help the Fedayeen Saddam against them. I heard the Fedayeen will start kill-
> ing British troops soon.

He was shaking with anger, and it was hard to know how seriously he meant his threat. 'People in Basra are burning inside but we are not asking the British army to leave until the security problems are solved,' he went on. There had been a huge increase in crime and kidnappings since Saddam's fall. Like many other Iraqis in those early months of the occupation, he expected the occupiers to clean up the mess that Iraqis felt the foreigners had created. They could not just walk away. Yet at the same time this retired officer's fury at the assault on his dignity was a sign that his mood could quickly change. He might call for the troops to go home immediately or be faced with a nationalist insurgency, which he would support.

The biggest problems the Americans had with the Shias in the first months of the occupation were with Sistani and Sadr. During the invasion Sistani had put out the word to Shias not to offer resistance. This was an enormous plus for the coalition, even though Sistani did not call for Shias to welcome the invaders or to work with them. His line was essentially one of waiting and seeing.

Unlike Ayatollah Khomeini in Iran, Sistani represented the 'quietist' tradition in Shia Islam, under which the clerical authorities kept out of government and away from direct contact with officials. They concentrated on moral and social issues. His first post-invasion utterances were to condemn looting and call on people not to start revenge killings of Baathists.

The pressures of the occupation and the growing mood of ordinary Shias forced Sistani to modify his strategy. He adopted an increasingly political role, as people asked him for guidance on security matters and how to react to what the Americans were doing. Bremer was stunned and dismayed when Sistani issued a fatwa at the end of June 2003, denouncing Bremer's intention to nominate a group of Iraqis to draft a new constitution. Only elections would be acceptable, he insisted.

The fatwa had an immediate effect, prompting Mohammad Bahr al-Uloum, a leading Shia cleric who had spent ten years in exile in London, to draw back from joining the governing council because it was a US-nominated body. Bremer had to work frantically to persuade Uloum to change his mind.

Sistani's mantra was elections, elections, elections. The ayatollah saw himself as the voice of all Iraqi Shias and he wanted to ensure they got the power to which their majority share of the population entitled them. He suspected the CPA of having secret plans to re-install the Sunnis in power. He would not get into the minutiae of how elections would be held, but refused to give way on the principle. In exasperation Bremer at one point asked, 'Are we going to let a 75-year-old cleric decide what our policy is going to be in Iraq?'[17]

Bremer's failure to appreciate Sistani's authority and the loyalty he commanded from Shias sounded very similar to the dismissive views of Gertrude Bell, Britain's oriental secretary in the 1920s. She had described the *mujtahids*, the Shia religious leaders, as 'alien popes' who were 'obstructing the government at every turn'.[18] Other British officials of the time sneered at their authority, claiming it rested 'on an intimate acquaintance with accustomed knowledge entirely irrelevant to human affairs and worthless in any branch of human activity'.[19]

If Sistani was difficult for the USA, 29-year-old Moqtada al-Sadr was a nightmare. Here was a Shia cleric with a large following who continually denounced the occupation in stark and fiery language – yet US officials appeared uninterested in understanding why he was so popular. They preferred to demonise Sadr, the only issue being whether he was a 'Bolshevik' or a 'Fascist'. Bremer wrote in his memoirs:

> I'd received increasingly disturbing reports about Moqtada from our able regional co-ordinator for the Centre South, Mike Gfoeller. He described Moqtada as a 'Bolshevik Islamist' who understood only one thing, raw power, and who would stop at nothing to get it. Mike's analysis was that while Moqtada currently lacked broad popular support, this was irrelevant. He relied on a small fanatically loyal gang of armed followers, totalling no more than two hundred men.[20]

Larry Diamond, who was one of the more liberal CPA officials, described Sadr's followers as a 'malignant cancer': 'There was a fascist tone to all the street action and thuggery, which was meant to terrorise enlightened people, persecute ethnic minorities, cow opponents,' he claimed.[21]

In reality, Sadr was a more complex figure than either of these characterisations suggest. The fourth son of Ayatollah Mohammad Sadiq al-Sadr, he had had no higher education, having given up after completing pre-graduation research at the Hawza, the main Shia institution for religious teaching based in Najaf. He probably would have remained in obscurity if his father and two eldest brothers had not been murdered by Saddam's agents in 1999. Their death seemed to awaken a sense of duty in Sadr. He decided to follow their model of social activism and political defiance. He was also conscious of the legacy of his distinguished relative, Ayatollah Baqir al-Sadr, who was murdered in 1980 and became known in the family as the 'first martyr'.

The elder Sadrs had played a distinctive role in Shia religious history. Under the Hawza tradition the leadership style was collegial, and the content of clerics' advice to the faithful was restricted to daily problems of social and family life. Baqir al-Sadr broke with that, as discussed earlier in this chapter, by founding an Islamist political party, the Dawa.

Moqtada's father, Mohammed Sadiq al-Sadr, was Baqir's cousin and pupil. Although he did not join the Dawa party, he took a similarly activist route. He was briefly put under house arrest after Baqir was killed, but Saddam later decided he could be relied on not to cause trouble. The dictator did not try to block his emergence as a leading figure in the Shia clerical establishment and allowed him to run religious schools and publish a journal. This eventually led to his recognition as a man of sufficient scholastic authority to be called a 'grand ayatollah'.

If Saddam thought these concessions would buy Sadiq al-Sadr's silence and cooperation, he was wrong. The grand ayatollah used his teaching position to launch an attack on the Hawza's quietist traditions. The Hawza should be *natiqa* (vocal and militant),[22] and champion the cause of the poor and oppressed, he argued. It should get closer to ordinary people by setting up bases in local prayer houses, a process begun by Sadiq himself. This gave him a network independent of the state. Sadiq also restored a practice not used by Iraqi Shias for decades. Instead of going to the mosque for individual prayers, Shias in Sadiq's mosques would be urged to pray communally on Friday and hear a political sermon commenting on the week's events. This was a practice that had developed in Iran during the 1979 revolution and became standard there afterwards. Saddam saw it as potentially subversive since it could lead to radicalised crowds taking to the streets as they left the mosque.

Shias traditionally discouraged communal Friday prayers. They believe the Twelfth Imam, the Mahdi, is 'hidden' but will one day return to end earthly oppression. Communal prayers with a sermon, on the pattern of the Sunnis, were considered wrong since, until the Mahdi's Messiah-like coming, they would be taking place with the sanction of a temporal ruler, who is by definition illegitimate. Sadiq's decision to revive Friday prayers as a congregational event was revolutionary, if not heretical. To justify it, Sadiq promoted the concept of *wilayat al faqih*, the government of the jurisprudent, which meant that a religious figure should oversee the secular government. It was the same notion that Ayatollah Khomeini had instituted in Iran in 1979.

Sadiq's activism and bold ideas posed a triple challenge: to the Hawza quietists, who did not believe in clerical government; to Iran, since he was rejecting their ayatollahs' claim to leadership over all Shias; and to Saddam.[23] It was no surprise when the dictator organised gunmen in February 1999 to kill him and his two sons in their car.

After the US invasion of 2003 four elements in Sadiq's teaching became especially important. His son Moqtada followed them faithfully. As a committed Islamist, but unlike the Hakim family, Sadiq had always attacked the West: 'No, no to America; no, no to Israel; no, no to the Devil' was one of his favourite ways of opening his Friday sermon. So Moqtada's hostility to the US and British occupation from its very first moment followed a long family tradition. It was not a youthful gimmick or a cynical ploy to win popular support.

Second, in spite of being a Shia, Sadiq always argued in favour of Muslim and national unity. 'There is no Sunni and no Shia; Yes to Islamic unity' was another common slogan. During the huge pilgrimage march to Kerbala in April 2003 crowds shouted '*Akrad, Sinna wa Shi'a; hatha al-Wattan menbi'a*' (Kurds, Sunni and Shia, this homeland we shall not sell). Third, Sadiq attacked those Iraqi leaders, clerical or secular, who had fled the Saddam regime and sought refuge abroad.

The final part of Sadiq's legacy which Moqtada took over was its social base. Sadiq had addressed himself mainly to the poorest urban Shia, the young unemployed men whose parents or grandparents had moved to slums in Baghdad and Basra from desolate rural areas. They were known as the *mustazafin* (the dispossessed). Better-off urban Shias and the bazaar merchants viewed Sadiq's plebeian following as a threat. There was also a geographical divide. Tribes in the more fertile lands around the holy cities of Najaf and Kerbala feared Sadiq's power to mobilise the masses. The poorer tribes in the marshes along the Iranian border, however, particularly around Amara (a city where the British were to have trouble after 2003), adored Sadiq.

Moqtada inherited these militant constituencies, while middle-class Shia tended to support the Hakim family's SCIRI movement. The eastern Baghdad slum known as Saddam City was quickly renamed Sadr City after the invasion, while Baghdad's leafy Karrada suburb across the Tigris from the Green Zone became a SCIRI stronghold.

Occupation officials rarely seemed to understand Iraq's class politics, preferring to see everything in sectarian terms. The Shias were one block, the Sunnis were another, and each would inevitably oppose the other. It was not until the autumn of 2005 that occupation officials took serious note of intra-Shia disagreements, when the question of disarming militias and reducing 'Shia-on-Shia violence' became a priority. If CPA officials did refer to class issues, at least indirectly, it was usually to write off Sadr's street followers as 'lumpen' thugs for hire. There seemed little awareness of the extent of Sadr's support, even though it was not hard to find. You only had to go to Sadr City at midday on Friday, as I often did in the early months of the occupation when it was still safe for a foreigner to do so. Stretching across two roads separated by a patch of gravel as wide as a football pitch, row after row of worshippers prostrated themselves on the ground in a vast open-air prayer meeting. They listened intently as provocative political sermons crackled out from loudspeakers.

Moqtada was not his father's expected heir. Sadiq had nominated two older men, both distinguished religious scholars. But the American invasion created an unpredicted political environment which favoured radical activists over elderly thinkers. Young imams, helped by armed volunteers, took over mosques, welfare centres, schools, and clinics. The initial aim was to prevent looting, but it quickly became a form of long-term control, and in some cases a kind of protection racket.

However, in crowded Sadr City Moqtada was viewed as a symbol of hope. The area was home to close to 3 million people, living in appalling conditions, and with access to only two general hospitals. Unemployment was 70 per cent. It was easy for Moqtada to find supporters by paying people a small daily allowance, raised from donations in the mosques. He filled the vacuum after Saddam's collapse with great energy and organising skill, pushing himself forward as his father's heir. He even made an issue of being the runt of his family and having minimal education, so that uneducated youth could better identify with him. In the words of one analyst, 'the upheaval caused by the occupation emboldened the more disadvantaged Shias and handed them a historic opportunity to achieve their goals.'[24]

In the occupation's early days Moqtada was still feeling his way. He was not in control of the outburst of street activity, either of the looting or the vigilante efforts to stop it by young imams from his father's Sadrist movement. Much of the chaos and violence was spontaneous. Similarly, there is doubt over Moqtada's role in a notorious incident, the murder of a distinguished scholar, Abdul Majod al-Khoei, in Najaf. Khoei had lived in London for years where he worked closely with the British and Americans in the run-up to the invasion. If Chalabi was the Pentagon's favourite secular Shia in exile, Khoei was their favourite religious one. Both men were helped to fly back to southern Iraq by the coalition a week before the regime fell, apparently in the hope they would have a head-start over other exiles.

A fracas developed in the precinct of the Imam Ali shrine when a crowd of Sadrists saw Khoei and his entourage. They may have feared he was trying to take it over, especially as he was accompanied by Haidar al-Rufaie al-Kilidar, the shrine's custodian in Saddam's time whom some considered a collaborator. There was an exchange of bullets lasting over an hour between Khoei's group and the crowd. Some witnesses claim Khoei was captured and stabbed. Others say he died in the crossfire. Khoei's supporters accuse

Moqtada, who was not present at the time, of giving orders for Khoei to be killed but there is no conclusive proof that he had contact with or control over the crowd.

Whether he had any responsibility for al-Khoei's death, the controversy did not lessen Moqtada's support. The pilgrimage to Kerbala turned him into a nationally recognised figure, shown for the first time on the foreign Arabic-language TV channels, which Iraqis were watching in the absence of any Iraqi ones. His picture was carried by countless marchers or stuck on the windows of cars and minivans.

The obvious response to this mass phenomenon would have been to try to talk to Moqtada, but Bremer seemed unable to find any way to handle the issue other than by strong-arm attempts at ostracism and violence. He made no attempt to have his officials contact him.

Demonising Moqtada only made the young cleric more popular. It strengthened his nationalist credentials and his role as the Americans' main Shia opponent. In July 2003, Moqtada took his criticisms a stage further when he used a sermon at the mosque in Kufa, about five miles west of Najaf (which had been his father's headquarters), to urge volunteers to join an Islamic army. He called it 'jaish al-Mahdi', the army of the hidden imam, or Mahdi. His call to arms came in response to rumours, broadcast on a newly opened local TV station, that US troops had surrounded his house in Najaf and were planning to arrest him. Sadr was seen asking people to come to his defence and several thousand people converged on the house. Significantly, they included Sunni demonstrators from Fallujah and Tikrit.

In the holy city of Najaf a few days later I tried to discover what Sadr wanted to do with this army. Unlike Baghdad's teeming Sadr City, Najaf is a relatively small town whose life and economy revolve entirely round the burial shrine of Imam Ali and the adjacent hotels for pilgrims, as well as the vast necropolis of tombs, some as large as a house, where Shias come from all over Iraq as well as Iran to bury their relatives. In the narrow alleyways of the bazaar every woman wears the *abbaya*, and shops sell posters of the ayatollahs murdered by Saddam along with pictures of Iran's former leader Ayatollah Khomeini, who spent years of exile in Najaf. At any time of the day small groups of people can be seen alighting from vans, carrying coffins draped in green into the shrine's vast courtyard. Farsi-speaking pilgrims from Iran wander past the stalls selling cold drinks and pictures of the imam.

Moqtada's office was in one of the crowded alleys. Sheikh Aws al-Khafaji, one of his spokesmen, was cryptic. 'I can't say what weapons the army will have. It will not fight with sticks and it is not just a large crowd of protesters. It is an army,' he told me. As a crowd of young men, many in black Shia turbans, milled about in an ante-room Khafaji summarised Sadr's anti-occupation message in relatively moderate terms. They sounded very similar to what I had heard from Sunnis in Falluja. Iraqis were still waiting for the Americans to get electricty and the water system back in action; the Americans ought to fix things before they left. Khafaji explained:

> Moqtada wants them to get out of the cities, but not out of Iraq now. Having troops in the cities frightens people. For the time being Moqtada is not considering calling for jihad against the occupation. We want to prove we are peaceful if they are peaceful.

At the lightly guarded US marine base on the edge of Najaf, Col Christopher Conlin took a relaxed line. There had been no fatal attacks on US forces in Najaf or any other southern Iraqi town, he pointed out. The recent protests outside Moqtada's house were a minor affair. US troops had never surrounded the house nor intended to do this. All that had happened was that the US had put extra troops on the main streets because Deputy Defense Secretary Paul Wolfowitz was making an unannounced visit.

There were two weaknesses in the colonel's position. Like Bremer, he underestimated Sadr's potential, claiming he was 'immature and manipulated by others'. He also told me he had sacked the local Iraqi TV director for incitement and broadcasting untruths. Under Bremer's draconian decrees on public order the colonel had the right to do that. It was both a sign of the occupiers' extraordinary powers as well as an action that could inflame Iraqi anger and resentment if it persisted.

Moqtada's anti-occupation line was shared by many other Shias, including secular professionals who were not radical politically. On 3 July, shortly before going to Najaf, I visited the town of Balad. Situated 50 miles north of Baghdad, it has a small Shia shrine and a largely Shia population of around 60,000. The surrounding farming area is Sunni but the town is one of only two or three compact Shia communities between the capital and Saddam's home base of Tikrit.

In an air-conditioned side room in Balad's only hospital a group of doctors described their links with the military hospital the USA had set up in the nearby base when they occupied it two months earlier. The doctors had sent many of their sickest patients to the US hospital because it had better facilities. In most Iraqi universities medicine is taught in English and many doctors speak the language well. It was therefore natural that professional contacts between Balad's doctors and their new American neighbours turned into social get-togethers. The Iraqi doctors occasionally ate at the US base and in return invited the Americans to join them at restaurants in town.

Not any more, one of the older doctors told me. 'We can't invite them to eat with us now. People wouldn't like it and they might accuse us of being collaborators,' he said. 'I won't give you my name because I'm afraid to. I'm an Arab and I will not accept disrespect.' None of his colleagues matched the vehemence of his words but there was no dissent from his views. The doctors' attitude to the Americans had changed three weeks earlier, they recounted. US troops from the base had conducted an offensive north of Balad, allegedly to hunt down armed insurgents loyal to Saddam Hussein, who was still on the run. The Americans killed and wounded several farmers. They were brought to Balad hospital where the doctors saw their terrible injuries and talked to their families.

Operation Desert Scorpion, as the US forces called it, gave a big push to a mounting wave of Iraqi disappointment. Like the Sunni town of Fallujah, Balad had liberated itself. Its Baathist leadership had fled before US troops came in after toppling Saddam in Baghdad. Dr Mustafa Mahmoud, an ear, nose, and throat specialist in his thirties, told me:

> It's not true that only pro-Saddam people are attacking US troops. I don't think it's only that. When a man has lost everything, his job, electricity, fuel, and water, he may develop feelings against them. The US response to any attack is very violent and brutal.

On the previous day US troops had killed another 11 Iraqis who were said to be trying to ambush a military patrol near Balad.

Roadside bombs against US convoys in the Balad area mounted a few weeks later, and the base and its large airfield soon became the target for almost nightly mortar rounds. Within a few months of the invasion, travel on the road from Baghdad to Tikrit was too risky for foreign journalists. The attackers were probably Sunnis from the adjacent farmland or further afield, but the anti-American anger I had heard from Balad's Shia doctors suggested that they too felt the occupation was insulting their national pride.

The Americans also met resistance from Shia tribal sheikhs. When US marines attempted to restore the police force in the town of Kut a hundred miles south-east of Baghdad in the first days after Saddam fell, half the force of two hundred dropped out. Local people had told them people who collaborated with the Americans were traitors. Shortly thereafter the police station burnt down. It was still smouldering when I drove to Kut the next day.

A small port on the Tigris, the town was a key site in imperial British history. British troops captured it in 1915 after a lightning advance from Basra but the Ottomans recovered, returned, and put the British under siege. With food running scarce and malaria taking its toll the British spent four months trying to break out while 7,000 soldiers died. The surviving 13,000 then surrendered to the Turks in one of the severest defeats the British army has ever suffered. The British cemetery off a backstreet – smaller than a football field, surrounded by houses and obviously uncared for – still smelt of defeat in 2003. Half the gravestones were fallen or covered by weeds. Goats grazed between the few that remained upright.

If there was a warning here for the Americans, it passed unnoticed. Finding the almost hidden cemetery was not easy and most occupation troops had barely heard of Babylon, let alone more obscure historical places. In Kut, the Americans had more immediate issues to handle. They were just beginning to realise that governing a foreign nation is harder than defeating one.

Several hundred Iraqis were guarding the gates of the governor's office to block the Americans from entering. 'No, no to America. No, no to Israel. Yes, yes to unity. Yes, yes to Islam,' some were chanting. The reference to Israel was prompted by rumours going round Iraq at the time. Word had it that Ahmad Chalabi, the Pentagon's favourite, was going to be named by the Americans as Iraq's new ruler, and that one of his first acts would be to recognise Israel.

Volunteer guards were allowing journalists into the barricaded building. Upstairs, Saeed Abbas, a retired schoolteacher and tribal sheikh who had taken over as governor, was holding court with about two dozen other men in flowing white robes:

> American troops want to appoint their own administration and not listen to the opinion of the people in the street. The people they have appointed so far were in the Baath party and the previous regime. People mistrust them. They will not cooperate with anything the troops do.

It would make no difference if the Americans succeeded in evicting him. 'I can manage these people from the mosque,' he warned.

At US marine headquarters in Kut, Major Michael Griffin said Saeed Abbas was self-appointed and represented only a minority of Kut's citizens. He had walked into the room when the unit commander, Brig Gen Rich Natonski, was halfway through a meeting with the advisory council of local leaders five days earlier. When Abbas shouted out, 'I want to inform you that half the people here are Baathists', he had been shouted down, Griffin said. He went on:

> It is virtually impossible to find someone who is not a Baathist. We identify the top person in a department, then go to his deputy and the man below that and ask what the top man was like. It is hard for people to understand that. They think being a Baathist is automatically bad. We want to show that by working with us you can get things working the way they were before, minus Saddam.

At one level the major's goals sounded praiseworthy. It was hard for outsiders to discover the truth about people's past in the welter of claims and counter-claims after Saddam fell. It was especially difficult in Shia areas, as the British were finding in Basra and the south-eastern provinces, which the Americans had given them to run. In Kut the issue was temporarily solved when the Americans managed to break into the governor's building a few days after my visit. Saeed Abbas and his followers fled. However, the Kut episode was not isolated. In Najaf in June the Americans had arrested and sacked the governor, a former army colonel, whom they had themselves appointed. Local people had denounced him as corrupt. In December 2003, the Americans sacked the governor of Hilla, another largely Shia province.

The mess over these appointments confirmed the lesson in democracy that Sistani had tried to give the Americans in his fatwa calling for elections. The best way of weeding out prominent Baathists, crooks, and thugs, and preventing them from returning to power, was to let local people use the ballot box, he had argued. It was not just a matter of legitimacy and allowing Iraqis rather than foreigners to decide who should rule Iraq. It was a practical issue. Iraqis knew better than outsiders what people had done under Saddam.

It took the Americans more than six months to get the message. Bremer initially favoured a long period of transition in which the Americans would rule through appointed governors at the local level, and nationally by decree. The length of the transition period was not spelt out. As late as November 2003, he was still resisting elections. Then, under pressure from Sistani, Bremer partially gave way. In mid-November he announced there would be an Iraqi national assembly whose task would be to draw up a constitution. But it would not be chosen by popular vote. Instead, a complicated system of caucuses would be set up. A 15-person organising committee in each of the country's 18 provinces would select representatives who would then meet to choose members for the national assembly. At each stage the occupying authorities, the Coalition Provisional Authority, would supervise the process, giving them the right to weed out candidates they did not like.

CPA officials produced numerous reasons why they did not favour quick elections. Some were technical: Iraq had no up-to-date electoral register, and it would take months to choose an electoral commission to prepare a register and certify parties and candidates. Some reasons were political: the experience of other societies coming out of prolonged conflict or dictatorship was that if elections were held very soon citizens tended to turn to identity-based parties, representing ethnic, sectarian, or linguistic interests. This squeezed out the moderate, secular, and national parties who needed time and a secure climate to organise and present their case. The arguments were fine, but the flaw was the occupation. If the country were under an impartial UN administration or trusteeship, delay might have been acceptable. As long as the election delay was being imposed by foreign occupiers with no announced limit to their own term in the country, it was bound to arouse suspicion.

The Americans tried to meet the point by announcing they would 'transfer sovereignty' to an Iraqi government in June 2004. They still did not spell out when the troops would leave. It also meant the Americans would be in charge of appointing the allegedly sovereign government.

Sistani promptly denounced the plan. He was not alone. Thousands of demonstrators took to the streets of Baghdad, shouting 'Yes, yes to Sistani. No, no to selection.' Many Iraqis who were sympathetic to the Americans found it insulting. Larry Diamond, who served as a senior adviser to the CPA, described their anger: 'I realised that Bremer and his most trusted CPA advisers simply did not grasp the depth of Iraqi disaffection, suspicion, and frustration, even among many of our partners and philosophical allies within the Iraqi political class.'[25]

In desperation the Americans turned to their old enemy, the UN, to broker a compromise. After much argument and an exchange of letters with Kofi Annan, the grand ayatollah won the principle he wanted. The caucus idea was scrapped and there would be elections for the national assembly. However, they would only be held in January 2005. In the meantime there would be an appointed 'interim' government.

Although he had lost out on the election principle, Bremer got his way on one major issue. He ordered US officials, in consultation with the governing council, to rush to draw up an interim constitution, called the Transitional Administrative Law. It was meant to provide the framework for Iraq's future with a privatised economy and a federal structure. Bremer's hope was that the TAL would be the basis for the eventual constitution. Larry Diamond found the issue as embarrassing as the row over whether to have elections:

> For the fourth or fifth time – I was losing count – the United States was finding itself on what appeared to be the less democratic side of the argument with Iraqis over transitional procedures. Sistani had called for an elected constitution-making body. Bremer said an appointed body would do. Iraqis wanted to conduct direct elections for local governments. Bremer and the top (US) governance officials vetoed them. The CPA proposed an opaque, convoluted process for choosing a transitional government and Sistani, along with many Iraqis, again demanded direct elections. Now the CPA and the governing council were saying to Iraqis, and I myself was saying, 'Here is your wonderful interim constitution' and a great many Iraqis were responding, 'Don't we have a voice in shaping the rules that will govern us?'[26]

While the rows over elections and sovereignty were raging between Sistani and the occupying authorities, Moqtada al-Sadr was quietly developing his political base. He supported Sistani's call for early elections but sharpened it with demands for the withdrawal of foreign troops, first from the cities, but eventually from Iraq altogether. He also widened his critique of the Americans by reminding poor Iraqis that the US occupiers intended to dismantle the system of subsidised food supplies and leave them worse off. Tens of thousands of families in Baghdad's Sadr City depended on it to survive. All the while, he was recruiting hundreds of unemployed young men into his Mahdi army, turning it into a full-fledged militia which could match the better-organised force run by his political rivals SCIRI and the Hakim family.

Moqtada's radicalism and his anti-occupation stance worried both the Hakims and the Americans. Since joining the governing council the Hakims had become increasingly close to the American project, in spite of incidents in which the Americans raided their Baghdad offices and removed computers. Ayatollah Muhammed Baqir al-Hakim was killed by a massive car bomb just outside Najaf's Ali shrine on 29 August. Unlike the murder of al-Khoei by a Sadrist mob in Najaf in April, no one blamed Moqtada for the car bomb. It came soon after the bombing of the UN headquarters in Baghdad and responsibility was later claimed by Al-Qaeda. Whether the aim was to create chaos or warn Hakim not to work with the Americans, it had the opposite effect: SCIRI became a fulltime partner with the Americans. Its leaders were sure to be given a role in any government the Americans proposed or approved.

Moqtada, by contrast, was outside the tent. The longer the occupation went on and the more it failed to deliver on its promises of jobs and better public services, the easier it was for him to increase his support on the street. After initially ignoring him, the Americans began to develop plans to try to break him.

They chose their moment on 28 March 2004. Moqtada's weekly newspaper, *Al-Hawza*, was ordered to shut for 60 days on the grounds that it had violated regulations banning incitement and hatred. It was an odd move, since the paper's latest issue was no more radical than previous ones. It also contradicted Bremer's line that the USA was bringing freedom to Iraq. Now it was bringing censorship against people who criticised the occupation. Simultaneously, the Americans published an arrest warrant for Moqtada which they said a US-approved Iraqi judge had issued some time earlier in connection with the Khoei murder.

The move against Moqtada backfired. Thousands of young Sadrists took to the streets of Baghdad to denounce the arrest warrant and *Al-Hawza*'s banning. Over the next few days armed members of the Mahdi army seized police stations in Sadr City as well as the holy cities of Kerbala and Najaf. In Sadr City, Mahdi army gunmen clashed with US troops for the first time since the invasion, killing seven members of a US patrol.

In response the USA sent in Apache helicopter gunships, a significant escalation which was damaging psychologically. Here was an image that evoked memories of Vietnam. Instead of Vietcong fighters in black pyjamas, US television viewers and Arabs throughout the Middle East saw black-shirted and black-robed militiamen, fighting a high-tech foreign enemy with simple weapons but the same indomitable nationalist fervour as the Vietnamese. The pictures also drew comparisons with Israeli gunships swooping over Gaza. Suddenly, the Middle East was spawning a second intifada.

The uprising coincided with the annual celebration of the Shia festival of Arbain. Whereas in April 2003 the millions of Shia pilgrims who marched to Kerbala and Najaf had been relaxed as they tasted their first freedom for decades, the mood in April 2004 was one of vigilance, anti-American anger, and preparation for martyrdom. Teenagers with rifles stopped cars and searched them for car bombs. There was not a single official policeman on duty.

As the Arbain pilgrimage wound down, the Americans stepped up their attacks in Sadr City. They were also in action in Fallujah. The twin battles produced dramatic scenes of sectarian solidarity, belying the stereotype of Sunni-versus-Shia animosity. Up to 200,000 people crowded into Baghdad's largest Sunni Mosque, Umm al-Qura, as mentioned in Chapter III.

Like the Tet offensive in Vietnam in March 1968, the Sadrist uprising in April 2003 was a major turning point in the war. Militarily the USA won, if body counts are the measure. The militias lost more men than the US army. The USA also showed it could not be defeated in a pitched battle. The psychological victory, however, went to Moqtada and his Mahdi army. The uprising attracted hundreds of new recruits and had shown that police loyalty to the occupation was shaky. In the USA, people who had supported the invasion began for the first time to question whether it had been worthwhile. Car bombs could be put down to Al-Qaeda and foreign jihadis, but the Sadrists were obviously Iraqis who were attacking Americans and sometimes the Iraqi police. The Iraqi intifada raised the spectre of a resistance movement that might never end. In the Middle East, Al-Jazeera and the new TV station Al-Arabiya showed the militias in a broadly positive light while concentrating on heavy Israeli-style US firepower.

The Sadrists' victory was sealed by an agreement brokered by mediators from several Shia Islamist parties as well as from Ayatollah Sistani. The Americans dropped their demand for Moqtada to be arrested and tried. He agreed to let the police back into the old section of Najaf and not to have his own militias carry weapons openly. Security would be shared between the police and a local security force. The final US concession came a month later when Moqtada's weekly newspaper was allowed to reopen.

One unfortunate side effect of the Sadrist intifada and the violent American reaction was a long-term increase in tension between the Islamists and Westerners, which vastly complicated foreign journalists' work. I learnt that lesson the hard way on a trip to Najaf in the last week of June to see how the Sistani-brokered agreement was working out. Our car was stuck in traffic on the edge of the old town. Suddenly two men in white robes walked out in front of us and took pistols from the pockets of their *dishdashas*. Opening the car's front doors, they forced my driver and translator out and ordered them to squeeze into the back with me. They then sat in front as a third gunman appeared and got in beside us. Twenty yards away traffic police watched but did nothing.

It was the moment feared by everyone in Iraq, whether foreigner or Iraqi. Were we on our way to some lonely 'safe house' to be dumped in a windowless cellar, ready for execution? Crammed four in the back, I was next to one of the doors. I had a fleeting instinct to jump out as the congestion eased and our new driver inched slowly up the street but quickly scotched the thought. Bullets would surely have followed me.

At the first roundabout the driver turned the car back towards the centre of town. A small surge of relief came over me. Wasn't it more likely that a safe house to hold us hostage would be out of town in a less heavily populated area? There was no reason why it should, but somehow the fact that we were heading back towards Najaf's old town seemed comforting. Perhaps our captors were plain-clothed 'detectives' from the Mahdi army rather than a ransom gang, I wondered. Maybe our activities had aroused suspicions.

I cast my mind back towards the events of that morning. On arrival from Baghdad we had gone to the Imam Ali shrine to interview Sheikh Ahmed al-Shaibani, one of Moqtada's deputies, about the deal reached with US forces at the end of the April clashes. We wanted to know how it was working out. Shaibani was an articulate man in his early thirties, who told us he was the first person in his family to choose a religious life. He became an Islamist student after finishing his conscription in Saddam's army.

Shaibani's line on the occupation was critical but relatively measured. He told us:

> The image of liberation forces has become one of occupation. We only get four hours of electricity a day. Food rations are being reduced all the time. We don't feel these forces have any credibility. They should leave Iraq tomorrow.

108

As many people have been killed over the last year as in Saddam's last five years. Bremer's tragedy is that he's allowing the Baathists back.

Then he turned to the deal with the Americans over Najaf. US troops were to remain outside Najaf except for the governor's office and the main police station. 'We have nominated the streets on which the US can patrol. We don't accept joint US–Iraqi police patrols. We agree only on patrols by the Iraqi police,' Shaibani said.

Later, I drove with my translator to two US bases just outside Najaf to get the American version. Security was tight and because we had made no prior appointments we were refused admission. Sitting in the car with the men who had hijacked us, I began to think our visits must have been spotted by the Iraqi cigarette-sellers who hung about near the entrance to the bases. They could have been Mahdi army informers who reported us to headquarters.

By now the car had reached Najaf's old town. At a checkpoint our captors showed their ID cards to guards wearing *dishdashas*. I relaxed a little more. This must mean they were indeed linked to the Mahdi army. They drove us to the shrine of Imam Ali and stopped by a low building at the back. Stripped of our mobile phones, they interrogated us about our trip to the bases, hinting we were spies. We pointed out that we had not been allowed in, which surely showed we had no relationship with the Americans. We also explained that we had talked to al-Shaibani earlier in the day. Why not contact him? He would vouch for us. After some discussion among themselves, the kidnappers consented. Thirty minutes later the young sheikh appeared, sternly ticked the gunmen off, and assured us this was not the way the Mahdi army normally behaved towards journalists. We agreed the episode was an unfortunate misunderstanding and all shook hands.

Back in our hotel, I drew three conclusions from the brief but scary encounter. The first was that Moqtada's Mahdi army was a powerful force, a state within a state, but capable of discipline. Lesson two was that normal reporting where you visit the 'other side' of a story was no longer possible on the same day. The third point was that insurgent attitudes towards Westerners were changing. More than a year into the occupation the Sadrists were beginning to see all Westerners through the same prism. It did not matter whether you were a journalist, a contractor, a civilian official, or a soldier – you were part of an enemy occupation, and would be treated at best with suspicion, at worst with outright hostility. A pattern was emerging which would not change without an end to the occupation.

A month later, trouble erupted in Najaf again, not just between the Americans and the Sadrists but this time with the new Iraqi government playing a key role alongside the USA. The main issue was the same as in April – who would control the streets? The April truce had been broken when Sadrist forces captured a police station and US troops surrounded Moqtada's home in an area outside the old town.

Iyad Allawi, the new Iraqi prime minister, wanted to confront the Islamist challenge and have Iraq run by secular professionals. He decided to make his mark with an American attack on the Sadrists. For three weeks battles raged on the edge of the old town and in the vast cemetery nearby, where gunmen could hide among the burial chambers. Hundreds of Sadrists were killed by rocket and gunfire from US helicopters. Over three dozen Americans died.

Sistani and the Sadrists worked out a new truce. Its terms differed little from the earlier one, except that the Iraqi government was asked to pay compensation to the victims and their families. The deal was a triumph for Sistani and a boost for Moqtada as well as his rivals, SCIRI, who benefited from Sistani's enhanced status.

The main Iraqi loser was Allawi. The Najaf deal marked a watershed. Millions of Shias did not understand how Allawi, himself a Shia, could have ordered foreign occupiers to mount an offensive against fellow Shias in a city that housed one of Islam's holiest shrines. Apart from the bloodshed, the offensive was an assault on Shia pride. The Najaf drama did enormous damage to Allawi and may have ended the last chance that Iraq's secular politicians had to turn the Islamist tide.

The national elections in January 2005 illustrated the point. Moqtada urged several of his supporters to run as independent candidates on the united Shia Islamist list that Sistani endorsed. The list included all the Islamist parties. It easily topped the poll, leaving Allawi's party far behind.

The Americans treated the elections as a victory. They emphasised the high turnout and the fact that Iraqis had the historic opportunity of a free choice, trumpeting these aspects of the poll as proof that they had come to Iraq as liberators bringing democracy. Behind the spin, however, the results were a disaster for the American project. The USA had succeeded in creating resistance among the Shias as well as the Sunnis. Their ally, Allawi, was perceived as an American puppet. Iraq's Islamists were on the threshold of gaining power, and the invasion had done far more to help Tehran than it had achieved for Washington.

V

LEAVE IN TIME OR GET
BOGGED DOWN

The longer the US presence is maintained, the more likely violent resistance will develop.

US Army War College, February 2003[1]

We've got to be certain the new Prime Minister won't ask us to leave the day after sovereignty.

George Bush, May 2004[2]

Poor Donald Rumsfeld. He got one big thing right. Yet by the time the defense secretary was sacked shortly after Bush's Republicans took a drubbing in the 2006 midterm elections, he was the most reviled man in America.

A chorus of recently retired generals had dared to demand his resignation, joining more predictable critics in the media and the Democratic party. He was blamed for sending too few troops for the invasion, and not reinforcing them rapidly afterwards. He was pilloried for his cavalier reaction to the orgy of looting in Baghdad – 'stuff happens'. He was accused of micro-managing the conduct of the battle against the insurgency even as he refused to admit in public that there was an insurgency. He was ridiculed for his remorselessly upbeat comments in the face of Iraq's slide into sectarian violence. Happy-go-lucky to the last, Rumsfeld turned his sacking into a joke. 'I have benefited greatly from criticism, and at no time have I suffered a lack thereof,' he said with his trademark half-smile and deliberately pernickety grammar as he stood alongside the president shortly after his departure was announced.

No one in Washington was willing to give Rumsfeld credit for the one issue where his instinct increasingly looked correct. The defense secretary sensed that any US occupation of Iraq had to be short-lived. If it was going to succeed, it must be measured in months rather than years. 'We do not want to be in a position where the failure of somebody to do those things ties our forces down indefinitely,' he said shortly before the invasion.[3] By 'those things' he meant working out in advance how Iraq's politics and reconstruction should be run.

US neoconservatives seemed to want a prolonged occupation of Iraq on the model of post-war Germany or Japan. Other officials preferred the Afghan model: to bring a cross section of prominent Iraqis together and let them choose a leader, provided he was secular and pro-American – the Hamid Karzai of Iraq. By his own account Rumsfeld took that line before the invasion, telling an interviewer: 'I tilted to the quicker handover ... I've always felt that foreign troops are an anomaly in a country, that eventually they're not natural and not welcomed really. There's also the concept of declining consent.'[4]

With the invasion successfully complete barely three weeks after it began, Rumsfeld and his close associates were even more sure of their view. On the day after marines toppled Saddam's statue in Firdous square, Larry Di Rita, Rumsfeld's special assistant on Iraq, briefed US officials in Kuwait as they prepared to fly to Baghdad to run the country. 'We went into the Balkans and Bosnia and Kosovo and we're still in them. We're not going to let this happen in Iraq. By the end of August we're going to have 25,000 to 30,000 troops left in Iraq,' he told them.[5]

Di Rita was accurately articulating Rumsfeld's policy (though not that of Rumsfeld's deputy, Paul Wolfowitz, who strongly advocated the neoconservatives' imperial ambitions of controlling Iraq for the long term). In 2007 it emerged through a Freedom of Information request that General Tommy Franks, the US force commander, issued guidelines to his staff on 16 April 2003 to prepare to reduce US troops in Iraq to about 30,000 by September.[6] Around the same day Rumsfeld made a similar commitment when he was coming out of the White House as Saudi Arabia's ambassador, Prince Bandar bin Sultan, was going in. He knew the Saudi prince was concerned that US troops would stay in Iraq too long and thought it would be better to let the Iraqi army and police handle security in post-war Iraq once its top pro-Saddam layer had been removed.

Rumsfeld sought to re-assure him: 'We'll accelerate the withdrawal. Don't worry,' he said.[7]

In a video message on 30 April Rumsfeld told Iraqis, 'Let me be clear. Iraq belongs to you. We don't want to own or run it.' He then added a sentence that would later become the catchphrase for Bush and the other neoconservatives who wanted to keep troops in Iraq on an open-ended basis, although Rumsfeld perhaps did not anticipate this. 'We will stay as long as necessary to help you do that, and not a day longer,' he promised.[8]

At first sight Rumsfeld's comments may seem out of character. But Rumsfeld was a hawk, not a neoconservative. He did not share the views of the Bush team's so-called 'defense intellectuals', like Wolfowitz and Richard Perle, who wanted to turn Iraq into a model of liberal democracy for the Middle East as well as a strategic launch pad for further crusades. Rumsfeld was a realist, perhaps even an idealist, to judge by his view that the occupation of Iraq should and could be short.

The trouble was that Rumsfeld never pressed his line with Colin Powell, the secretary of state, and Condoleezza Rice, the national security adviser, let alone with the president. In February 2003 he made a widely reported speech saying the USA should not be involved in 'nation-building'.[9] But his position seemed to be either confused or hypocritical. Once the invasion of Iraq was complete he took no action in pursuit of his argument for an early withdrawal of US troops. As a result, the case for a short occupation never took off within the administration.

Instead, the history of US policy in post-Saddam Iraq became a classic example of how one line of action becomes ever more entrenched without any key decision-maker daring to propose alternatives. A narrative is established that every official has to follow, or otherwise risk being marginalised, ridiculed, or sacked. The danger of this happening exists in any bureaucracy. It was particularly high in an administration where the president never asked probing questions or called for a wide range of options, but expected uncritical support from his staff on the grounds that 'If you're not with us, you're against us.'

It took three more years before the idea of a timetable for a US troop withdrawal re-emerged into the elite debate. When a handful of Congressmen began to raise it, Bush pilloried it as 'Cut and Run' as opposed to 'Stay the Course'. Even the bipartisan Baker-Hamilton commission, which was asked to look at ways of stemming the relentless increase in US battle casualties and Iraq's worsening insecurity, flunked the test. Its November 2006 report talked of 'precipitate withdrawal' and 'premature withdrawal', using loaded and negative epithets to distort the case.[10] Why didn't it consider the pros and cons of an 'early withdrawal'?

If Rumsfeld's instinct for a quick pull-out had been seriously considered in April 2003 the alternatives might then have been posed, tendentiously (but no more so than the 'Cut and Run' smear) as 'Leave in Time' or 'Get Bogged Down'. Of course, it would be naive to imagine there was any serious chance of a policy debate, let alone that it might have resulted in a decision to withdraw. Flushed with the rapid toppling of Saddam, the neoconservatives were extremely unlikely to bring home US troops in any foreseeable future, even if there had been no insurgency. Once resistance began, however, the issue was put in macho terms of 'not letting the enemy win'.

The war was designed to send a message to the region and the world that the USA was the Number One power, able and willing to project force to any part of the globe with or without UN approval. The message to Arabs was that the USA would occupy the country, set up a client government, and maintain bases indefinitely. As many Iraqis had suspected before the invasion, it was not just a crusade to create a pro-Western democracy. It was also a strategy for giving US oil companies control over Iraq's resources and for threatening Iran. The neoconservatives' model was the US occupations of Germany and Japan in 1945 – long-term projects to reshape a country emerging from authoritarian rule and to make it a permanent geopolitical ally.

When the Americans started to talk about transferring sovereignty to Iraqis and thereby 'ending the occupation', they always decoupled this from the question of a troop pull-out. In his memoirs Bremer describes the notion of a short occupation as a 'reckless fantasy', which would require 'careful work' if its Iraqi and American proponents were to be disabused of it.[11] He records that on the eve of his departure for Iraq to take up his job as US overlord he gave Bush what sounds like an insufferably patronising lecture about civil society. He explained to the president that there are 'shock absorbers' that help to cushion the individual from an overpowering government, like a free press, trade unions, political parties, and professional organisations. All this would take time to build, he told Bush.

A year later, with Iraqi impatience rising, Bremer's concern was that the Iraqis he had nominated to the IGC and whom he was going to appoint to be Iraq's government might call for a troop withdrawal. He told senior CPA officials he feared 'the potential for this body to pass resolutions that could be very harmful to coalition interests, such as calling for the withdrawal of the coalition'.[12] Other US officials worried that Iraqi ministers and the parliamentary representatives who would be elected the following year might 'veer out of control and challenge the US presence in Iraq', as one Bremer adviser put it.[13]

Bush was even more explicit about the danger. When he and his advisers talked to Bremer in a conference call to Baghdad shortly before the Americans were due to hand sovereignty to an appointed interim prime minister, the president told the meeting: 'It's important to have someone willing to stand up and thank the American people for their sacrifice in liberating Iraq. I don't expect a Yes man. But at least I want someone who will be grateful.' Bremer was deputed to meet potential candidates individually and check their loyalties. After he reported back to the White House a few days later, Bush was still nervous. 'We've got to be certain the new PM won't ask us to leave the day after sovereignty,' he insisted.[14]

Bush's refusal to contemplate an early withdrawal and set a timetable for a full pull-out was entirely consistent with the neoconservative imperial ideas. Yet it was, in my view, the cancer that undermined the occupation from the first day. It aroused Iraqi suspicions. It ignited nationalist anger and produced the insurgency. It reminded Iraqis of their long history of living under foreign rule. It affronted their sense of dignity. It made many Iraqis feel uncomfortable about taking senior jobs with the coalition. It turned Iraq into a magnet for jihadis from across the Muslim world, as well as for Al-Qaeda's terrorists. As an official for the Association of Muslim Scholars told me with a cold smile a year after the invasion: 'We say a double thank you. Thank you for coming here and removing Saddam. Thank you for coming here and making yourselves easier targets.'[15]

Some key Iraqi intellectuals who had enthusiastically campaigned for the USA to invade their country later realised what a disaster occupation was. Kanan Makiya, a long-time exile, a professor of Middle Eastern Studies at Brandeis University, and a former friend of Ahmad Chalabi, was one of the architects of regime change. His 1989 book about Saddam's atrocities, *Republic of Fear*,[16] was often quoted by the neoconservatives and Vice President Dick Cheney. He had met Bush in the White House. However, on the fourth anniversary of the invasion he had advocated for so long, he was in despair at the blood-letting: 'I want to look into myself, look at myself,

117

delve into the assumptions I had going into the war,' he told an interviewer. The Americans had to take much of the blame: 'Everything they could do wrong, they did wrong. The first and the biggest American error was the idea of going for an occupation,' he said.[17]

A few experts close to the US government saw the danger in advance. Conrad Crane and W. Andrew Terrill were in charge of a team at the US Army War College that came out with a far-sighted analysis in February 2003, a month before the war was launched, entitled 'Reconstructing Iraq'. The Pentagon released it with a disclaimer that their views did not necessarily reflect government policy. 'The longer the US presence is maintained, the more likely violent resistance will develop,' the analysts proclaimed in their opening paragraphs.[18]

They warned of the 'deep religious, ethnic, and tribal differences which dominate Iraqi society'. They pointed out that Iraqi politics had been 'considerably bloodier than usually seen in the rest of the Arab world'. Iraqi history was riddled with coups and counter-coups and armed clashes between factions in the streets. There was a high degree of volatility, with 58 Cabinets in the 37 years of the monarchy. Massive purges of the army were frequent long before Saddam Hussein. As a result, they advised: 'Understanding Iraq is a much greater challenge than considering the political culture of most other Arab nations.' They argued that post-Saddam politics would be characterised by the rise of ethnic and sectarian parties, and that even if democratic elections were held, there was no guarantee that the new government would be pro-Western. They pointed out that Yasser Arafat was the only Arab leader chosen freely and fairly, and he was no friend of the USA.

Above all, they warned that most Iraqis and other Arabs would assume that the USA intervened for its own purposes and not to liberate the population. Regionally the occupation would be viewed with great scepticism, which could only be overcome if Iraqis were quickly seen to be enjoying a secure and prosperous new life. It concluded:

> A US military occupation of Iraq will involve a number of special challenges and problems that relate directly to Iraqi political culture and wider regional sensitivities about the military domination of an Arab Muslim country by a Western power. Despite a relatively short experience with French and British occupation, the Arab world today is extraordinarily sensitive to the question of Western domination and has painful memories of imperialism.

Yet even this illuminating study did not bite the bullet by recommending that a US-led invasion should be followed by an early military withdrawal. In spite of its warning that suspicion of US motives and resistance would develop, it plumped for an occupation of three years. It hinted that things would be better if the USA handed over to an international force, but it did not make this a condition for success.

The Pentagon's initial instinct for a short occupation, as well as studies like the War College report, appear to have rubbed off on General Jay Garner, the first US overlord in Iraq. Unlike Bremer who succeeded him, Garner was not a neoconservative. The job the Pentagon asked him to do was to head something called the Office for Reconstruction and Humanitarian Affairs, a title that suggested his role was to handle a relatively short-term emergency. Garner told his family he would be back home by August.

In spite of the narrow title of his office, Garner realised a key component of his job was to find Iraqis to whom government could quickly be delegated, at least partially. Before the invasion the Bush administration had been torn over whether to nominate a government-in-exile. The neoconservatives wanted one, with Ahmad Chalabi at its head, but the State Department killed the idea on the grounds that it would look too much as though Washington was foisting its friends on the Iraqi people undemocratically. Under-Secretary of State Marc Grossman told the Senate Foreign Relations Committee in Washington DC on 11 February 2003: 'The Iraqi diaspora is a great resource but not a substitute for what all Iraqis will need to do together to work towards democracy in their country.'

Garner's plan, soon after he reached Baghdad, was to call a 'Big Tent' meeting of Iraqi civic and political leaders to discuss how the country should be governed. A meeting of around 70 Iraqis had already taken place under US military auspices in Nassiriya before the invading forces reached Baghdad. Garner's meeting on 28 April was more representative, however. It took place in the Green Zone in a large, low building, shaped like an oyster. About three hundred Iraqis turned up, well over half of them people who had spent the Saddam years at home, in prison, or underground. Their average age seemed to be around 60. It was hard not to be moved by the sight of these men (it was mainly men) emerging from the hall. Here was Iraq's civil society (the one which Bremer was to claim would take years to create) pottering collectively back into the sunlight after a quarter-century of repression.

I asked one short, elderly man in a brown suit what he felt about the meeting. He turned out to be Nasir al-Chadirchi, the son of a respected prime minister under the monarchy. A typically secular Baghdadi lawyer, who had belonged to the Communist party in the early 1960s, he pointed out that Iraq had many Islamist groupings, including the Hawza, the Shiite religious school in Najaf. They had a right to take part too, he said tolerantly. He went on:

> Chalabi had some support but not the majority here. There was no majority for any of the exiles. There will be a chain of meetings. We don't know when a government will be formed, but things may begin with elections for people to represent Baghdad.

Dominic Chilcott, a British official from the Foreign Office, and Larry Di Rita, Rumsfeld's adviser who was seconded to Garner's staff, briefed the media on their plans for the next step. Chilcott said there would be a 'national convention to determine the core of an interim authority'. Di Rita said the meeting had begun to discuss what the principles for this interim authority should be. Everyone recognised that today's meeting had not been representative enough to form the new authority, and it was never the intention to form it at the first get-together. Nevertheless, Iraqis had shown 'a clear sense of urgency' to have some form of decision-making process to interact with the coalition.

The national convention that Chilcott had predicted never happened. Within days of his 'Big Tent' meeting, Garner learnt he was to be replaced by Bremer. The new overlord was a neoconservative whose attitude to Iraqi politicians was perceived as condescending and arrogant. His memoirs drip with irritation at their opposition to his schemes and their slowness to reach decisions. He was reluctant even to bring Iraqis into the picture as advisers and he hoped to delay the transfer of sovereignty as long as possible.

The fact that he created an Interim Governing Council (IGC) in July was in no small measure thanks to two foreigners: John Sawers, a former British ambassador to Egypt and Saudi Arabia, who had been appointed as the top British civilian in the occupation; and Sergio Vieira de Mello, the UN secretary general's special representative in Iraq. De Mello, in particular, was highly sensitive to Iraqi views, and he made a point of meeting a wide cross section of civil society as soon as he arrived in Baghdad in June.

This included not just politicians and clerics, but representatives of women's groups, trade unions, and all the professions.

I first met de Mello when he served as the UN's man in Kosovo after Yugoslav forces withdrew. He was a man of enormous charm and energy who saw his role as a political administrator as one of listening to and including as many different interest groups as possible. In the few weeks he spent in Pristina before being transferred to East Timor, he worked hard to get representatives of the Albanian and Serbian communities in Kosovo to sit down together. He hoped to banish the triumphalism of the victorious Albanians and disarm the resentment of the defeated Serbs, so that they would stop taking their lead from Belgrade.

De Mello was one of the brightest men in the UN bureaucracy, and frequently tipped as a future secretary general. Born to a well-off Brazilian family, he had a doctorate in philosophy from the Sorbonne and was fluent in several European languages. A handsome man, he dressed elegantly without being ostentatious. Like many very bright men, his manner was sometimes aloof, but in conversation he was alert and an attentive listener – qualities not usually found in people who are arrogant. I got to know him better in East Timor where I spent a month researching a magazine article on the UN's performance.

In his short time in Baghdad he received me for two long discussions, in which he expressed a mixture of frustration with the Americans and optimism about Iraq. When he died a slow and painful death, trapped under concrete by a bomb blast, it was odd to think I had sat just a few days earlier on the sofa in his second-storey office, which was now a dusty pile of rubble. Three other people I interviewed in those first months of the occupation were later assassinated.

De Mello saw his priority as helping Iraqis recover their independence. Under the Security Council resolution that authorised the UN presence in occupied Iraq, his job was to work with Iraqis in restoring representative government. He interpreted this as part of a process that would get the Americans to leave. Only if Iraqis began to feel that the occupation of their country was coming to a speedy end would there be a reduction in the sense of humiliation which was creating the resistance, he believed.

The Americans had just killed Saddam Hussein's two sons, Uday and Qusay, after being tipped off they were in a house in Mosul and there was much speculation that Saddam would soon be cornered too. US officials assumed this would cut the resistance dramatically. De Mello took a different view. He was convinced that armed attacks on the Americans would go on being condoned rather than condemned by most Iraqis as long as the occupation continued. (At that stage the overwhelming number of resistance targets were Americans. Iraqi and other civilians were rarely attacked, and suicide bombing had barely started.) If foreign tanks appeared on the streets of Rio, people would resist, de Mello had told a Brazilian newspaper. To me, he put it like this in early July: 'Security can only get worse. Iraqis' impatience and exasperation with such a massive force is likely to increase and is psychologically understandable.'[19]

In the report he drafted for Kofi Annan to give the Security Council in mid-July, de Mello pointed out that in talking to Iraqis he heard 'an overwhelming demand for the early restoration of sovereignty and the message was conveyed that democracy could not be imposed from outside.'[20] Iraqi political, religious, and civic leaders were discussing 'an Iraqi-led transition agenda.'[21]

None of these hopes were fulfilled by Bremer and his masters in Washington. It was to be almost a year before sovereignty was transferred, and then only on paper. The transition agenda remained US-led. But de Mello had done what he could within the limits laid down by the occupation authorities. Creating a governing council was an essential, if small, part of giving Iraqis some form of ownership in the new Iraq. If there was not going to be a Garner-style national convention to elect an interim 'authority', de Mello wanted the small group of Iraqis Bremer intended to appoint at least to have some dignity. Bremer initially wanted them to be called an advisory body. De Mello got the name changed to 'governing council'. It was not entirely cosmetic, because the council was given the power to nominate ministers and approve the budget.

In East Timor de Mello had devised a system of double elections. First, there would be a nationwide vote for a constituent assembly. This would write a constitution that would be put to a referendum. If passed, elections for a parliament and president would follow. Apart from not having a directly elected president, the model was the one that the Americans ended up following in Iraq.

In spite of his strong views, de Mello managed to retain a close working relationship with the prickly Bremer. In public he was always careful to say he saw his role as complementary to Bremer's CPA. The UN man also performed a useful function by consulting Ayatollah Sistani (who refused to receive occupation officials) and by persuading men like Hakim to join the governing council. 'I decided it was best to keep a low profile,' he told me in early July. 'I've been trying to relay Iraqi frustrations and aspirations to the coalition in a manner which was found useful.' A touch boastfully, he added, 'I've been giving advice to Bremer on how to manage Iraqis' hurt pride.'

The best way was to show the occupation was not open-ended, he argued:

> I've told the CPA that it's important for Iraqis to realise this is a finite process. Iraqis complain that they're completely in the dark. They don't know if there's a calendar or road-map or when this will come to an end.

He tailored his case to Bremer for greater Iraqi inclusion, he said

> by stressing the utilitarian value of my advice in terms of the success of his project rather than any notion of international legitimacy. Bremer doesn't care about international legitimacy. He's a true neo-con.

Three weeks on, by which time the IGC had been established, de Mello's view of Bremer had shifted. He felt the US proconsul had become more aware of the need for international backing. Perhaps de Mello had also changed, and was now a more intimate part of the occupation team. He certainly showed he could be a good manipulator. The first crisis over Moqtada al-Sadr had erupted. True to his principles of inclusivity, de Mello took the view that the coalition should open contacts with the young cleric. It was not shared by Bremer or any other senior coalition official, including John Sawers, the British representative, who told me the senior Shia clerics he talked to saw Moqtada as 'an over-energised young man who hasn't properly grown up and is not anchored'.[22] Sawers made it clear he agreed. De Mello took a different line, though it sounded cynical:

> We should talk to Moqtada and the last thing we should do is to ostracise him. The problem is we don't control him. He's not one of us … It's always useful to have an enfant terrible, as long as you can control him.[23]

A few days later, de Mello was dead. The men who launched the bomb attack on UN headquarters in Baghdad were linked to Al-Qaeda. In November 2004, intermediaries from one of the main mosques in Fallujah gave me a tape purportedly made by the group, led by Abu Musab al-Zarqawi, the leader of Al-Qaeda in Iraq. It claimed the driver of the massive truck bomb that had killed de Mello and 21 other UN staffers was Abu Farida al-Masri, an Egyptian who, the tape said, had already killed several Coptic Christians. De Mello was targeted because he had 'dismembered' Indonesia by removing East Timor. The UN building was full of 'agents', according to the tape. Was this the real reason why the UN headquarters was targeted by the truck that drove into the lightly guarded car park and detonated close to the side of the building? Did the murderers feel the UN had become too close to the occupation, and was helping it to entrench itself? Or did the atrocity, which was bound to reduce the UN's influence and force Kofi Annan to pull the remaining UN staff out of Iraq, have other aims? Perhaps Al-Qaeda wanted to create chaos by leaving the Americans without any legitimising or restraining advice from the UN.

The UN had a good reputation with most Iraqis – although it was hard to find any US or British officials in Baghdad who admitted or knew that. Bremer himself thought the opposite, writing in his memoirs that 'I knew many Iraqis believed the UN had turned a blind eye to Saddam's brutality'[24] and 'I wanted our coalition, not the United Nations with its murky political agendas, to take the lead.'[25] Sawers' line was similar. 'The UN doesn't have the standing and authority it has in many countries', he told me in July 2003. Their comments sounded like a classic case of confusing the UN with the major powers that sit on the Security Council and give the UN its instructions. The Western veto-wielding nations supported Saddam during his war on Iran in the 1980s. In the 1990s it was they who imposed sanctions, which the UN had to administer.

Although a majority of Security Council members dared to thwart Washington and London in early 2003 by not passing a resolution to authorise an invasion of Iraq, their backbone softened once Saddam was ousted. It was as though one battle with the USA was enough. They were not prepared to fight US and British efforts to get a UN resolution to approve their post-invasion role as Iraq's administrators. The Russians played little part in modifying the US/UK draft but, as usual, the French tried hardest. They wanted the UN to take charge of post-war Iraq and set a timetable for a US and UK troop withdrawal. French diplomats say the aim was not to embarrass Washington and London but to create a basis of international legitimacy for peacekeepers to come in and prepare a rapid handover to an Iraqi government: 'We did not want to make the disaster more disastrous,' in the words of one senior official.[26] Before the invasion, they had predicted that Iraq's ethnic, sectarian, and tribal complexities would make it hard for a new government to establish its authority and create stability. The French line was not adopted, and Paris went along with the US/UK draft.

UN officials were divided. Senior members of Kofi Annan's political staff, including Kieran Prendergast, a former British Foreign Office official, were cautious about getting involved in Iraq. They saw trouble ahead. Others like Jan Egeland, a former Norwegian foreign minister who was the UN's humanitarian coordinator, wanted to move in. Annan came down on the latter's side. He felt the UN had to show Washington goodwill and prove the UN could be relevant. The new resolution would lift sanctions and the UN would take part in reconstruction in post-war Iraq.

Resolution 1483, which emerged on 22 May, was a lop-sided compromise that gave Washington most of what it wanted. The only concession it made was that the USA and UK were referred to as 'occupying powers'. They had hoped to get a text which would either call them liberators, or at least use a neutral term like administrators. In every other way the resolution satisfied them. It effectively authorised their presence on an open-ended basis, merely stating the situation would be reviewed in a year's time. There was no mention of a timetable for withdrawal or of replacing the US-led coalition with UN peacekeepers. Instead, other countries were invited to send troops to join the US-led coalition.

There was also no date for the establishment of an Iraqi government. Under international law, occupying powers are supposed to confine themselves to preserving law and order and taking care of the population's humanitarian needs. They are not supposed to govern or change the country's government system. Resolution 1483 gave the USA and UK that right.

The UN role in post-war Iraq, although it was described in the resolution as 'vital', was in fact only peripheral and advisory. It was confined to reconstruction, humanitarian affairs, and help in bringing about representative government. After his appointment as Annan's special representative, de Mello met Annan and other senior UN officials in New York to be briefed by the UN's top legal adviser on how much executive authority he would have. The resolution used vague phrases about the UN being in Iraq to 'facilitate', 'encourage', 'promote', and 'help'. 'At the end of the meeting, we were more confused than when we started,' one participant recalls.[27]

UN resolution 1483 was a watershed from which most of Washington's subsequent problems flowed. Had there been a transfer of peacekeeping to the UN in May 2003, the insurgency could have been avoided. With the UN rather than the US in charge, Iraqi suspicions that their country was a pawn on Washington's imperial chessboard would have been stillborn. This was the greatest missed opportunity of the post-invasion period.

In the summer of 2002, nine months before the invasion, Blair had urged Bush to 'take the UN route', and seek international approval for US and UK actions. In February and March 2003 he pressed hard for a UN resolution to authorise the invasion, even though he later claimed it was not legally required since in Britain's view resolutions from 1990 already permitted one. After Saddam was ousted, Blair lost interest in pressing for a handover to the UN. Bush would not have it, and Blair did not try. In the words of a senior official in the British Foreign Office who asked to remain anonymous, 'The Americans were not suddenly going to say, "We'll hand over to the UN." It wasn't practical politics.'[28]

Edward Mortimer, Kofi Annan's speech-writer, eloquently described the compromise behind UN 1483 in a newspaper article a few months later. Writing in a personal capacity, he warned that the Security Council's willingness to let the USA and the UK run the occupation would doom it to violent resistance:

The Security Council, when it passed Resolution 1483, struck an implicit bargain: accept the occupation as a temporary expedient, whatever you think of its origins, in order to be able to work for a better outcome. In doing so, it deliberately skated over the issue of legitimacy – not an airy-fairy concept, but what makes people obey a government even when it is not standing over them with a gun.

Legitimacy is crucial because no government – and especially not a foreign government – can deploy enough guns to coerce all of the people all of the time. Unless Iraqis themselves are given the power, and have the will, to confront the forces of violence and disorder in their society, those forces will not be checked … If Iraqis will accept any outside help in reorganising their state and confronting the forces of disorder, it surely must be from people who derive their legitimacy not from the right of conquest but from a UN mandate.[29]

Iraqis from various political groupings whom I spoke to at the time, as well as non-political people, made it clear they preferred a UN presence to occupation by the USA and the UK. Amar Hakim, Ayatollah Mohammed Baqir al-Hakim's nephew and official spokesman, told me in Najaf in early July 2003:

> It would really be an achievement if power can be taken from the CPA and given to the UN … Any government chosen by Bremer cannot be defended in front of the Iraqi people, and won't be able to bear responsibility … It is the UN which can help to minimise differences among Iraqis and take care of their demands.

Moqtada al-Sadr's spokesman in Najaf, a young cleric called Sayed Mustafa Jaafar al-Yaqoubi, made the same point to me on the same day, albeit more obliquely. He contrasted the UN with the USA: 'The UN is a humanitarian international organisation representing the whole world. We consider the United States as occupiers.'[30]

Most relevantly, perhaps, Sunni clerics had a positive view of the UN. In the early weeks of the occupation the chances that an insurgency would develop were strongest among Sunnis. In April, when Garner was still in charge of the occupation, I visited the Abu Hanifa mosque in Adhamiya, a northern suburb of Baghdad. It was outside this mosque that Saddam made his last known public appearance before the Americans reached Baghdad. Wearing army uniform and a beret, the dictator had had himself filmed briefly talking to a few dozen people in the street.

The imam, Dr Rashid al-Obeidi, told me he wanted to believe the best of the Americans. He hoped Garner would help to form an Iraqi government, as his 'Big Tent' meeting seemed to be proposing. 'They should do that, and then go. The United Nations could do good if they come. They're not an army,' he said. The mosque's Friday preacher, Sheikh Moayed Azami, took the same line: 'Garner says they will leave Iraq after they've formed a government. I hope so, and I believe it. We don't want more damage.'

From the Abu Hanifa mosque I drove a short distance to the home of Wamidh Nadhmi, a professor of political science at Baghdad University. He was an Arab nationalist from the Nasser era and one of the most interesting secular Iraqis who had never gone into exile under Saddam. That fact made some Iraqis suspect him, especially as foreign journalists and other visitors had been allowed to see him in the latter part of the Saddam era when all such contacts were controlled. But he had been elected president of the Arab Association of Political Scientists, which gave him some international protection, and he carefully stepped back from any political organising during the Saddam period. He confined himself to intellectual criticism, and this was tolerated. The authorities gave him permission to subscribe to the *Guardian Weekly*, which arrived regularly by post un-tampered and with no articles cut out by Iraqi censors. Nadhmi even got the edition that contained pictures of the aftermath of Saddam's use of gas against Halabja in 1988. When Nadhmi told me that story, I was reminded that South Africa's prison authorities had let Nelson Mandela receive the *Guardian Weekly* in his cell on Robben Island. Maybe our paper was not as radical as some of us liked to think.

In his sixties and with a PhD from Durham University, Nadhmi rarely failed to charm his European visitors. He took a lively interest in world politics and knew the subtleties of most countries' systems. I found chatting with him provided a welcome escape from the intensity of the Iraqi debate, though when he got back to local politics his analysis of the various players' motives and ambitions was detailed and acute.

Nadhmi recalled his excitement at the huge pre-war demonstrations against Bush and Blair in London, Paris, New York, and other cities. 'Tony Blair faces more opposition in Britain than he does from Arab rulers,' he commented wryly. He accepted that Islamists would be strong in the new post-Saddam Iraq, but that was not the main issue. The priority was to have national unity against the occupation. 'What we're faced with now is not a choice between secularism and religion. We're facing an invasion and foreign rule,' he argued.

He refused to join Garner's 'Big Tent' on principle:

> Garner represents an occupation force and an aggression that went against UN resolutions and has no legitimacy. It's led by an administration which is trying to impose US hegemony all over the world, and is being confronted by people and governments in many countries. It's especially hostile to Arabs and Muslims.

There was nothing wrong with hospital directors or university administrators having practical contacts with the Americans. That made sense. But political dialogue was another matter. He and his fellow Arab nationalists in Baghdad were boycotting Garner. 'It's unfruitful and pointless, as well as humiliating and unpatriotic. We won't take part in this conference or any other which the US authorities call,' he told me.

Nadhmi had always had good contacts with the Kurds. He had been out-raged by Saddam's anti-Kurdish atrocities. Since Saddam's fall, when it be-came possible to meet Kurdish politicians again, he said he had urged them to unite but not be too dependent on the Americans:

> I've told them: 'We don't ask you to fight the Americans. That would be ridic-ulous and you're threatened for the time being by Turkey. But please stand by the Arabs, and understand the attitude of Arab patriots. You are the only group which is justified in accepting US protection.'

Among the Shias, Nadhmi reserved his praise for the Dawa party, though he called it fundamentalist. Although some leaders had escaped abroad, it was the only group that had left people inside Iraq to conduct armed re-sistance to Saddam, in spite of massive repression. He had doubts about Hakim's SCIRI, which he thought was 'playing a game'. They appeared to be opposing the Americans or at least distancing themselves, but he was not sure whether they would stick to that line. The Sadrists were interesting because they represented the 'Iraqi Arab tendency' among the Shias while SCIRI represented the 'Iraqi Iranian tendency'.

When it came to a role for the UN, Nadhmi took a moderate position. He favoured a UN peacekeeping force, into which US and British troops would integrate, saying, 'To ask for US and UK troops to leave is unrealistic. But bring UN troops in and they can be part of it.'

The politicians most conflicted about how to respond to the occupation in those crucial early weeks were Iraq's Communists. They were torn in at least three or four directions. Founded in 1934, they prided themselves on being Iraq's oldest political party. In the 1950s and 1960s they enjoyed sub-stantial popularity among Baghdad's secular and professional intelligentsia, as well as in Kurdistan and the towns of the Shia south, except the holy cities of Najaf and Kerbala. They were never so strong among Sunnis.

The Communists' relationship with the Baathists was always tense and difficult. They saw the Baathists as latecomers who were competing with them for the same constituency. After the first short-lived Baathist coup in 1963, they suffered massive repression. At least 3,000 of their members and supporters were tortured and executed. In 1973, after the Baathists were back in power, the Communists signed an agreement called the National Action Charter. They approved the Baathist government's apparent com-mitment to socialist goals as well as its good links with the Soviet Union.

The party was legalised again, allowed to organise, and invited to contribute two ministers to the government. However, as Saddam began to take control of the Baath party in 1977 and 1978, the Communists once again lost out. There was another wave of arrests and executions, the party was banned again, and by 1979 most of its surviving leaders had had to flee Iraq or move to Iraqi Kurdistan where they set up armed partisan units.

This bitter legacy put the Communists in a fearful quandary when they re-surfaced in Iraq in April 2003. They had boycotted the London conference of exiles and come out against the invasion. But they also hated Saddam, having suffered so many murders of their party cadres at his hands. As a result, they were vigorous advocates of extensive de-Baathification, although they opposed the way the Islamist parties politicised it. Many senior members of the party were Kurds and the party had its own branch in Kurdistan, where it had operated freely since 1991 and had been in government in Irbil with the Kurdish Democratic party, under the protection of the US-enforced no-fly zone.

Finally, there was the issue of power. The Communists had been unable to campaign easily in the quarter of a century since they had last been a legal party. They knew they had lost a good deal of support. Meanwhile, the Islamists had become much stronger. To support armed resistance against the Americans offered no prospect of progress or reconstruction, the Communists argued. But could they afford to go into non-violent opposition? Would this not lead to their marginalisation?

The Communists decided the way out of the dilemma was to stay in the game, suspend competition between the parties for the time being, and try to form a national unity government with representation from all the secular and religious groups. I stopped in at the party's new headquarters in Baghdad's suburb of Karrada the day after it opened on 19 April. The building used to belong to the *mukhabarat* (the security service) and the Communists simply broke in and took it over in the same way that other parties were grabbing abandoned regime property throughout the capital and in the major towns. A team of party members was painting out the slogans from the Saddam period that covered the walls. One quoted the dictator: 'Keep the enemy in your sights and don't let him get behind you.' Another team had just had time to hang red flags on the building's facade along with a banner celebrating 'A free homeland for joyous people'. In the foyer, frail-looking elderly men, some of them released from prison little more than a week earlier, were embracing long-lost friends. There were tears and hugs. Hundreds of party activists who had fled to Kurdistan were already back in Baghdad, giving the Communists initially a bigger presence than other parties. Others had emerged from clandestinity in Baghdad.

Faris Faris, a member of the party's Central Committee, told me as we sat on metal chairs in an otherwise unfurnished room that Iraq needed unity after the Saddam years. The priority was to get the Americans to accept there should be an independent Iraqi government, and to have it in place soon. At the same time it was clear the Communists were preparing for the looming competition with their Islamist rivals:

> We are suspending our ideological differences. The ballot box will decide. We're in a very difficult situation. We've got to start building a democratic society. We must build new structures for workers, farmers, the intelligentsia, artists, and young people.

When it came to the party's attitude to the Americans, Faris took what sounded like a militant line: 'I would like the Americans to leave now. We want Iraq's reconstruction to take place under the patronage of the United Nations,' he said. The issue of whether formally to ask the USA to go would be up to the new Iraqi government to decide, he added. In the meantime the party would not cooperate with Garner's consultation process. He explained that 'Some people want Iraqis to bow down to foreigners. Others are like us and think we should build an independent national government made up of all parties on a temporary basis.'

I was back at the party's headquarters three months later. It was 14 July, the 45th anniversary of the toppling of the monarchy, and for the first time for 30 years groups representing every kind of political line had been free to take part. A mile-long procession of banner-carrying men and women marched through Baghdad to Firdous square, where Saddam's statue had been situated. Many carried pictures of Abdul Karim Qassim, the army officer who led the coup against the king. Others had banners with implicit anti-occupation slogans: 'We want a transitional national government for the Iraqi people'; 'We want Iraqi sovereignty'; and 'There is no alternative to Iraqis deciding their future by themselves'.

Kawa Besarani, a Kurdish member of the party's leadership, had just returned from the march when I met him. A long-time activist and intellectual, he conceded the party was torn over what to do. The IGC that Bremer appointed had been inaugurated the previous day. A long and agonising meeting of the party's executive had decided that Hamid Mousa, the party's general secretary, should accept Bremer's invitation to join. Besarani conceded the IGC fell short of what the communists and many other parties wanted. It did not include all groups. For example, the Arab nationalists had decided to stay out. In spite of being called a 'governing' council, Bremer retained the right to veto any decision. There was also a real danger the council would be made a scapegoat for the coalition's failings: instead of blaming the Americans for electricity shortages, people would blame the IGC, even though it was the Americans who were in charge.

A slight majority of the IGC's 25 members, including its three women, had remained in Iraq under Saddam, but its inner core was the so-called Group of Seven parties, all but one of which had been in exile (the two Kurdish parties, Chalabi's Iraqi National Congress, Iyad Allawi's Iraqi National Accord, Dawa, SCIRI, and Chadirchi's National Democratic party). Besarani acknowledged that many Iraqis felt the IGC were US puppets who had tied their colours to the US mast in exile. He responded defensively:

> That's an emotional reaction ... I don't think people who feel that way appreciate what's going on in Iraq. We are in an occupied country. We and the other political forces need to operate in a new arena. There's a new environment for political struggle. We have to accept the complication of the moment.

The first issues the IGC had already had to decide were whether to send a delegation to New York to address the Security Council in a week's time when de Mello went there to give his first report, and what the team's mandate would be. The IGC chose a three-man team made up of Adnan Pachachi, a secular former foreign minister, Ahmad Chalabi, the Pentagon favourite, and Tariq al-Hashemi, who led the Iraq Islamic party, a mainly Sunni grouping that was banned during the Saddam period.

Besarani revealed that the delegation had decided not to raise the issue of UN troops replacing the Americans. Instead, it would recommend a gradual sequence of events – first to set up some form of representative Iraqi government, then to build a new Iraqi army, and to leave the question of a US troop withdrawal until later. The formula was exactly what Washington wanted. However, Besarani claimed there was no realistic alternative since the Security Council had passed Resolution 1483 in May. Any chance for

Iraqis, or other nations, to put pressure on the USA and Britain to hand over responsibility to a UN peacekeeping force and announce a timetable for withdrawing US and British troops had already been lost.

If the USA had wanted to leave Iraq soon after toppling Saddam, could it have done so? Some analysts say it was impossible, both legally and practically. Under international law, specifically the Hague Convention of 1907, occupying powers have certain obligations. One is to take all necessary measures to restore public order. They cannot abdicate until other peacekeepers or a new government emerge. The argument carries little weight, however, first because the USA singularly failed to restore public order from the first day of the occupation. By not stepping in to curb the postwar looting and only seriously defending one Iraqi government building, the oil ministry, US forces quickly broke their obligations as occupiers. There is also nothing in the Hague Convention that would have prevented the USA from announcing a timetable for withdrawal, by inviting alternative outside forces or the Iraqis to restore order, and acting as caretakers until they arrived.

Other analysts make a 'democratic' case for claiming the USA had to remain in Iraq. Many Iraqis wanted the Americans to stay, partly for security reasons since they feared the Baathists would fill the vaccum and return to power, and partly in order to get electricity and other basic services going. It is certainly true that many Iraqis, particularly in Baghdad, complained of constant power cuts and blamed them on the Americans. They could not believe a superpower managed to topple the regime within less than three weeks, using massive high-tech missiles and bombs, but was not able to guarantee a reliable supply of electricity. This was the 'You broke it, now fix it' argument.

Security fears were frequently expressed, mainly by Shias. 'There's no safety, no order,' Mohammed Abdul Salam, a young Baghdad barber whose father was executed by Saddam, told me. 'I used to close my shop at 1am. Now I have to close it by 7pm. I was walking home with my takings and was almost surrounded by a group of thieves. I just managed to run off.' He was also worried about a possible Baathist comeback: 'We're ready to eat bread and onions rather than have Saddam back. I don't want the US to leave. There will be confusion. We want security,' he said.[31]

Important though these views were, polling data showed that they were not shared by the majority. A national poll by the Iraq Centre for Research and Strategic Studies at the end of September 2003 found that 50 per cent opposed the presence of coalition forces while only 33 per cent supported them.[32] Asked who contributed most to their security, the number who cited the local police was four times higher than the number who cited coalition forces. Even the presence of local neighbourhood patrols was seen as more effective than US and UK forces.

As for the danger of a Baathist comeback, Sayed Mustafa Jaafar al-Yaqoubi, one of Moqtada al-Sadr's spokesman, told me in Najaf in July 2003: 'Even if Saddam tried to make a comeback, Iraqis have now tasted relative freedom. They wouldn't tolerate his return.' The argument sounded convincing, especially as Shias, who particularly hated Saddam, were growing increasingly confident of using their demographic majority to become Iraq's dominant political force. The Baathists were discredited and demoralised. It is true that, as the occupation dragged on, it became more common to hear Iraqis comparing life under the Americans to Saddam's rule, and saying that things used to be better. But in most cases this 'Saddam nostalgia' sounded rhetorical. It was a complaint against the invasion and the chaos it had brought rather than a sign of serious support for the Baathists to return to power.

Finally, there is an argument that Iraq after Saddam was a 'collapsed state', and that the Americans had to stay in Iraq to rebuild it. This is a version of the 'You broke it, now fix it' argument, but more far-reaching. According to this view, it was not just electricity and public services that needed repair, but all public institutions and the entire fabric of government.

One of the clearest expositions of the 'collapsed state' case is made by Toby Dodge, a British historian of Iraq.[33] He argues that the Iraqi government's capacity had been hollowed out under Saddam, first by years of sanctions and then by the regime's diversion of resources from official institutions to networks of patronage. The entrance of US troops into Baghdad in April 2003 destroyed it altogether. Dodge argued, 'The Iraqi state, its ministries, their civil servants, police force and army ceased to exist in any meaningful way in the aftermath of regime change.'[34] It would require decades of US commitment to reverse the process. 'Unless the US can commit to the generation-long project of rebuilding the Iraqi state – and this seems highly unlikely – then Iraq will continue to be a place of misery for its population and instability for its region,' he concluded.[35]

His argument, in my view, exaggerated the degree of collapse of the Iraqi state. It was certainly true that the army dispersed as the Americans advanced, and Bremer then declared it dissolved – but it could have been quickly restored had the Americans invited it back. Whole units were ready to return to duty, and the only change needed was the purge of a few senior Baathist officers. The army long pre-dated Saddam as an honoured national institution. It was not identified as closely with Saddam's repression as the newer forces he had created, such as the Special Republican Guard and the Fedayeen Saddam.

A similar story applied to the police force. Many of its men came back to work within days of the regime's removal, and if the occupation authorities had been quicker in announcing pay increases and other incentives, and had rapidly employed Iraqis to repair looted or damaged police stations, a revived police force could have been in action within weeks. I saw many functioning police stations in the first months of the occupation. Walls had sometimes been shattered by shelling or rockets during the invasion, furniture was rudimentary, and vehicles were in short supply, but the men were on duty. It is true that they did not return in time to fill the entire security vacuum. Criminal gangs operated with impunity and there was a surge in kidnappings and armed robbery. But it was another two years, with the onset of sectarian killing, before the police lost credibility and 'collapsed' as a force that Iraqis could trust.

Nor was the looting and destruction of ministries as serious a problem as is sometimes claimed. The CPA got the foreign ministry back in action in its original building within three months, and the same could have been done for other ministries. Not all were beyond repair. The Americans went into the defence ministry a month after the occupation and found thousands of highly classified files still intact.[36] Reports that Baath party activists and Saddam's security service people had been rushing round all the official buildings in Baghdad destroying sensitive documents were not correct.

In Iraq's smaller towns looting was less systematic than in Baghdad and Basra. In any case, for most Iraqis the symbols of governmental authority do not reside in ministry buildings in the capital city: they depend on functioning schools and hospitals. Hospitals remained open throughout the invasion, and thanks to their staff few were looted. Schools resumed rapidly in April 2003. They had closed during the invasion because of fear of US and UK bomb attacks, but started up afterwards.

A third factor of state activity that was crucial for most Iraqis was the continued supply of subsidised food rations. Every Iraqi family was listed on computerised records held at small warehouses in each neighbourhood. They were entitled once a month to pick up supplies of rice, sugar, cooking oil, flour, and other staples. Originally set up under the UN's Oil-for-Food Programme, these rations had become a lifeline for an estimated 60 per cent of Iraqis after the country's economy nose-dived under the pressure of sanctions. Bremer's team initially wanted to phase them out on the grounds they were a socialist hangover that went against market economics. De Mello's UN office successfully dissuaded Bremer from taking such a disastrous step, which would have alienated the entire population. So the subsidised food supplies continued under the same system of UN-run financing as before the invasion, a clear sign for Iraqis that the state had not collapsed.

The real issue was who ran the state. Was there a government that Iraqis felt was legitimate? How soon would Iraqis regain their sovereignty? Even though UN Resolution 1483 showed that the US intended to keep troops in Iraq on an open-ended basis, would power return to Iraqi hands rapidly and substantially enough for the nationalist element of the slowly growing insurgency to give up the fight against the occupation? Chapter IV has already described how the Americans created resistance, even among moderate Shias, by their initial delay in holding elections – a policy that made Shias suspect US intentions. But US reluctance to go down the electoral route served to alienate all Iraqi communities.

Early withdrawal had been ruled out, but could there be early sovereignty? Bremer was no enthusiast for it. Even before he appointed the IGC, he had made his imperious attitude clear. 'One thing you need to realise is you're not the government. We are. We're in charge,' he told the leaders of the main exile groups on 16 May 2003.[37] It was an extraordinarily arrogant and insensitive line that can only have alienated and humiliated the Iraqi elite, even as they still lacked the confidence or the will to call for the occupation to end. Gradually, too, many of them started to come to the view that the priority was to get an Iraqi government in place and leave the issue of the US troop presence until later.

Rumsfeld and the generals were keen to appoint an Iraqi government within months. Shortly before the invasion General John Abizaid, an Arabic-speaking Lebanese-American who was deputy head of US Central Command, had said: 'We must in all things be modest. We are an antibody in their culture.'[38] As the insurgency in Sunni areas began to grow, the Pentagon started to realise that part of it was fuelled by nationalist anger. By then the rate of attacks on coalition troops had reached 30 a day. On a trip back to Washington in October, Bremer was handed a plan by Rumsfeld. It called for sovereignty to be transferred on 9 April 2004, the anniversary of Saddam's statue being toppled. This, Rumsfeld argued, would remove the label that the US forces were occupiers. Bremer disagreed with the timetable. He thought 31 December 2004 was early enough. Instead of giving in, he started complaining to the administration's chief hawk, Vice President Dick Cheney, that there was no military strategy for victory.

At one level Bremer saw the point which Abizaid was making. In a broadcast to Iraqis in mid-August 2003 he had acknowledged it publicly, though rather patronisingly as though Arabs had not already sensed it for themselves: 'Dignity is hard to maintain when foreign troops, no matter how well intentioned, walk your streets', he said. The remedy he proposed was completely inadequate. Instead of setting out a schedule for withdrawing US troops from Iraq he merely offered a plan for building up Iraq's forces: 'In the months ahead you will see fewer troops on your streets as coalition troops are replaced by trained, effective Iraqi police.'[39]

Bremer realised that without a full withdrawal of troops from Iraq sovereignty meant little. Bob Woodward reports Bremer as telling Andy Card, Bush's chief of staff in October:

> We are kidding ourselves if we think it's the silver bullet that's going to end the opposition. It won't, because the average Iraqi's going to go outside his house and there's still going to be a Bradley tank sitting there.[40]

In his own memoirs, Bremer was blunter:

> I said no Iraqi, insurgent or not, would be fooled by such semantics. We would still have lots of forces in the country which would certainly look to most Iraqis like an 'occupying' army, whatever we called it.[41]

The answer should have been to plan for a full US withdrawal rather than make it conditional on Iraqi forces slowly being trained. It was not just a question of removing what Rumsfeld had called the 'label' of occupation, but removing the occupation itself. However, Bremer was not keen on an early end either to the occupation or his own role. He justified his case for delaying the transfer of sovereignty partly on the issue of what kind of government would take over. Would it be appointed or elected? Would there first be a new constitution, and who should draw it up? He wanted time to thrash these questions out.

Bremer felt the constitution was the most important problem since it would set the country's guidelines for years ahead, long after sovereignty was transferred. As a neoconservative, Bremer wanted it to enshrine the privatisation of the economy, including the oil sector, and to protect foreign investors. But Bush was beginning to worry about his re-election chances. As the Iraq triumph soured, with US troop casualties rising, he felt he had to create a sense of momentum towards his stated goal of democracy in the Middle East. He was not primarily interested in whether sovereignty would affect the casualty rate. But he hoped the transfer of sovereignty would help him to claim to the American people that his strategy of making Iraq a model pro-Western democracy was working. First topple Saddam, then give Iraqis back their country. He decided that the end of June would be the transfer date, later than Rumsfeld wanted but sooner than Bremer proposed.

Behind the nit-picking over dates a new dynamic was taking root in US policy – 'stay the course'. The more US troops died, the greater became the temptation to remain in Iraq so that there could be no perception of the USA giving up or retreating. The dynamic is as old as war itself. It was particularly hard to counter in the macho locker-room culture that Bush cultivated, where tough questions were not asked, difficult options were not put on the table, and the image of strong leadership in the 'war on terror' was made priority number one.

Bremer recounts a White House meeting on 27 October 2003. Bush was there along with Condoleezza Rice, Donald Rumsfeld, and General Abizaid. Bremer told the president most Iraqis supported Bush's vision of a peaceful, democratic Iraq. Abizaid discussed the new sophistication of the insurgents' methods. Bremer said how hard it was to find good Iraqi leaders since Saddam had killed or co-opted all of them. They talked about strengthening Iraq's security forces. Bush cut the discussion short with a typically simple message: 'Well, one thing is clear. We stay the course in Iraq. We don't show any weakness in the wake of these new attacks. There'll be no loss of resolve now,' he insisted.[42]

To a man with a mindset like Bush's, the insurgency was not only forcing the USA to stay. More usefully, it was also creating the pretext for it to stay – which is what the neoconservatives had always intended to do. And it was making it harder for any Democratic challenger in the 2004 election to call for the US to abandon the war. It was not until a sectarian bloodbath started in 2006 that members of the US Congress were able to develop an argument for leaving that would be acceptable to the political mainstream – 'you can't play a useful role in other countries' civil wars'.

The 'stay the course' mentality affected almost every US official. Here was another clash of cultures, American machismo versus an Iraqi desire to run their own affairs. Even liberals could not break free of it. Larry Diamond, a professor of political science at Stanford, served for four months as a CPA adviser in early 2004. He left disillusioned. In a confidential memo to Rice as he departed, he warned her that if the USA did not find ways to enhance the legitimacy of the political process in Iraq so as to 'ease pervasive Iraqi suspicions and anxieties about American motives and intent, we will face a widening resistance that we will not be able to defeat militarily'. He recommended that the USA should state clearly it did not want permanent military bases in Iraq. He proposed a target date for withdrawing US forces. So far, so good. But Diamond's target date was long into the future – 'three or four years down the line', as he put it. More importantly, he called for the USA in the meantime to send 'significantly more troops and equipment'.[43] This sounded like the 'surge' that Bush was to adopt almost four years later – hardly a convincing exit strategy.

In practice, the 'stay the course' policy was doomed neither to satisfy Iraqis and end the insurgency nor to reduce US casualties. Rather the opposite. Richard Armitage, a former senior State Department official who advised Colin Powell, asked Powell the following about Bush in 2004: 'Has he thought this through? What the president says in effect is we've got to press on in honour of the memory of those who have fallen. Another way to say that is we've got to have more men fall to honour the memories of those who have already fallen.'[44]

It sounded alarmingly like Vietnam. When Bush first announced his 'stay the course' strategy, the number of US troop deaths was 265. Four years later, it was 15 times higher, and the president was still refusing to name a date for US troop withdrawal.

VI

CREATING RESISTANCE:
HUMILIATION AND DEATH

We've even lost our right to get undressed for bed.
Saad al-Mahdawi, March 2004[1]

The resistance was born not only of ideological, religious, and patriotic convictions, but also as a response to the brutal actions of the occupation and its administration. It is a response to arbitrary break-ins, humiliating searches, arrests, detention and torture.
Haifa Zangana, April 2007[2]

I t was a warm, spring evening in May 2003 when US troops stopped the car in which 11-year-old Sufian Abd al-Ghani was riding with his uncle and a neighbour close to their suburban Baghdad homes. They were ordered out and told to lie on the road face down. Sufian's father heard the commotion and rushed out of his house to find the soldiers pointing their rifles at his son and the others. Claiming the uncle had fired at them, the troops started beating the three captives with their rifle butts, the father said later.

A neighbour confirmed that a shot had been fired, but described it as part of a row between the Ghanis and another family. 'In Iraq this is normal. Almost every household in Baghdad owns a weapon. One man was drunk. The Americans must have heard the shot as they were passing. It was not directed at them,' the neighbour, who preferred not to be named, told me when I came to investigate the incident.

The American soldiers searched the Ghanis' house while Sufian was kept on the ground with the two adults for three hours. Although the

Americans found nothing suspicious, they put hoods over their captives' heads, tied their wrists with tight plastic handcuffs, and drove them away. 'Why are you taking my son?', a desperate Abdullah al-Ghani pleaded. 'Don't worry. As he's a child, we'll send him back in a couple of days,' a Sgt Stark assured him.

The three were taken to Camp Cropper, a detention centre on the huge US army complex near Baghdad airport. It was less than two months since Saddam Hussein was ousted and the occupation was still young, but around 500 Iraqis were already being held in Camp Cropper.[3] They slept on the ground in large tents with inadequate water rations and not enough blankets to go round, according to former detainees with whom I spoke.

Sufian spent eight days with around 20 adults in these miserable conditions. They were given packets of ready-to-eat meals but no change of clothes. Then the hood went back over his head and Sufian was taken to the Salhiyeh detention centre for women and juveniles – a holding facility run by US military police in an Iraqi police station just outside the Green Zone.

Sufian's luck seemed to be turning at last. A woman prisoner realised he was much younger than the other inmates. As soon as she was released a few days later she went to see the Ghani family, who had been searching frantically for their son. It was now 17 June, almost three weeks after his arrest on 28 May. They brought the boy food and clean clothes, and four days later obtained an order from Mohammed Latif al-Duleimi, a US-approved investigating judge, for Sufian's immediate release. Elated, Sufian's father took it to the US military police who ran the Salhiyeh detention centre.

To his shock, they told him Iraqi judges' orders had no legal authority.

Now Ghani turned for help to the new US-founded police academy. There he met a Capt Crusoe, who was moved by the boy's story and took up the case. He rang a US army lawyer at Camp Cropper who ordered the boy's immediate release. Yet when Ghani returned to the detention centre, hoping to be able to take his son home at last, the military police still refused to act. Ghani went back to Capt Crusoe, who made more phone calls, but to no avail. Finally Crusoe, by now almost as frustrated as Ghani, went to the detention centre with Ghani. He walked in, demanded the boy be handed over, and brought Sufian out himself. 'Take your son,' he said.

The boy's ordeal was over after 24 days, but serious questions remained. How could an 11-year-old child be held for over three weeks without anyone in authority asking questions? Why did his freedom have to depend on his father having the luck to come across the goodwill and sympathy of an energetic American officer rather than on an efficient system of checking, charging, or releasing detainees?

The answer was depressingly simple. The US army had planned for war for almost a year but made no proper arrangements for policing Iraq and handling detainees after the fall of Saddam. It was an astonishing failure, given that one of the invasion's stated purposes was to remove a dictator and restore human rights.

Sufian's plight was experienced by thousands of other Iraqis. When US convoys and patrols began to come under sporadic attack in late April and early May, the troops' usual response was to round up any Iraqis they found nearby and keep them in prolonged detention. All Iraqis were to be treated as hostile unless they could prove otherwise. Politicians in Washington may have been referring to Iraqis as a 'liberated people' but, with a few individual exceptions, US soldiers and officers behaved as though they were a conquered enemy. Given that a majority of Americans thought Saddam was linked to the attacks of 9/11, many soldiers saw the occupation as 'payback time'.

Sufian's case highlighted the problems faced by many Iraqis: arrests followed by clumsy interrogation, or none at all; the lack of a prompt trial-or-release system; poor prison conditions; constant buck-passing; and sloppy paperwork by the occupation authorities. The result was that in almost every case of a detention relatives took weeks or months to find out where their loved ones were held. Hundreds of families were affected. It was yet another example of how the US occupation quickly became the problem, not the solution. First, the very presence of foreign troops on Iraqi streets created resistance. Then, through the mistakes of their counter-insurgency tactics, that resistance widened and deepened. To Iraqis, the American practice of mass arrest smacked of racism, Islamophobia, and revenge.

By March 2004 more than 10,000 Iraqi men and boys were in US custody.[4] The vast majority appeared to be innocent of any crime, if one batch of cases reviewed by US military judges that month was typical. They recommended that 963 of 1,166 detainees (82 per cent) should be released without charge, according to US officials.[5]

Ahmed Suhail, a final-year high-school student, was with his father, a well-known Baghdad vet, when they were stopped at a US checkpoint on 15 May 2003. His father had a pistol in the car. At the time this was not an offence. (The occupation authorities banned the carrying of weapons outside the home from 14 June.) The two were hooded and taken to Camp Cropper. Ahmed told me:

> We were in a tent for 150 people. We only got 25 litres of water a day for everyone, which means about a cupful per person, in temperatures of over 40°C … There was a small ditch in the open for a toilet, which meant you were naked in front of everybody. There was no shower. We slept on the sand. My father could speak some English and two soldiers gave us overalls as a change of clothes.

After three weeks, for no apparent reason, Dr Suhail was taken to Abu Ghraib, Saddam's notorious Baghdad prison that had already been pressed back into service by the Americans as the numbers of detainees sky-rocketed. A week later he was released, but his son remained at Camp Cropper before being transferred to Camp Bucca, another detention centre near Umm Qasr, close to the Kuwaiti border. For 11 hours he had to lie on the floor of a US army truck with 21 other prisoners as they travelled 400 miles, stopping for the night in Nassiriya.

The conditions at Camp Bucca were a little better than Camp Cropper, Ahmed said, with detainees having regular access to showers. After 33 days there, and 66 of detention in all, Ahmed was brought back to Baghdad and released. He told me, 'At no time was I questioned, interrogated, or charged. It was punishment without trial. When the Americans first came to Baghdad I was happy, but I don't want to speak about my feelings towards them now.'

These wild arrests naturally turned thousands of detainees against the occupation, while their families were angered by the humiliating efforts they were forced to make to find their loved ones. The pool of resentful Iraqis quickly grew. In increasing desperation they had to go from one US office or base to another in the hope of getting news. Saddam was a dictator, but at least he was Iraqi. Now people saw foreigners putting Iraqis in prison. The occupation authorities knew no Arabic and hired few interpreters so Iraqis were forced to use someone else's language to try to obtain information about missing husbands, sons, and brothers.

In her home in Mansour, a western suburb of Baghdad, Eftekhar Medhat described to me in July 2003 how her husband, Zakariya Zakher Sa'ad, was arrested the previous month. He worked as a gardener and nightwatchman at the Russian consul's residence. The consul had left Iraq during the American bombing and the house remained a target for looters and burglars long after the first turbulent days of the occupation.

Alerted one night by a neighbour who had heard a noise, Sa'ad went outside with his Kalashnikov rifle. He ran into an American patrol and was thrown to the ground and arrested. Partly in mime and partly in his minimal English he tried to explain who he was. The neighbour came out and assured the soldiers the man was the consul's watchman, not a thief or a resistance fighter. In vain. Sa'ad was taken away. Medhat explained:

> At first we went to Abu Ghraib to look for him ... There the Americans told us to go to the airport. At the airport they told us to go to the International Committee of the Red Cross. We went to the ICRC but got no help.

She then turned to the 101st Airborne's civil military operations centre, located in a disused local supermarket. In the early months of the occupation these urban centres offered some chance for Iraqis to contact Americans in a relatively normal, non-threatening environment. When the resistance grew, the Americans closed them for security reasons.

Carrying a photo of her husband, Medhat approached the centre with her 19-year-old daughter, Huda, feeling safer to have each other's company. They allowed me to come with them, thinking this might also help. The two officers on duty, Major Hector Flores and his sergeant, Paul Holding, took a sympathetic interest in the case. Unlike most American troops, who patrolled in armoured vehicles in conditions of increasing tension as attacks on convoys grew, Flores and Holding talked and listened to Iraqis on more or less equal terms. 'I'm the happiest man in the US army. We are in contact with ordinary Iraqis and we can really help them. We call them customers,' Holding told me proudly. His job included processing claims by Iraqis for damage after American troops shot at vehicles or homes, or when Iraqis were wounded by unexploded US bombs.

Trawling through long lists of badly transliterated Arabic names, often with the first names and family names in the wrong order, Flores finally found a reference to a detainee at Camp Bucca called 'Ahmed Mahjoub

Zakariya, born in 1948'. 'I think it is your husband,' he told Medhat. 'I'm going to fax a photo of him to Camp Bucca, and I hope they will then let him out.' She looked guardedly hopeful but after all the previous disappointments was not ready to relax yet. When I rang her some days later, she announced in delight that her husband had been found and released.

As with the 11-year-old boy, a system that required an individual act of kindness by an American officer to locate an innocent detainee was clearly inadequate. By July 2003 the abuses were already so numerous that Amnesty International and Human Rights Watch were starting to compile dossiers. The International Committee of the Red Cross (ICRC) was also in action, trying to fulfil its mandate of inspecting prisons and tracing missing people. However, it relied on the Americans and the British to keep accurate computerised lists of detainees' names, a requirement that was not being implemented. 'The lists provided by the coalition are not comprehensive and far from complete. The process needs to be improved,' the ICRC spokesperson Nada Doumani told me.

The CPA's own rules stipulated that suspects be allowed to consult a lawyer within 72 hours of reaching a detention camp. In practice, 'detainees appear to be invariably denied access to lawyers, sometimes for weeks', said an Amnesty report in July 2003.[6] A confidential report by the ICRC, which was leaked in early 2004, said that an effective system for notifying families about detainees still did not exist. US units making the arrests rarely identified themselves or said where they were based, and gave no reason for the arrest. Relatives often only learned where a loved one was being kept (as in 11-year-old Sufian's case) when other prisoners were released and told them:

> In the absence of a system to notify the families of the whereabouts of their arrested relatives, many were left without news for months, often fearing their relatives unaccounted for were dead. Nine months into the present conflict, there is still no satisfactory system ... even though hundreds of arrests continue to be carried out every week.[7]

In their defence, CPA officials pointed to the appalling legacy of the Saddam regime. 'In his time people had to scrawl their names on cell walls to get remembered. There was no list of any kind,' said Charles Heatly, an occupation spokesperson seconded from Britain's Foreign Office.[8] He assured me that work was almost complete on repairing cell blocks at Abu

Ghraib so that medium-security prisoners could move from tents into proper buildings 'comparable to UK prisons'. He told me in early August 2003 that a large prefabricated building for several hundred other detainees should be ready at Abu Ghraib in a week's time. The tents at Baghdad airport would then be emptied and its 500 prisoners transferred. In the light of revelations of what happened at Abu Ghraib later, this switch to repairing and using Saddam's old prison complex turned out to be less of a benefit than was presented.

Beside the sheer number of detentions carried out by occupation troops, Iraqis were angered by the insulting and humiliating methods used. Soldiers kicked down the doors of family homes at night, frightening residents out of their sleep. They arrested men in their nightclothes after forcing them to crouch and be searched, often in front of their wife, daughters, and children.

The indignity was massive, as I was told in graphic detail by Saad al-Mahdawi, a businessman in the town of Muqdadiya, about 50 miles north of Baghdad, in March 2004. He headed the local branch of the Iraqi Islamic party. Inspired by the ideals of Egypt's Muslim Brotherhood, the party was founded in 1960 in Iraq's brief political renaissance after the overthrow of the monarchy. Within two years it was banned and forced to go underground. It had sprung back to life only days after Saddam's fall, and Mahdawi claimed it already had 320 branches and was the main voice of Iraq's Sunni Arabs.

Under Saddam, Mahdawi recalled, he was put on a blacklist and forbidden to travel abroad. He was arrested five times and subjected to appalling tortures. They hung him from the ceiling, gave him electric shocks, and kept him in solitary confinement in a tiny cell to try to get him to give the names of party sympathisers.

Under the American occupation, Mahdawi was arrested on suspicion of links with the insurgency. His brother, along with the US-approved mayor of Muqdadiya, rushed to the Americans to complain. They managed to get him released after just 24 hours in detention.

I asked Mahdawi, could he compare the two experiences? 'Saddam's security police were angels,' he replied. The answer seemed absurd. It was only a few days since the incident, so it was still fresh in his mind. But surely he must be exaggerating. I inquired how the Americans could have been worse.

It's the way they arrest you. Saddam's security people used to send a paper saying I had to report to their office. Of course I complied. The Americans come into your home. Under Saddam they humiliated you in their gaols, not in front of our families. As men, we can take it, but for women and young girls it's terrible.

His claim that men could take it sounded a little hollow. Perhaps they could take the physical suffering, but I sensed what they really hated was the attack on their honour and dignity, and their image as patriarchs and men of authority. As if to confirm what I was thinking, Mahdawi went on: 'All those weeks of torture under Saddam were nothing compared to those seconds in front of my family. Now we always sleep in our clothes. We've even lost our right to get undressed for bed.'

Our conversation took place in the Islamic party's offices. Sheikh Aloui Farhan Hussein, the imam of one of Muqdadiya's mosques who also taught in a technical college, sat with us and nodded at Mahdawi's last remarks. He commented:

We used to have this idea about Western armies. We thought they were ci-vilised. As an Arab, take me to any gaol, but don't say to me in the bazaar or on the main street 'Hey, you'. You know, we are so disappointed.

He then launched into a set of graver complaints. US troops were attack-ing homes in the area round Muqdadiya and killing innocent people, he said. As a member of the city council, he had regular contact with the local American commander, Col John Miller. He recalled how the colonel had come to say farewell on his last day in the area. The sheikh seized the oppor-tunity to raise the case of several families who had lost loved ones recently when four shells landed on their village. Five people died, including a young woman who had celebrated her wedding only three weeks earlier. 'It was not a random attack. The shells were fired professionally. They landed in a line, with 20 yards between each impact,' he said he told the colonel.

He showed the colonel several pieces of shrapnel he had collected. The colonel acknowledged it was an American shell but suggested the fire may have been in response to mortars launched at the base from the village. 'Ev-eryone knows no one attacks you during the daytime,' the sheikh said he had replied. Colonel Miller asked what the sheikh wanted him to do. 'Compen-sate the people,' he said.

The colonel offered to go to the village and the sheikh said he would go ahead 'to prepare the people to receive you properly'. At 4pm the colonel arrived with a group of troops, but it was the sheikh who accepted the apology on the families' behalf. 'It was too hard for local people to take the apology from the Americans directly,' he explained.

The incident was not yet over. The villagers wanted compensation and the sheikh described to me the bargaining he had with the new US commander, a few days later. The Americans offered $6,000, to be divided up among the families of the five dead and five wounded. The sheikh tried to raise the figure but the Americans insisted he sign for it or lose it altogether. He had just come back from handing the money to the families when I met him and Mahdawi in the Islamic party's office.

It would be wrong to suggest that either Saad al-Mahdawi or Sheikh Aloui Farhan Hussein was an ally of the Americans before Saddam's fall. That was clear. 'Our party refused to take part in the London conference of exiles [in December 2002] because it was designed to give support to a foreign invasion,' the sheikh told me with pride. But it was the actions of the US forces since the invasion that were upsetting local people. He continued:

> Even though they removed Saddam, people are starting to hate the Americans because of their bad behaviour and mistreatment. It's the way they arrest people by surrounding houses. Everyone knows no one will resist them. It's never happened that a householder opened fire. It's a big mistake to arrest a man and put a bag on his head, and put his head on the ground and crush it with boots in front of his wife and children. Instead of asking the householder to open a cupboard, they just smash the locks.

In spite of their disappointment and anger, both men were willing to give the Americans a bit more time. The occupation was almost a year old when we spoke but they hoped it would end when sovereignty was transferred in a few months' time. 'We believe in political jihad, which means peaceful and non-violent resistance. We tell people not to use violence. We need peace in order to rebuild Iraq,' Mahdawi said.

The sheikh took a similar line:

> I can't say we want the Americans to go but at the same time I can't say we want them to stay. All Sunnis look on the Americans as occupiers, and according to our religion we have to fight foreigners. But our party has given

instructions to people to go along with the Americans as long as there is a clear date for them to give our sovereignty back. It's our duty in this period to go ahead with political work because non-violence is needed for reconstructing our state.

After leaving the two men, I drove five miles to the village of Zuham where the US shells had landed. We passed through a typical flat Mesopotamian landscape of date palms in fields that were cut through by small canals and sluice gates. Vines were beginning to bud on trellises. Farmers were steering carts pulled by donkeys along the bumpy dirt roads.

In spite of mounting anger against the occupation, Western reporters could still visit rural Sunni areas. The resistance considered us neutral rather than agents of the Americans or British, and hostage-taking had not yet become the modus operandi. Al-Qaeda supporters with their more virulent ideology were not yet numerous or influential. Within weeks the mood would change, however, and it would be too dangerous to travel through small towns like Muqdadiya, let alone into Sunni villages.

Even at this stage, I found the mood in Zuham more radical than the sheikh and his friend had indicated. Graffiti on farm walls said, 'Long live Saddam, long live jihad', although no one had been rash enough to write them on the side of a house, thereby inviting an American raid. We stopped at a mud-brick house where Emad Mehdi Khalaf Abd, a day labourer who works on his richer neighbours' land, described the day he heard a loud detonation nearby. He was at home with his family. He rushed across the yard and into the street to see what it was. There was a second explosion, and 50 seconds later what turned out to be a third artillery shell crashed into his yard where his family were standing rooted in fear. His wife and three-year-old daughter were killed outright. His small son and two other daughters received shrapnel wounds. Two of his adult sisters, and one of their children, also died.

According to US troops, the range of the largest mortar used by insurgents, the 120mm, is 7km. Zuham is at the outer limit of that distance from the base of the US Third Brigade Combat Team at Baquba, which acknowledged firing the four artillery rounds, allegedly in response to mortar attack. Zuham's villagers vigorously denied that anyone fired a mortar round. Emad Khalaf Abd told me, as he pointed to the crater in the hard-packed earth outside his ruined home:

The Americans patrol regularly by day and night. You can't even carry a stick when you walk in the fields ... When Saddam was president, we tried to keep away from politics. We wanted a quiet life. Nothing has changed for me in the year since he's gone, except the lack of stability and security, and now of course this. I have lost my family.

He did not hide the fact that he was upset at Saddam's capture by the Americans a few weeks earlier. 'His collapse was our country's collapse. We had expected he would defeat the Americans. We wanted him to defeat the Americans,' he said. 'I'd like the Americans to leave Iraq today or tomorrow. They weren't welcome even before they arrived.'

The raid that killed five innocent members of the Abd family was far from being an isolated case. As the US military began to hunt down insurgents who were laying roadside bombs or attacking police stations, reports of mistakes caused by badly aimed or indiscriminate fire mounted steadily. Some killings of civilians were described by witnesses as deliberate acts of revenge, like the killing by US marines of 24 people, including five small girls in one family, in the country town of Haditha along the Euphrates on 19 November 2005.[9] It happened shortly after a US marine was killed when a roadside bomb struck a convoy.

There was no accurate count of these needless deaths, since the US military did not keep one, and it was hard for other investigators to make complete tallies. The Iraq Body Count, a respected independent research group which collated and checked media and other reports of civilian deaths, calculated that occupation forces killed at least 266 civilians in the three weeks of April after Saddam's regime collapsed. In the 11 months from 1 May 2003 until the end of March 2004 they killed another 292. (The USA was responsible for 98.5 per cent of the killings by occupation forces.)[10]

If one assumes that every one of the roughly 550 civilians killed by US troops in the occupation's first year had five close family members, the degree of hatred against the Americans caused by these deaths becomes apparent. Over the next year, the number of civilian victims of US violence rose dramatically. Between April 2004 and March 2005, as they intensified their counter-insurgency campaigns, occupation forces killed 2,096 Iraqi civilians, almost four times the previous year's toll.[11] These figures do not include people shot in incidents where insurgents and US troops exchanged fire. They only cover unarmed people who died unambiguously at the hands of occupation troops or aircraft.

Western newspaper readers and TV viewers often had the impression that car bombs and suicide attacks were the main danger for Iraqis. As sectarian killings developed in 2005 and 2006, these atrocities did become the largest cause of death in Iraq. But it is important to go back to the first two years of the occupation, since this was the period that turned hundreds of thousands of Iraqis against the foreign forces in their midst. Terrorist car bombs were given prominent media coverage since most took place in Baghdad where photographers and reporters had immediate access to scenes of carnage. In fact, away from the cameras in the smaller towns and the countryside north and west of Baghdad, the Americans were taking more lives. The toll of victims of American fire in the two years after Saddam's regime collapsed is four times higher than the number of Iraqis killed over the same period by car bombs and suicide attacks by anti-occupation forces.[12]

The largest set of casualties in 2004 resulted from the two attacks by US marines on Fallujah. The first assault in April, as well as the attack on the Shia holy city of Najaf in the same month, was so fierce that it even worried Washington's British allies. An internal memorandum to ministers from the Foreign Office's Iraq directorate on 19 May, entitled 'Iraq: The medium term' and leaked to the *Sunday Times* of London, stated:

> Heavy-handed US military tactics in Falluja and Najaf some weeks ago have fuelled both Sunni and Shi'ite opposition to the coalition, and lost us much public support inside Iraq ... We need to redouble our efforts to ensure a sensible and sensitive US approach to military operations.[13]

Although the memo said the USA had learnt lessons from Fallujah and Najaf and was 'generally proceeding more cautiously', there was no evidence of this in subsequent months. The USA launched a second attack on Najaf in August and blasted its way into Fallujah in November, destroying more than half the town in a combined ground and air assault. There was also a high death toll from US air strikes on other Iraqi towns and villages. Using airpower against insurgents is a notoriously indiscriminate tactic since it inevitably kills and terrorises civilians, as is clear also from the conduct of the Sudanese air force in Darfur and NATO aircraft in Afghanistan. In just four months, between July and October 2004, the USA conducted 55 air assaults in Iraq. They led to the deaths of 547 civilians, according to the Iraq Body Count.[14]

If people were not safe in their homes, they were also at great risk on the roads. In the earliest days of the occupation, before the first roadside bombs or the attacks by suicide car drivers, jittery US troops were already taking an unnecessary toll of civilian life at checkpoints or on highways when cars came close to US vehicles.

One of the grimmest scenes in the days after Saddam's fall unfolded at Baghdad's Central Teaching Hospital for Children. The morgue was full and a small patch of grass between the car park and the railings along the main street had been turned into a graveyard. Plastic sheeting was strung along railings to prevent curious passers-by from seeing the bleak scene that was unfolding. Dozens of relatives were searching through the mounds of loosely packed soil to identify the bodies which lay underneath.

I visited the hospital on 13 April 2003, four days after Saddam's statue was brought down. A middle-aged man, Aboudi Kazem, was kneeling by one graveside with lines of anxiety etched on his forehead while a hospital orderly in a blue coat dug at the earth with his bare hands. Two other men joined in, moving the soil away in gentle scoops. Dark blue trousers emerged, first one leg, then the other. A small hand, its fist slightly clenched, was slowly uncovered. The dead boy's face was hidden by a red cloth. The orderlies hesitated for an instant as if they needed extra strength before they started to remove it.

By now Aboudi Kazem was lying above the grave on one elbow, drawing fiercely at a cigarette. Was this going to be his moment of truth? Were the diggers about to find the missing body of his son Ali, the 16-year-old he had not seen for seven months since the boy left home in Najaf to look for work in Baghdad and stay with his uncle there? As the cloth was unwound, the father's face tensed and then suddenly relaxed. The teenage boy whose eyelids the orderlies were carefully clearing of dust was not Ali.

Aboudi Kazem knew his son was dead, victim of an American marine at a Baghdad checkpoint. He even knew Ali must be in this hospital since this is where his uncle brought him before he died. Aboudi Kazem desperately needed to find Ali to give him a decent burial and say goodbye. Yet when discovery was imminent, Aboudi Kazem flinched at the horror of seeing his boy's face emerge from the grave.

He dragged himself to his feet and lit another cigarette while orderlies tossed earth back on to the 'wrong' boy. They moved towards another grave to dig again. The only clue was a label stuck in the ground: 'grey T-shirt, blue trousers, no name, 11 April'. This one also failed to produce Ali.

Roughly 50 new graves could be seen in the patch of grass. Hospital officials said some contained victims of shoot-outs as neighbourhoods defended themselves from looters, but the vast majority of the dead had been killed by US fire. 'The Americans can stay here one week, and no more. If they stay longer, we will screw them. They only want our oil,' said one man in anger when he realised we were Western reporters.

Ali Kazem's uncle, Mohammed, was with the boy when he died and had no doubt his nephew's death was unnecessary. During the three weeks of the US 'shock and awe' bombing campaign the family rarely left their home. When it was over, they thought it was safe. Ali had gone out with his uncle to have a look around. 'We had a white flag on the car to show the Americans we came in peace,' Mohammed said. 'We got out at the checkpoint and put up our hands. Ali died with his arms raised. A bullet hit him in the side just below his left shoulder.'

What ought to have been a rare accident had become so routine a year later that Jameel Ghani Hashim, manager of homicide statistics for the Iraqi interior ministry, admitted that he was as terrified of US checkpoints as any other Iraqi. 'These soldiers are so nervous, that whenever I see a checkpoint, I drive the other way,' he said. 'And that's me. I work with Americans. I'm still scared.'[15]

In the early weeks of the occupation Iraqi drivers would often drive close behind slow-moving Humvees and hoot to tell them to stop blocking highways by taking up all the lanes. People complained that the Americans were behaving as though they, rather than Iraqis, owned the country. A number of lethal incidents in which Iraqis were shot by the Americans stopped Iraqi drivers letting their road rage bring them so close to convoys, however. Humvees started to carry menacing signs in Arabic warning people to stay a hundred yards back or risk being shot. Iraqis then began to complain that troops in American vehicles behaved as though every Iraqi was an enemy.

Yahia Said, an Iraqi political scientist based in London, vividly described one moment of fear on his first trip back in December 2004. He wrote in an email to me and other friends:

> We were driving home with some friends on my first night in Baghdad. Suddenly we stumbled on a US ambush in the middle of a dark alley. I noticed red dots of light moving across my fellow passenger's face. The laser sights

were bouncing off us like in action movies. The soldiers began to wave unintelligible signs. The driver was confused and thought she should drive closer to be searched – a mistake which cost many an Iraqi their lives. After a lot of panicked screaming and confusion we drove off shaken but unscathed. Many Iraqis did not make it home that day. The father of a Baghdad student we met the next day was shot in an incident not unlike ours.

There were many reasons for the Americans' quick resort to excessive force. One was the absurdly high premium that US commanders put on 'force protection'. The manuals might call for troops to get 'positive identification' before pulling their triggers but in panicky situations soldiers tended to fire immediately if there was the slightest danger of their unit taking casualties. Bush's war on terror had also created a general sense of anti-Muslim prejudice and Islamophobia, which devalued Arab lives. This was hard to counter at the mess-hall level since there were very few Muslim soldiers in the US forces.

Army training gave US soldiers no preparation for peacekeeping. It was all about combat rather than winning hearts and minds. Failing to paint out names like 'Carnivore', 'Blind Killer', and 'Bloodlust' that had been stencilled on the barrels of Abrams tanks during the invasion hardly created the right climate for dealing with 'liberated' Iraqis, even if most of them, fortunately, could not read English. One retired British defence chief recounted his amazement at being told about the 'warrior ethic' during a visit to West Point, the US army's elite war college:

> They were going on about how the soldier is a fighting machine. I couldn't believe it … There's an American arrogance, kicking down doors, searching homes in an excessively aggressive way. The time when they needed to be aggressive, i.e. to stop the looting, they weren't.[16]

In April 2007 the American Civil Liberties Union (ACLU) managed to obtain US army documents about civilian killings under a Freedom of Information request. They covered 479 cases in Iraq, and 17 in Afghanistan, where relatives had asked for compensation.[17] Some 198 were denied because the military found that the incidents arose 'from action by an enemy or resulted directly or indirectly from an act of the armed forces of the United States in combat', which the military calls 'combat exclusion'. In 164 cases, just over half the non-combat events, the US made cash payments to family members. In approximately half of the cash payment cases, the USA accepted responsibility for the death of the civilian and offered a 'compensation payment'. In the other half, US authorities issued 'condolence' payments. These – as in the case of the Abd family described earlier in this chapter – were discretionary payments capped at $2,500 per person and offered 'as an expression of sympathy' but 'without reference to fault'. [18]

The ACLU described the released files as offering 'a window into the lives of innocent Iraqis caught in conflict zones'. In one file, a civilian from Salahuddin province stated that US forces opened fire with more than a hundred rounds on his sleeping family, killing his mother, father, and brother. The firepower was of such magnitude that 32 of the family's sheep were also killed. The US army acknowledged responsibility and made a compensation payment. [19]

Almost one in five of the 496 killings took place at checkpoints (50 cases) or near American convoys (42 cases). In a typical incident a civilian said his son drove up to a checkpoint in Kirkuk, was shot at through the roof of the car and hit in the abdomen. He later died from his wounds. An email in the file from an army sergeant stated: 'How was he supposed to know to get out of the vehicle when they fired warning shots? If I was in his place I would have stayed put too.' [20]

The documents did not make clear whether the 479 cases amounted to a small or large percentage of the total claims made by Iraqis. Nor was there any way to know how many cases, if any, led to prosecutions of troops or disciplinary action.

Until 1 May 2003, when Bush declared major combat operations over, most checkpoint killings were considered combat-related and not covered by claims legislation. This exemption would have included the killing of Ali Kazem, whose distraught father was looking for his body in the makeshift graveyard at the Baghdad Children's Hospital. It was only after strong pressure from relatives and tribal leaders that the US widened the basis for claims.

Brutal and humiliating US search operations and the widespread deaths of Iraqi civilians during counter-insurgency attacks or at checkpoints were blights on normal life that Iraqi Arabs had not suffered during Saddam Hussein's regime. It was not surprising that Iraqis compared life under occupation with life under Saddam, and said security had been much better in the past. Political repression casts a pall of fear over any society, but it is a factor that most people, barring a small percentage of courageous rebels and dissidents, accept and internalise. Foreign troops, by contrast, are a visible and daily reminder that a country has lost its independence. If those troops are a source of constant fear because of occasional careless and violent behaviour, people's resentment is bound to grow.

Barely a year after the invasion a USA Today/Gallup/CNN poll conducted in March–April 2004 found a majority of Iraqis had a negative view of the behaviour of US troops. It was not just the fact of the occupation they disliked but the way it was conducted. As many as 58 per cent of Iraqis claimed US forces behaved fairly badly or very badly.[21] A retired US colonel, Douglas A. Macgregor, put it succinctly:

> Most of the generals and politicians did not think through the consequences of compelling American soldiers with no knowledge of Arabic or Arab culture to implement intrusive measures inside an Islamic society. We arrested people in front of their families, dragging them away in handcuffs with bags over their heads, and then provided no information to the families of those we incarcerated. In the end, our soldiers killed, maimed, and incarcerated thousands of Arabs, 90 per cent of whom were not the enemy. But they are now.[22]

Once detained, hundreds of Iraqis were subjected to further abuse by US military guards. This became another major source of anger for Iraqis. Although the issue was highlighted by the scandal of Abu Ghraib, independent human rights organisations had already expressed alarm several months earlier. As early as May and June 2003, Red Cross officials came across 52 cases of maltreatment during visits to Camp Cropper, the US detention centre at Baghdad airport. As is their normal practice, they did not publicise their concerns except to US officials. They were confirmed, however, when an internal ICRC report was leaked in February 2004, as mentioned earlier in this chapter.

In complaints presented to the Americans in July 2003, ICRC officials mentioned the case of a prisoner who said he had been beaten during interrogation as part of an ordeal in which he was hooded, cuffed, threatened with being tortured and killed, urinated on, kicked in the head, lower back and groin, force-fed a baseball which was tied into the mouth using a scarf, and deprived of sleep for four consecutive days.[23] The mistreatment was linked to interrogations overseen by the 205th Military Intelligence Brigade, based in Wiesbaden, Germany. They were subsequently put in charge of interrogations at Abu Ghraib.

It was later revealed that in September 2003 Lt Gen Ricardo Sanchez, the top US commander in Iraq, gave permission for US officials at Abu Ghraib to use dogs, temperature extremes, reversed sleep patterns, sensory deprivation, yelling, loud music, and diets of bread and water on detainees whenever they wished.[24] They did not have to seek approval from authorities outside Abu Ghraib.

After some officers at US Central Command complained, Sanchez modified the list so as to require prison officials to obtain his direct approval for the remaining high-pressure methods. Among the tactics apparently dropped were those that would take away prisoners' religious items, control their exposure to light, and inflicting 'pride and ego down', which means attacking detainees' sense of pride or worth.

When the Abu Ghraib scandal was exposed, US officials sought to play it down as the work of a few rogue soldiers, rotten apples in the barrel. But Sanchez' modified list permitted several techniques that involved mistreatment. These included manipulating a detainee's diet, imposing isolation for more than 30 days, using military dogs to provoke fear, and requiring someone to maintain a 'stress position' for as long as 45 minutes.

The US army refused to confirm how often these techniques were used. They were similar to methods approved by Donald Rumsfeld for use on prisoners at the US detention centre at Guantanamo Bay in Cuba. The ICRC reported being told by several military intelligence officers at Abu Ghraib that:

> it was part of the military intelligence process to hold a person deprived of his liberty naked in a completely dark and empty cell for a prolonged period, to use inhumane and degrading treatment including physical and psychological coercion against persons deprived of their liberty to secure their cooperation.[25]

The issue that made Abu Ghraib internationally notorious was the grotesque sexual humiliation of Iraqi prisoners revealed in souvenir photographs taken by a group of US guards. The vile acts that naked Iraqi prisoners were forced to perform and the smirking and gloating by US soldiers, including a young woman in uniform, caused shock and revulsion. The images raced round the world via television and the Internet in April 2004, making the name of Abu Ghraib as notorious as Guantanamo Bay. The humiliation and abuse of Iraqi detainees, which had previously been known only to the victims themselves and their extended families, was now shared by millions of people.

Bush promptly went on television to apologise and try to contain the damage. In the Middle East the pictures were shown repeatedly on Al-Jazeera and Al-Arabiya, as well as other TV stations. Surprisingly, the initial reaction from commentators in the Arab media was not as fierce as might have been expected. Al-Jazeera's first editorial response was not so much to denounce the Americans as to turn the spotlight onto abuses in Arab prisons. A programme chaired by its popular talk show host, Faisal al-Qassem, called attention to torture in several Arab countries. His restrained and reflective lead was followed by commentators in Egyptian papers who asked about conditions in Egypt's prisons.

For the wider Arab and Muslim public, however, Abu Ghraib symbolised everything that was wrong about the US occupation of Iraq. It was seen as a deliberate Western assault on the dignity and values of a different culture. For example, in the Middle East dogs are normally treated as unclean. They are scavengers that carry disease and roam around rubbish tips, yet here they were being used to intimidate and threaten defenceless people. Arab men were stripped naked and forced to crouch in front of a young woman so she could laugh at a pyramid of male bodies. Others were made to smear themselves with excrement or perform humiliating homosexual acts, again in the presence of a woman, and everyone knew the pictures were taken so that they could be paraded as trophies before other leering soldiers in the barracks afterwards or in bar-rooms back in the USA. The fact that all these indignities were applied to Arabs by ill-educated and low-ranking foreigners on Arab land could not but anger people across the Muslim world.

Rami Khouri, the noted Lebanese commentator for Beirut's *Daily Star*, expressed the point eloquently on the openDemocracy website:

Abu Ghraib, in the final analysis, is for most Arabs not only about American soldiers abusing Iraqi prisoners; it is a symbol of the much wider, older abuse of Arab citizens as a whole by power structures dominated by western armies, Israeli occupiers, and indigenous Arab dictators – and of their own sense of themselves as disempowered, colonised subjects.[26]

The antidote to this racism and occupation was

the same as it always been: resistance that aims for liberation. It is not surprising, therefore, that most Arabs silently cheer the armed resistance against the Anglo-American occupying forces in Iraq and against Israeli occupying forces in the West Bank and Gaza; nor that politically Islamist and other non-violent opposition movements that challenge existing Arab regimes attract large followings in their own societies.[27]

In his memoirs, Bremer described being outraged by the Abu Ghraib pictures. However in a meeting with the governing council he tried to minimise it by contrasting the scandal with the 'far more savage torture' that was carried out under Saddam as a matter of policy and with impunity. Bremer reported that a number of council members concurred, adding that the Arab media had ignored Saddam's cruelties.[28]

What Bremer and the council members were saying was partly true but their reaction showed a failure to understand how most Iraqis in the Arab 'street' saw Abu Ghraib. Iraqis did not compare it to Saddam and the past. They saw it in the context of the current occupation that affronted their dignity and was humiliating and abusing fellow Iraqis. The internal British Foreign Office memo mentioned earlier in this chapter understood Iraqi feelings better, acknowledging that 'The scandal of the treatment of detainees at Abu Ghraib has sapped the moral authority of the coalition, inside Iraq and internationally.'[29]

An opinion poll conducted for Bremer three weeks after the scandal broke showed it was a major turning point. People who up to then were still willing to show some respect for the USA were disillusioned. The poll found 71 per cent of Iraqis expressing surprise at Abu Ghraib: they had expected better things from Americans. Once they realised what had happened to Iraqi detainees at US hands in Saddam's old prison, they lost faith. Less than a third expected justice or that any American would be punished for the outrage. Most of the minority who thought someone might be punished expected it to be reserved for the small fry. Higher-ups would escape, they said.[30]

Many Iraqis who still supported the occupation changed their minds. 'I used to say to my family that it's OK for the Americans to stay because they will bring prosperity,' said Noor Alan, an 18-year-old female student at Baghdad University. 'The other day I started to say it when I saw on TV the pictures from Abu Ghraib, but I couldn't finish my sentence. My family said, "What are you talking about? It's getting worse."'[31]

Shocking as the Abu Ghraib pictures were, the abuse they portrayed was only the tip of an iceberg of widespread mistreatment, wrongful imprisonment, and excessive use of force by US troops against Iraqis. The fact of a foreign occupation was the major factor that provoked resistance from Iraqis, whether they were motivated by nationalism, Islamic pride, or a combination of both. But the heavy-handed manner in which the USA conducted its counter-insurgency campaigns played a large part in increasing that resistance, and making it more determined and stronger.

VII

BRITAIN AND BASRA

The people of England have been led in Mesopotamia into a trap from which it will be hard to escape with dignity and honour.

T.E. Lawrence, 1920[1]

The British have essentially been defeated in Basra.

Anthony Cordesman, 2006[2]

A year after the Iraq invasion 52 retired British diplomats, most of them career specialists on the Middle East, wrote an extraordinary open letter to Tony Blair. Problems in Iraq were mounting fast, and the diplomats deplored the British government's lack of proper pre-war analysis. They described Iraq as the region's most complex country and said it was naive for the Americans and British to think they could create a democratic society, however much some Iraqis might want one:

> All those with experience of the area predicted that the occupation of Iraq by the coalition forces would meet serious and stubborn resistance, as has proved to be the case. To describe the resistance as led by terrorists, fanatics and foreigners is neither convincing nor helpful.[3]

The letter caused a political sensation. Retired diplomats rarely go on record in direct opposition to their former employer, or in such numbers. Here was the voice of a generation of senior Foreign Office Arabists, ranged against a prime minister who did not understand the region.

It would be nice to think it was echoed by their colleagues still in government service. Many observers assumed it was. What the 52 were saying must surely be an on-the-record distillation of what Foreign Office officials had told Jack Straw, their minister, and Downing Street in private.

Astonishingly, this was not the case. Interviews I conducted with top Foreign Office diplomats as well as Arabic-speaking British ambassadors in the region reveal a stark and damaging vacuum in the department's pre-war advice. The predictions that the 52 claimed were made by 'all those with experience of the area' may have been shared privately by people inside the Foreign Office's grand Italianate mansion in Whitehall, but they did not circulate as official thinking nor reach ministers.

While a few officials in Britain's intelligence agencies told their bosses they had doubts about the reliability of the evidence on Saddam Hussein's weapons of mass destruction, no serious qualms were raised by the government's foreign policy experts about the equally important issue of whether an occupation of Iraq could work. Analysing the likely consequences of having Western armies occupy one of the major Arab states should have been a crucial element in judging whether it was in the British interest (let alone that of Iraqis) to launch an invasion. Yet such analysis was simply absent. Ministers never asked for it. Officials never offered it. This failure to ask the right questions on the eve of a war was arguably the biggest foreign policy blunder in recent British history since Suez.

Neither of the Foreign Office's top two officials, Sir Michael Jay, the permanent under-secretary, and Sir Peter Ricketts, the political director, were Arabists. In Downing Street Blair's top foreign policy adviser, Sir David Manning, had been Britain's ambassador in Israel from 1995 to 1998 but never served in an Arab capital. No one in Whitehall rang alarm bells by recalling the difficulties of Britain's imperial involvement with Iraq and the long years of nationalist resistance to British occupation, particularly in the south. No one suggested there might be an insurgency if occupying forces stayed in Iraq too long. No one pointed out that Saddam's removal would very probably led to the Shia Islamists taking power, thereby strengthening parties that were closely allied to Iran. This would make nonsense of US and British hopes for Iraq to become a liberal, secular, and pro-Western democracy and remain, as Saddam's Iraq was, a regional bastion against the mullahs in Tehran.

In 2004 the government appointed an inquiry under a former Cabinet secretary, Lord Butler, to look into the intelligence services' findings on Iraq's supposed weapons of mass destruction (WMD). Hearings by the House of Commons Foreign Affairs and Defence committees in 2003 and 2004 also looked into the intelligence lapses on WMD, as well as Britain's pre-war diplomacy at the UN, and the failure to prevent looting after the invasion. However, there were no parliamentary hearings to examine what advice, if any, the British government received on the politics of post-war Iraq.

By 2007, as Iraq sank further into disaster with British casualties rising remorselessly, opposition parties in Britain began to press for a full-scale public inquiry into the government's failure to foresee the difficulty of running an occupation. They wanted something akin to the inquiry that examined the mistakes that led to the Falklands war in 1982, which was led by distinguished former diplomat Lord Franks. However, first under Blair and then under Brown, the government played for time, claiming it would be wrong to hold such an inquiry as long as British troops were still in Iraq.

If an inquiry into the quality of the British government's pre-war analysis is ever held, the results of my interviews with senior officials suggest it will uncover grave lapses, both at expert level and by the prime minister and his staff. With blithe self-confidence, Blair assumed the invasion would be welcomed by Iraqis and therefore it would be easy for the USA and UK to run the country after Saddam was toppled. His style was not to encourage his policy preferences to be questioned, or to call for assessments of possible consequences. He seemed to think that any problems that emerged after the invasion would be technical and uncomplicated, and could be played by ear.

Of course, it is unlikely that Blair would have refused to send British troops to Iraq alongside the Americans even if he had heard from his officials that an occupation would meet serious resistance from Iraqi nationalists and that Islamists would fill the vacuum after Saddam was removed. Blair was set on going to war at Bush's side under any circumstance. MI6 and the Joint Intelligence Committee did warn him that invading Iraq would help Al-Qaeda find new recruits and increase the terrorist threat to Britain, but this was not enough to deter Blair.

While the expected increase in Al-Qaeda or other jihadi activity after a Western invasion of a major Muslim country would be damaging for the

British homeland, armed resistance by Iraqi nationalists and the transfer of political power to Shia Islamists who were backed by loyal militias would endanger the occupation and put British and American soldiers' lives at risk. This surely should have provided pause for thought. In fact, the two trends merged. After the invasion jihadis took their anger out both inside Britain as well as against British troops occupying Iraq.

Even if Blair was by nature hostile to opposing arguments, questions still need to be asked as to why the government's analysts did not do a better job of predicting the invasion's disastrous aftermath inside Iraq. If they had warned ministers that an occupation would be a hazardous affair, which would not lead to a secular pro-Western democracy, there might at least have been a fuller debate in Cabinet and Blair would have been under much greater pressure not to send British troops to war.

Unfortunately, once he had decided on the principle, Blair was not interested in the problems an invasion might throw up. His lack of attention to detail was well known in the Foreign Office and Downing Street. Britain's key ambassadors saw it for themselves when Blair summoned them back to London in January 2003 as war fever mounted in Washington and arguments over a second Security Council resolution to authorise an invasion heated up at the UN. In a lengthy speech the prime minister outlined British policy on Iraq and the Middle East in general, naturally without conceding that a decision to invade had already been taken. He was telling the ambassadors how to sell the line rather than seeking their advice.

'Blair basically harangued us. I don't remember anyone giving any feedback,' I was told in March 2007 by one ambassador who came back from the Gulf for the occasion, and has since retired. Like several other officials I interviewed, he requested anonymity. The following day Mike O'Brien, the Foreign Office minister responsible for the region, held a smaller meeting with British heads of mission in the Middle East. He recalled:

> He told us they were trying to impose democracy in the Middle East. I said I didn't think it would work, but we were not asked for our advice and we didn't give any ... The issue was not posited in the context of should we invade or not.

Another British ambassador who attended the meetings and talked to colleagues about the looming invasion said 'everyone was unprepared for the aftermath'. He admitted to me that:

to my shame I was in the complacent camp. We underestimated the insurgency. I didn't hear anyone say, 'It'll be a disaster, and it'll all come unstuck'. People felt it was a leap in the dark but not that we were staring disaster in the face.

After the invasion he recognised that the leader of the country where he served had been far more perceptive about post-Saddam Iraq than the Foreign Office's Arabists. 'He predicted it would all fall to pieces on sectarian grounds. He was unhappy about the invasion, even though he was a host to US forces and the top US brass came through regularly,' the ambassador said.

It is often argued that the occupation stumbled because of a lack of pre-war planning. The assumption is that it could have succeeded if proper plans had been made. But the real problem was a lack of political analysis, and in particular a lack of awareness that Western armies cannot successfully take over Arab countries and force them to run along Western lines.

There was plenty of pre-war planning, both in Washington and London. The Foreign Office set up a special Iraq Policy Unit in the run-up to the war. Its brief was to concentrate on contingency planning for the invasion's immediate effects, according to a diplomat who attended its meetings. What would happen if Saddam's forces used chemical weapons and British forces took heavy casualties? The government had plans to commandeer hospitals in Britain's National Health Service if army hospitals were swamped. What if hundreds of thousands of Iraqis fled the bombing? Plans were made for huge tented camps and emergency food supplies, to be run with the UN. The Department for Trade and Industry tried to guess what would happen to oil prices in the event of war. The Department for International Development focused on humanitarian assistance to refugees, and reconstruction.

However, no discussions were held on vital issues such as: How would troops be received if the occupation lasted many months or years? What political forces would come out on top in post-Saddam Iraq? How should Iraq's future government be chosen after the fall of Saddam, and what role should the occupiers play? Would Iraqis or the Americans be in charge?

A few of these questions were briefly touched on when Blair and his closest advisers first became aware, about a year before the invasion, that Bush had determined on regime change. A series of secret papers, later known as the 'Downing Street Memos', were leaked to Michael Smith, then the defence correspondent of the *Daily Telegraph*, in September 2004. They revealed the state of American and British thinking at the time of Blair's visit to Bush's ranch at Crawford in April 2002.[4]

There was a miserable lack of detailed foresight. In a note to the foreign secretary, his political director Peter Ricketts talked about the 'end state' that might follow Saddam's removal. The only scenario he mentioned was that a Sunni general might replace Saddam. A memo from the Overseas and Defence Secretariat of the Cabinet Office saw Saddam's successors as either a Sunni general or a 'representative government', but it did not suggest that this might involve a government led by Shia Islamists. To 'impose a new government' would involve nation-building for many years, it warned. 'The greater investment of Western forces, the greater our control over Iraq's future, but the greater the cost and the longer we would need to stay,' it said. There was no hint that occupying Iraq would produce resistance or that the cost mentioned in the document would not just be financial but would include a cost in terms of coalition forces' lives.

The memo described one benefit of getting rid of the Iraqi dictator. 'While in power Saddam is a rallying point for anti-Western sentiment in the Arab and wider Islamic world, and as such a cause of instability,' it said. Astonishingly, it did not see that his forcible removal by means of a US/UK invasion would also be a rallying-point for Arabs and other Muslims and an even greater cause for instability.

On the question of what sort of government would follow Saddam, the overseas and defence secretariat said, 'We need to consider what sort of Iraq we want.' The option of a Sunni military strongman was not desirable, it commented, since he might re-acquire weapons of mass destruction. The better option was a 'representative, broadly democratic government'. The memo predicted this would be 'Sunni-led', though it would give Shias fair access to government. The memo claimed – again, quite wrongly – that Shias had no wish to control Iraq's government.

A note from Manning to Blair about meetings he had with Condoleezza Rice, then the national security adviser, said, 'There is a real risk that the Administration underestimates the difficulties.' He made it clear that the only difficulties he had in mind were the public relations strategy for explaining why the USA and UK were going to war, how to handle the UN, and the conduct of the invasion itself. Manning's note made no mention of how an occupation would be viewed in Iraq and around the Middle East, or who would take power post-Saddam.

Perhaps the most perceptive of the various internal documents was one from Jack Straw to Tony Blair. This said the prime minister would have to convince sceptical Labour MPs (on whom Blair would have to rely for a House of Commons vote for war) on a number of key issues, including 'whether the consequence of military action really would be a compliant, law-abiding, replacement government'. Straw doubted whether any replacement regime would be better than Saddam since 'Iraq has had no history of democracy so no one has this habit or experience'. Yet even these doubts about Iraq's post-Saddam future, as expressed in the foreign secretary's confidential note to Blair, can only be described as sketchy and not well informed. As with all the other secret Downing Street discussions, there was no appreciation of the chances of nationalist resistance to an occupation and no hint of any risk in having Western armies try to impose their will on an Arab country by force. The idea that this would be a massive flouting of Arabs' sense of dignity and honour just did not come into British or American calculations.

Four months later, the level of analysis had not advanced. The report of a meeting which Blair chaired with his top advisers on 23 July 2002 stated that British contacts with the administration showed there was little discussion under way in Washington of the 'aftermath' of an invasion. However, neither Blair nor any of his team, which included the foreign secretary and the head of MI6, expressed serious concern or suggested what the aftermath might be. Their meeting centred on the various US battle plans and how Britain could be involved in the military campaign.[5]

As the clock ticked towards the invasion, analysis and advice on post-Saddam Iraq remained rudimentary and inaccurate. According to Clare Short, the secretary of state for international development who resigned from the government soon after the occupation started, the wisdom of invading Iraq never came up formally at Cabinet meetings. 'There were never any papers or proper analysis of the underlying dangers and the political, diplomatic, and military options. The whole crisis was handled by Tony Blair and his entourage with considerable informality,' she recorded later. Her worry was that without a UN resolution the occupiers would have no legal right to make political changes in Iraq after Saddam was removed.[6]

Peter Hain, another minister, confirmed that the Cabinet saw no papers on post-war Iraq. 'In Iraq the failures of covert intelligence were compounded by the absence of political intelligence: a comprehensive lack of understanding of the sectarian forces and fault lines present across the country,' he disclosed, although not until four years after the invasion.[7]

Even if he had been aware of how serious the post-war political environment in Iraq would be, Blair was not the kind of person to make an issue of it with Bush. He took the view that it was in Britain's strategic interest to go along with whatever Bush decided. Civil servants and senior British military sources repeatedly complained that he never raised difficult problems with Bush, even when he had been briefed to raise them before going to Washington. He either lacked consideration for the consequences of an invasion, or perhaps he feared risking his friendship with Bush by sounding like a sceptic or a wimp if he questioned the war plans. He thought he had considerable influence in the White House, and his various trips to Washington, which always culminated with a press conference at Bush's side, were designed to give the impression that as a major contributor of troops he was an equal partner in decision-making.

British officials were under no such illusions. As I was told by one senior diplomat, 'We weren't plugged into the State Department's detailed planning exercise. We tried but couldn't get into it. It was the first warning sign that we weren't part of it.' In the words of another, 'The UK supplied 10 per cent of the invasion force. We provided 10 per cent of the staff of the Coalition Provisional Authority. We had 10 per cent of input into policy.'[8] In the final weeks before the invasion the Pentagon wrested control of post-war planning away from the State Department, leaving British ministers even more in the dark. A senior British officer was attached to US Central Command in Florida but the main issues of Iraq's post-war arrangements were not discussed there. Even in Washington among the neoconservatives who were leading the drive for an invasion there was no clear idea whether to appoint Iraqis to run the country or to put a US overlord in charge. This was only decided after Saddam was toppled.

Unlike France, Germany, and Italy, the British had no embassy in Baghdad in Saddam's final 12 years of rule. This left them bereft of good, on-the-ground intelligence. It also meant there were few people in the Foreign Office with direct experience and knowledge through having served in Iraq. As a result, the British did not predict the rise of Iraq's Islamists, whose strength destroyed the American neoconservative project for a model US-friendly democracy. As Christopher Segar, who took part in the pre-war discussions and headed the British office in Baghdad immediately after the invasion, told me:

The conventional view was that Iraq was one of the most Western-oriented of Arab states – with its British-educated, urban, and secular professionals. I don't think anyone in London appreciated how far Islamism had gone, not just among the Shias, but the Sunnis too.[9]

One of Britain's diplomats who kept a special watch on Iraq's Shia Islamists admitted he did not foresee their post-war rise. He told me:

The issue of secularism versus religion was discussed but none of the leaders of SCIRI [the Supreme Council for the Islamic Revolution in Iraq] seemed very strong. I don't think anyone could have formed a view of the relative appeal of SCIRI and Dawa. We didn't know how Sistani would react to an invasion. Moqtada was unheard of.[10]

Yet in post-invasion Iraq the two Islamist groupings, SCIRI and Dawa, became the biggest electoral parties. Dawa produced the first two prime ministers, and Moqtada al-Sadr became a key anti-occupation player.

Thanks partly to their Baghdad embassy, the French were better informed. They saw the potential for tensions between religious and secular forces in Iraq if Saddam were toppled. They also sensed an occupation would create resistance. Dominique de Villepin, the foreign minister, alluded to it in diplomatic code in a speech to the UN Security Council in New York on 7 March, two weeks before the invasion:

These crises have many roots. They are political, religious, economic. Their problems lie in the tumult of centuries. There may be some who believe that these problems can be resolved by force, thereby creating a new order. That is not France's conviction. On the contrary, we believe that the use of force can arouse rancour and hatred, fuel a clash of identities, of cultures – something that our generation has a prime responsibility to avoid.

In an interview with *Time* magazine, the French president, Jacques Chirac, argued that the war would be perceived in the Arab and Muslim world as an attack on Islam:

Among the negative fallout would be inevitably a strong reaction from Arab and Islamic public opinion. It may not be justified, and it may be, but it's a fact. A war of this kind cannot help giving a big lift to terrorism. It would create a large number of little bin Ladens. Muslims and Christians have a lot to say to one another, but war isn't going to facilitate that dialogue. I'm against the clash of civilizations; that plays into the hands of extremists.[11]

Chirac saw clearly that Saddam's removal would lead to Shia Islamists taking over in Iraq. During a phone call with Bush in September 2002 he asked Bush, 'Tell me what you're going to put in Saddam's place?' He told an interviewer later that he then warned Bush of 'the fragmentation of Iraq, and turmoil throughout the region with Shias being in charge in Baghdad and Tehran'.[12] As the war drew closer, he repeated the point more strongly to the Americans: 'You say you want democracy. Very well, democracy means elections. If there are elections, the Shias will win because they're the largest community and having Shias in power is not democracy. So your reasoning doesn't work.'[13]

Without an embassy in Baghdad, the Foreign Office should have tried to make up for the gap by canvassing the views of the Iraq experts in Britain's universities and elsewhere outside government. Blair held a brief meeting (as mentioned in Chapter I) with six British academic specialists in November 2002. It was never repeated. Charles Tripp of the School of Oriental and African Studies, and author of the standard work *A History of Iraq*, spoke to me at length about this meeting when I interviewed him in London in April 2007. He said that apart from this meeting in Downing Street, 'I can't remember participating in any meaningful seminar on Iraq with the Foreign Office. We were not asked to brief officials in the Middle East department.'

At the Downing Street meeting he was struck by a marked contrast of styles between Blair and his foreign secretary, Jack Straw. 'Straw asked interested questions, who, what, why, and so on. Blair didn't seem that interested. He wasn't focused. I felt he wanted us to reinforce his gut instinct that Saddam was a monster. It was a weird mixture of total cynicism and moral fervour,' Tripp recalled.

The discussion on Iraq did not last long, but like his colleagues Tripp focused on the complexity of Iraqi politics. He stressed the issue of tribalism and Islamic nationalism, and how they were already reviving in Iraq under Saddam. 'You get rid of Saddam but you don't get rid of Iraq's problems,' he told Blair and Straw. George Joffe, one of the other academics, said Iran would take advantage of an invasion of Iraq. Tripp added, 'I said Iran knows more about Iraq than anyone else, and they'll be there for a long time.'

Blair became more animated when the discussion turned to Palestine. According to Tripp, it was couched in terms of 'What do we have to do on Palestine to make what we do in Iraq swallowable – how do we prevent an attack on Iraq being seen as an attack on the Arab world?' Blair realised that

Arabs throughout the region would not welcome the invasion but failed to see that their feelings would be shared by many Iraqis. He was taken in by the liberation myth, and the notion that Iraqi delight at getting rid of Saddam would override any resentment about being occupied by foreigners, or any other negative reactions.

Tripp gave a warning that there would be 'disorganised forms of resistance' after Saddam fell. 'I thought there might be lots of people with their noses out of joint and people who resented foreign invaders and the people they'd bring in, and they would use force,' he said.

The Foreign Office's failure to assemble reasoned advice on the effects of an invasion resulted from several factors, according to several former officials I interviewed. Some had to do with long-term changes in the Foreign Office's management and culture, they said. In recent years it has suffered a series of staff cuts, with the result that there is a dominance of short-term crisis management, less time for strategic thinking, and a reduction in policy planning. Officials see their role vis-à-vis ministers differently from the past. 'Officials have become less independent-minded than they were, and more willing to rally round the cause,' a recently retired ambassador complained.

The Foreign Office was aware the Americans were in total control of the pre-war planning and were set on regime change. This meant the British government's energy in early 2003 was devoted to getting a UN resolution to authorise the war. Everything flowed from that, British diplomats say. They wanted UN cover for the invasion, and spent great effort to get the Security Council on board. Sir Jeremy Greenstock, Britain's UN ambassador at the time, explained: 'We were so focused on trying to avoid a war. That's why the UK didn't focus 100 per cent on post-war planning.'[14]

Denis McShane, who had been a minister in the Foreign Office, saw a historic shift in the department's role. Officials' time was increasingly taken up with spin and policy presentation rather than with analysing policy options and their likely consequences. He told the Iraq commission that:

> There was no planning or thinking about what would happen in Iraq once Saddam was gone … The Foreign Office was too busy on the minutiae of UN language or managing UK public and parliamentary opinion to devote resources to offering Washington a blueprint for a post-Saddam Iraq.[15]

These factors help to explain why the British government got so many things wrong before the war. Nevertheless, they are not an excuse for the lapses. A senior Foreign Office official, who saw the few position papers that were written about the invasion's likely consequences, told me, 'The basic assumption which turned out to be false was that Iraqis felt themselves more Iraqi than Sunni or Shia.' The papers also predicted that 'in the South there would be a welcome and it would be less difficult than in Baghdad where it would be harder to manage a transition'. The official conceded that 'We underestimated the difficulties. No one realised how difficult it would be.'[16]

British ambassadors in the region concentrated on telling London what support the invasion was likely to receive, publicly and privately, from the Arab governments to which they were accredited. The Gulf states and Jordan would back the use of force to remove Saddam. Syria would not. The ambassadors sent London little analysis of what their contacts expected the fallout to be inside Iraq or what the 'Arab street' would feel.

British diplomats at the UN appear to have failed to tap the expertise of their Arab colleagues. They passed no warnings to London. In this they were less efficient than diplomats from the countries that were on the Security Council but not as permanent veto-bearing members. Juan Gabriel Valdes, a former foreign minister of Chile who served as his country's UN envoy in 2003, represented one of the ten countries whom the British wooed hard for support for a second UN resolution. Valdes said later:

> We decided to have talks with every one of the members of the Arab group at the UN, but particularly with Jordan and specially with Saudi Arabia and other countries that were good friends of the USA but who told us, in private, exactly what has happened historically in Iraq ... It was not very difficult to get that information, that if the war happens, Iran would take an enormous role, that the situation would be absolutely catastrophic, and that the turn of events would leave the USA and Great Britain to be involved in an atrocious situation.[17]

A senior Foreign Office official admitted to concern that Iran would benefit from the invasion more than other countries in the region, but he chose not to communicate this to ministers. 'I remember saying to myself that we might be in a position of having destroyed Iraq and leaving a resurgent Iran. We should be more careful that Iran doesn't become a problem state,' he told me. He agreed that British diplomacy was dominated by the debate at the UN. 'We put a huge amount of effort into trying to get a second resolution. The focus was on process rather than substance,' he said.[18]

The invasion's legality was the central issue for the British government and its officials. This meant that all discussions of US intentions to invade regardless of whether the Security Council passed a UN resolution had to be kept highly confidential. Minutes of Blair's conversations with Bush, and of meetings between Condoleezza Rice, the national security adviser, and Manning, the Downing Street foreign policy adviser, were restricted to an extremely narrow group in London. In the Foreign Office they usually went only to Straw. A few other papers went to the top two officials, Jay and Ricketts, while a third category could be read by the head of the Middle East department while he sat in Jay's office (he was not permitted to make a copy).

Foreign Office officials say the demand for this level of secrecy came from the White House because they didn't want things to get back to the Defense Department and State. Several British officials were unhappy when Lord Goldsmith, the attorney general, changed his advice on the eve of the invasion and said it was legal even without a second UN resolution. But only one, Elizabeth Wilmshurst, who worked in the Foreign Office's legal department, resigned. An ambassador to one Middle Eastern country told me he contemplated resigning on the eve of the war. In the end he decided it would be a dereliction of duty at a time when British casualties might require help in the country where he was posted. Sir Michael Jay met three times a week with about two dozen senior staff, and said, 'I could sense there was real concern and there would be a very lively debate, but I didn't get the impression that top people would walk out.'[19]

Another reason why both Downing Street and the Foreign Office failed to analyse the invasion's probable aftermath was that it was not envisaged Britain would play a major post-war role. This deprived the issue of some of its urgency for British officials. A senior British diplomat, Sir Hilary Synnott, was seconded to the CPA in Baghdad in May 2003, but this was not arranged in advance since the very concept of a CPA, with an all-powerful US overlord at its head, only emerged after the invasion.

The political responsibility that Britain assumed in Basra came about by chance. Far from being handed control of Iraq's south-eastern provinces by Washington because this had been the centre of British colonial rule in the First World War – as many in Britain imagined – the initial US plan foresaw no leadership role for Britain in Basra's civilian administration. The official who was appointed by Washington to head the CPA's Basra office was Ole Wohlers Olsen, a former diplomat from Denmark. The Americans only decided to put in a British civilian as Basra's CPA boss as an afterthought, after Olsen criticised the US in a newspaper interview for failing to provide southern Iraq with enough financial support. Infuriated, L. Paul Bremer, the CPA chief, sacked him and offered the post to Britain. This suddenly gave Britain a bigger say in Basra than it had expected.

While the civilians in Whitehall had little time or motive to think about post-war Iraq, this was not the case in the Ministry of Defence. They were preparing for the invasion and what would come afterwards more fully than their Downing Street and Foreign Office counterparts.

The original idea was for Britain's main ground forces to invade Iraq from the north, coming in through Turkey with the Americans, as part of a two-pronged assault which would include US forces from Kuwait in the south. The British would move through the Kurdish region and go south toward Basra but remain under command of the US 4th Infantry Division.

Less than three weeks before the planned invasion, everything changed. The Turkish government was run by a moderate Islamic party. Under massive US pressure it reluctantly agreed to let US and British troops come through Turkey. However, feelings among its own backbenchers exploded and by a narrow margin parliament voted to block access for US and British invasion troops.

In haste, the USA changed tack. Its ground force would be smaller because one division was still stuck in ships off Turkey. The troops invading from Kuwait would race to Baghdad, bypassing the main Iraqi towns on the way. British naval and special forces would capture the Fao peninsula on the Gulf, and the British would then take Basra.

Although no political role was envisaged for the British in Basra, it was planned that the British military would be in charge of security and policing for an unspecified period in southern Iraq. Their job was to provide 'containment' and create a stable environment while reconstruction got under way. This role in the invasion and its aftermath gave senior British officers a vital stake in how the war was conducted and what policies should be pursued when Saddam's regime fell.

Unlike the Americans, they did not expect the invasion force to be seen as liberators. 'I've been around the Middle East quite a bit,' I was told by one of the most senior officers in Britain's invasion planning. He reluctantly prepared for the invasion because he saw it as his duty. 'In France in 1944 the invading armies were liberating the country from another foreign invader.

This war was liberation from another Iraqi. The whole philosophical stance was shaky from the start. It's like a family row. You don't intervene.'[20]

Admiral Sir Michael Boyce, the chief of the defence staff (Britain's highest military post), recalled the visits he made to the Pentagon before the war:

> There seemed to be a huge reluctance in the US defence hierarchy to accept that the invasion forces wouldn't be seen as a liberating army except in the very initial stages, and that therefore they would face a fairly hostile population.[21]

Senior British officers were surprised when the USA disbanded the Iraqi army. During the invasion, British ground force commanders were ordered not to capture Iraqi units if they came across them during the approach to Basra unless they were putting up resistance. One reason was that the British army did not want to have to guard and feed hundreds of prisoners, but commanders also expected they would soon need Iraqi troops as allies in maintaining security once Saddam fell. This message of 'Surrender and you'll be free' was put out to Iraqis before the invasion, 'but it wasn't just propaganda. It was true,' a senior military source said.[22]

The idea that the Iraqi army would be needed after the war was one of several points British commanders wanted Blair to raise with Bush. To their disappointment, he backed off from raising tough issues. After the decision was taken to disband the army, British ministers publicly defended it even though the top brass were furious and believed that by creating massive Iraqi resentment it caused needless US, British, and Iraqi deaths.

Without any Iraqi military help, the British army found itself in lone control of security in Basra and the three nearby provinces. The USA ceded the area to the British military to run in partnership with the CPA under its Danish head. In line with old colonial traditions, British commanders took a generally pragmatic view of their mission in Iraq. While neoconservatives like Bremer held to an ideological vision of imposing a Western-style democracy and a privatised economy, the British were mainly interested in stability. They sought out the region's power holders and let them take the leading role, albeit initially under close supervision and control. 'You had to let it go with the indigenous flow. We took that for granted,' a senior British officer told me.[23]

Basra, the centre of Britain's area of occupation, was once a flourishing city, and it had a long association with the British. Its position on the Shatt al-Arab waterway leading to the Gulf gave it great strategic value as a port and trading hub as well as making it the most multi-cultural city in Iraq, certainly more so than Baghdad. During the Ottoman period, besides its Turkish rulers it had large Christian, Armenian, and Jewish communities. The British first set up a consulate in Basra in 1764. The city was also a key link in Britain's overland communications chain between London and the empire in India – the so-called 'British Dromedary Post'. Travel by camel across the desert was often more reliable than going by sea.[24]

The Indian connection remained strong when Britain invaded the Fao peninsula south of Basra within months of the start of the First World War and then moved on to occupy Basra in 1915. The city became the head-quarters for occupying the whole of Iraq, a task that took the British four years to complete, mainly using Indian troops. Most colonial administrators in Iraq were veterans of the Indian civil service, moving up from Calcutta rather than down from London. In contrast to dusty inland Baghdad they liked Basra's coastal setting with its grand mansions along the canals and the corniche, as the avenue beside the waterway was called.

Centred on Basra and the provinces of Dhi Qar, Maysan, and Muthanna, Iraq's 'deep south' retained a separate cultural identity from Baghdad and the north, thanks to the predominance of Shias among the Arab population. Even under Saddam Basra retained a different and more cosmopolitan feel than the rest of Iraq.

Its decline started with the eight-year war against Iran. Although the city was never occupied by the Iranians it came under artillery bombardment. During the 1991 uprising against Saddam it suffered again. The dictator punished the damaged city by neglecting it and funnelling post-war recon-struction money elsewhere. The draining of the marshes to the north of the city between the Tigris and the Euphrates forced hundreds of thousands of poverty-stricken peasants to look for survival in the city. By 2003, with a population of 1,300,000, Basra was in a poor state of repair, run-down, overcrowded, and with a tenuous economy that derived little benefit from its nearby oil fields. Profits went abroad or to Baghdad.

This history of oppression under Saddam led the British to believe that, although invasions are rarely popular, the Shia of the south would accept occupation more readily than the mixed Sunni/Shia city of Baghdad. These hopes were not borne out. A 2003 poll by the Iraq Centre for Research and Strategic Studies found even greater suspicion of foreign troops' intentions in Basra than Baghdad. Some 52.3 per cent of people in Basra took the view, just after the invasion, that the newly arrived foreign troops were occupiers rather than liberators. By October 2003 that view was shared by 75.7 per cent. The kinder view of the British as liberators was down to 7.7 per cent.[25]

In July 2003 I visited a girls' primary school in the centre of Basra, less than a hundred yards from the coalition's headquarters. Tony Blair had spent 15 minutes there a few weeks earlier on his first visit to Iraq. Suad al-Lami, the headmistress, produced a ledger with his autograph. 'Thank you. You are wonderful. Tony Blair', it said. Many local residents and parents had come out to thank Blair for helping to topple Saddam, the headmistress recalled. However, a number of other parents had strongly objected to the fact that she had received him.

While stressing that everyone was glad at Saddam's downfall, she produced her own list of complaints against the British. It echoed what I and other reporters heard in Baghdad every day about the Americans. She explained that she had not felt it right to make any complaints to Blair during his brief visit. 'We had electricity from 8am to 9am yesterday. Today it came on at 9am. The security situation is getting worse all the time. Car thefts are going up. At my home there's been no water for three days,' she said.

In a tone of sorrow more than anger, the headmistress said, 'The coalition forces don't know the nature of the people here. The environment and culture is not the same as in Europe.' She cited the case of her husband, who was a military engineer and a colonel in the Iraqi army. Although he never joined the Baath party, he was now barred from government jobs because of his army rank. 'We know army lieutenants who were devoted to Saddam but they are not barred,' she said.

Her comments about the lack of security were repeated by several other Basra residents. In a middle-class suburb of large homes I talked to Thamer Hamdan, a well-known orthopaedic surgeon with a degree from Edinburgh University. His brothers were keeping guard in the front garden as a stream of neighbours, relatives, and other well-wishers arrived and filed into the guestroom. Dr Hamdan had just returned home after a kidnap ordeal lasting several days. He was released after his brother put together a ransom of around $25,000.

The captors had seized him as he was locking up his city centre clinic one weekday afternoon. He recognised them as members of the al-Karamishi, a particular tribe of Marsh Arabs who were being blamed for much of Basra's burgeoning crime. Although he was well treated and came out after only a few days, his ordeal sent fear through Basra's wealthier households. Many neighbourhoods started to put up barriers of earth and date-palm trunks across their roads to control entry by strangers. In Baghdad, ironically, similar barricades were being taken down as the post-invasion waves of looting came to an end.

The surgeon's kidnap was a hint of the more brutal, numerous, and lethal abductions that were to come, though no one predicted how bad they would get. 'There have been between 10 and 15 kidnappings in the last fortnight,' Col Ronnie McCourt of the British army in Basra told me. 'It is partly for money, partly tribal disputes, and sometimes people taking a hostage to swap for one of their own who has been taken.' Other British officials reported a spate of revenge attacks and murders of former regime officials.

By July 2003 the British military and the CPA were concentrating on getting the Basra police back in action after initially accepting a security vacuum. In the early days of the occupation British forces had been as unwilling to try to stop looting as the Americans were in Baghdad. In Basra much of it was probably done by Kuwaitis taking revenge for the wholesale theft and vandalisation of their own country by Iraqi forces in 1990. After Saddam fell it was easy for trucks and other vehicles to drive the short distance from Kuwait to Basra and load up with everything they could find in government offices, hotels, banks, shops, and abandoned private homes. The British wanted to maintain a 'light footprint', so they imposed no curfews or checkpoints to search cars and trucks. By 11 April they were already withdrawing their heavy-armoured vehicles from Basra, little more than a week after they had entered the city centre.

They began patrolling on foot, without flak jackets and with berets instead of helmets so as to give a less menacing image. The trouble was that symbols became confused with substance. Local people did not know whether the British really intended to provide security or whether they were only going through the motions until Iraqi police could do the job. One British officer told a reporter in April 2003: 'We can't provide law and order. Only a police force can do that. No one's actually started planning how it's going to go after the war. There's a real vacuum.'[26]

By mid-summer the CPA had started to vet old police personnel and take on new recruits. It repaired damaged police stations and supplied new uniforms. In July, three months after the invasion, half the pre-war compliment of 1,500 police were on duty again in Basra's central district, which has a population of 750,000 according to Col Ali Abdullah Najim, the chief of police.

At this early stage of the occupation, tension between local people in Basra and the British troops was still low. As Col Najim put it to me, 'People feel relaxed and quite comfortable with British troops. I don't expect any attacks on them.'[27]

Nevertheless, there were signs of political difficulties that could lead to bigger problems as the various Shia groups started to jockey for position. Acting on the advice of the British commander, the CPA appointed an interim council for Basra in May. It had to be disbanded a few days later after merchants in the city and Islamist politicians complained it was run by a tribal leader who was a former Baathist. The initial British policy of picking a tribal leader, which they also followed in nearby Maysan province with its provincial seat in Amara, was based on classic colonial practice as well as a feeling that tribal sheikhs were secular and had good hierarchical control of their people.

The opposition to the British appointee showed how the power of the commercial leaders in Basra was growing. They resented the tribal sheikhs who held sway in the countryside and smaller towns. But now there was a third element, the Islamist politicians, whose views also had to be recognised. They felt strongly about former Baathists, and freely used the accusation that any secular professional who had prospered during Saddam's period must have been a regime supporter. It did not matter if they were Shia. Sectarian divisions were not an issue at the local level. The pressure led to hundreds of middle managers not returning to work after Saddam's downfall, or for many, resigning their jobs under pressure. Some were even murdered for having been members of the Baath party. This settling of scores greatly complicated the British effort to find competent local Iraqis to work with.

A second British attempt to produce a city council was equally difficult. It coincided with Blair's visit to Basra on 1 June and produced a major embarrassment when a crowd marched on the building that the CPA had turned into a town hall. They carried banners denouncing the occupation and saying, 'We can manage ourselves, by ourselves'. They pushed past a cordon of British military police. Two sheikhs who led the demonstration,

Ahmed al-Maliki and Khazal al-Saedi, who were both linked to Moqtada al-Sadr's movement, were allowed into the town hall. There they persuaded the other Iraqis present that the British plan to run the council with an appointed Iraqi as co-chair was unacceptable. In any case, the council was merely focusing on water, electricity, and other technical issues and had no real authority, they pointed out. To the frustration of the British the meeting broke up in disarray after they left. Initially excluded from the meeting, the sheikhs had managed to spoil a process that had been designed specifically to limit their and other politicians' influence.[28]

The episode showed how hard it was for foreigners to try to run another country's politics. Iraqis were willing to accept the British as service providers, provided the occupation produced security, electric power, and money for wages. They would not allow them to dominate or manipulate the political scene.

Because the British military worked with and for the CPA, the Foreign Office in London had no direct contact with Basra. Sir Hilary Synnott, a recently retired ambassador to Pakistan who was sent out in July to replace the CPA's Danish head, found the Foreign Office in the dark about Basra when officials briefed him before he took up his post. 'It became clear to me that London knew very little about what was going on. "The political scene is a mess. It's an emerging situation. Tell us what is going on,"' he recalled being told.[29]

A key issue that angered the Islamist political parties was whether, in the absence of a fully functioning police force and with crime on the rise, the British military would allow armed militias to fill the gap. The high level of criminality was one of the main issues ordinary people complained about. SCIRI, which had a large militia organisation known as the Badr brigade, wanted to use it to guard public buildings. The British refused. SCIRI's Basra leader, Salahal Batat, made it clear he resented that when I spoke to him in July 2003 in a sports complex that his party had commandeered:

> This is a blow against Iraqis. We have told the British their forces are too small to protect us, and people don't respect the ordinary police ... They told us they'd make Iraq an ideal country in the Middle East. They've made it a symbol of looting and destruction.

The two problems – policing and the struggle between the various Islamist parties, each with its own militia – would dog the British throughout their time in southern Iraq. They never managed to handle either of them successfully. Warning signs emerged in Basra in August 2003 at the height of a typical summer of blistering 45-degree heat. In an excellent study, Michael Knights and Ed Williams, two researchers for the Washington Institute for Near East Policy, called it the 'summer of discontent'.[30] Electricity went down for two days at the same time a shortage of fuel saw long and increasingly angry lines at petrol stations. Thousands of protesters came out on the streets, burning tyres and throwing stones at British troops who used techniques adopted from Northern Ireland, firing rubber bullets. Three Iraqis were killed.

Iraq was a much tougher environment than Northern Ireland, however, as Brig William Moore, the British commander in Basra that summer, later admitted. He told a parliamentary committee that

> Iraq is the most volatile and violent place in which I have served. The population as a whole possessed a lot of weaponry, with at least two weapons in most households. In addition, the tribes and criminal gangs were very well armed, with heavy machineguns, rocket-propelled grenades and bomb-making kits.[31]

The worst incident for the British in the early months of their occupation came on 24 June 2003, when six Royal Military Police officers were gunned down in a police station in Majar al-Kabir, just south of Amara in Maysan province. The town had put up strong resistance to Saddam during and after the 1991 uprising and, like the rest of the province, liberated itself from Baathist rule before British forces arrived. To some extent Majar was the Fallujah of the Shia south. Both were proud towns, one Shia, the other Sunni, with long traditions of local independence, which they had demonstrated by toppling Saddam's officials without outside help. It was not surprising that people in Majar resented the appearance of foreign armoured vehicles and soldiers on their streets, in this case from a nation that had occupied them in an earlier generation.

What triggered Majar's uprising was a move by the British to round up weapons. People were outraged. As a local police recruit put it:

> After three months and more, they still don't understand us. Guns are precious to these people. We didn't give them up to Saddam Hussein and we won't to the British. The attitude of men here is, 'kill my son, but don't take my gun'.[32]

British troops had already infuriated people by searching houses and coming in with dogs to look for explosives. Arabs consider dogs unclean. The searches sparked attacks on a number of British patrols, and the murder as mentioned of six military police in June. In the words of two Washington commentators:

> the brutality of the incident cut through an air of complacency that had developed in the relatively quiet south-east area of operations and exposed some uncomfortable truths. The local population was neither patient nor harmless. Consent for occupation was exceedingly fragile. Despite their reputation for more enlightened 'community soldiering' British soldiers had crossed local red lines without knowing it. Put plainly, they did not know enough about the cultural environment they were operating in.[33]

When I visited the town a few days later, it was clear that Islamist parties were gaining strength. The British may have flouted tribal customs, but it was the Islamists who were profiting from the discontent to gain support. To the background clatter of caterpillar tracks as British troops trundled their Warrior armoured vehicles down the main street, Salam Abdul Wahed, an intense man in his early thirties, received me in a bare office to explain the popular mood. He described himself as head of the town's 'cultural committee' that had been formed a few days before Saddam's downfall 'to handle cultural and religious issues'. He was linked to the Hawza in Najaf, he said, an indication that he was a follower of Moqtada al-Sadr.

At the beginning the British troops had not angered people, he claimed. They cooperated with the 'emergency guards' who had been appointed by locals to protect public buildings. He was referring to the embryonic militias that Sadr and other movements were forming. The atmosphere changed when the troops started to confiscate weaponry, he said. As if to reinforce the point the young cleric pointed to a sign on his wall, in English and Arabic, which said 'We request the postponement of weapons searches until an independent Iraqi government is formed, and there is legal sovereignty.' If that was not a clear enough rejection of the occupation, a second sign was completely explicit: 'Where is Iraq's freedom?', it asked.

By the time of Iraq's first elections in January 2005, the Islamists were in near-total control of south-eastern Iraq. They had used the intervening year and a half to impose their conservative social values, particularly in Basra, the region's most liberal area. Cinemas and shops selling music, videos, and alcohol were raided and shut down. Barbers were ordered not to shave people's beards. Militants patrolled the campuses instructing women to wear the veil and preventing men and women from walking together.

In spite of SCIRI's public anti-British noises that I quoted above, SCIRI officials courted the British privately. They sought to persuade the occupation authorities that SCIRI provided the best guarantee of security in Basra. Their campaign was successful and the British gradually turned a blind eye to the militia's expansion. SCIRI officials were given top positions, as heads of customs, intelligence, and police. This allowed SCIRI to start infiltrating the police by putting their own followers into uniform and thereby making the distinction between the police and the militias increasingly unclear.

SCIRI had several affiliates. Besides the Badr brigade, its armed wing, SCIRI ran an organization called Thar Allah (Revenge of Allah), which murdered opponents under the guise of punishing former members of the Baath party. Financed by Iran, SCIRI was able to speak directly to people in Basra through the radio stations it had set up in exile in Iran. Taking advantage of Bremer's privatisation programme, SCIRI bought controlling shares in electricity companies, flour mills, and oil services companies, as well as farms, commercial businesses, and factories.[34] Before terminating the CPA at the end of June 2004, when sovereignty was nominally transferred to Iraqis, the British felt they had no option but to put Basra's provincial council into the hands of the two strongest local parties, SCIRI and Dawa (both of which had spent the last decades of Saddam's rule in exile in Iran), as well as a new Islamist party, Fadhila (Virtue). A moderate secular governor, Judge Wail Abdel Latif, was replaced by an Islamist.

For Basra's secular middle class the British policy of submitting to the Islamists was a deep disappointment. They expected the British to back them in putting professionals in charge after Saddam's downfall. But the British found the Islamists' charges that many professionals were enthusiastic Baathists too hard to challenge. Through pressure, confidence, and violence the Islamists had shown they were Basra's dominant force, and the British accepted it.

Nevertheless, as Iraq's first elections approached, the secular groups still hoped to use the ballot box to reverse the Islamist tide. I encountered some of them in the Writers' Club in a narrow alley close to Basra's central market on 28 January 2005. The atmosphere was cosy and civilised, but the dark and shuttered rooms suggested that they belonged to a breed of people whose time had past. Later they took me off to a suburban home to meet more of their friends. Communists, Christians, and representatives of two parties calling themselves independent democrats explained how they had put together a coalition, called the United Democratic Forces (UDF), to fight the elections for an Iraqi national assembly and also a new provincial council.

Shadowy Islamist forces were assassinating opposition politicians, the UDF people told me. A retired oil company employee who felt too nervous to have me use his name in print told me:

> My relative, Ahmed Hamid, a well-known athlete here, was shot and killed when he was leaving his office for lunch ten days ago … He was a liberal man who wanted to block those who are putting limits on normal life here. The religious extremists want to eliminate all the technocrats and secular people in this city.

A Christian said his four brothers had recently fled to Kurdistan to escape the mounting pressures. He was out of work after extremists looted his liquor store, killing his brother-in-law who was working there. His daughter had resigned from her job as a cleaner with the British occupation forces after two other Christian employees were murdered. Perhaps the angriest was a retired headteacher. He blamed the British for giving power to what he called 'the people who came from Iran'. 'How is it that the British allowed the religious parties to run this region?', he asked in a tone of deep bitterness. He felt the British had handed Basra to the Islamists on a plate. I heard similar comments from Tariq al-Ibresan, the Basra head of the National Democratic party, one of the six parties in the UDF. 'The British haven't helped democratic forces establish themselves in the governing council. They're only concerned with their own security,' he told me. In spite of their disappointment, this small group of secular professionals wanted the British to remain in Basra for fear of worse to come if they withdrew. 'British troops are our assurance of safety in the south. It is Iran that wants them to leave,' the retired oil company employee told me.

Other secular professionals in Basra were supporting the list headed by Iyad Allawi, the US-appointed interim prime minister. He projected himself as a national non-sectarian politician but many Iraqis despised him for authorising US troops to use force against the Sadrists in Najaf and Sunnis in Fallujah.

Faced with this competition, the Shia religious parties – SCIRI, Dawa, and the Fadhila party – put aside their rivalries and drew up a combined list of candidates for the national election. The aim was to urge all Shias to vote as a block and thereby maximise their strength in the National Assembly vis-a-vis the Sunnis, Kurds, and the non-religious parties.

The Sadrists played a cunning game. Moqtada al-Sadr could have called for a boycott, arguing that the elections were taking place in the shadow of a foreign occupation and were therefore illegitimate. Or he could have called on his followers to vote so as to give his line a voice in parliament. In fact, he did neither. He would not himself cast a vote, he said, but he gave no instructions on what other people should do. Meanwhile, he quietly encouraged a number of his key lieutenants – such as Salam al-Maliki, the deputy governor of Basra – to approach the organisers of the combined Shia Islamist list and get themselves put on it as independents.

The results came as a shock to the secular parties and their liberal middle-class supporters, as well as to the non-Muslim minorities. The UDF won little more than 2 per cent of the vote in the provincial ballot. Allawi's party did somewhat better, but the big winner was Islamic Basra, the combined ticket of SCIRI and Dawa, which took 33 per cent. Fadhila, which represented the moderate wing of the Sadrist movement, did well with just over 20 per cent.[35]

With the elections over, the British saw no reason to change their policy of giving the Islamists free rein to run the city and province. Regardless of whether they were liberal or conservative on social issues, most Shias had used the election to express their sectarian identity in the first free vote they had ever been allowed in their lives. It was like a collective open-air census, a way of tabulating Shia strength vis-a-vis Iraq's other communities. Polling day had the air of a Shia festival as huge queues waited in the soft January sunshine, with women separated from men to go one by one into tents to be searched for weapons or bombs.

No serious incidences of violence marred the poll. British forces congratulated themselves on the precautions they had taken, but the truth was there had never been a threat. Every Islamist party and militia had candidates running on the ballot so why would they want to target voters? Nor had there any been any Al-Qaeda activity in south-eastern Iraq. As for sectarian violence between Sunnis and Shias, this was minimal in the Basra region. The region's total Sunni population was small, and Sunnis who felt under threat from Shia domination tended to flee rather than fight. At least 40 per cent were estimated to have gone by 2007.

In other words, the British had it far easier than the Americans in Baghdad and Iraq's north and west. During the whole of 2004 only ten British troops died from hostile military action in Iraq, compared with 719 Americans over the same period. Extrapolating for the much larger US force, the British death rate was under a quarter that of the Americans.

The calm election campaign, the low level of anti-British violence during the previous year, and the fact that people in Basra were able to express their preferences through the ballot box suggested to many mainstream British politicians that the time had come for Britain to leave Iraq. A large percentage of Britons had felt that way ever since the invasion, but by January 2005 the pressure to leave was mounting. Three of the most respected British politicians – Robin Cook, who had resigned from Blair's Cabinet on the eve of the invasion; Douglas Hurd, a former Conservative foreign secretary; and Menzies Campbell, the Liberal Democrat party's foreign affairs spokesman – issued a joint statement calling for US and British troops to leave Iraq by the end of the year:

> We must recognise that the longer the occupation has continued, the stronger the resistance to it has grown. There can be no credible programme to reduce support for the resistance unless we convince the Iraqi people that we have an exit strategy within a realistic timeframe.[36]

Their advice was not taken, and British troops remained in south-eastern Iraq. The British government refused to name a timetable for complete withdrawal. It was an absurd policy since there was little positive the British could do in Basra or indeed in Maysan where the Sadrists had topped the poll. The region was in the hands of the Islamists, a position that had been approved by Iraqi voters in an election the British described as fair. If tensions continued to mount between the various Islamist militias, the British could only intervene at their peril. This was an intra-Shia civil war, which outsiders might exacerbate but could not control.

With local politics now in Iraqi hands, the British confined their own role to 'security sector reform', which meant training the police and Iraqi army. In the case of the police, this meant giving advice on forensics and intelligence work. The policy met little opposition since the militia leaders were keen to get more of their people into uniform and they happily supplied recruits. This had a double benefit for the militias. It gave them an offi-cially sanctioned share in security duties; it also offered a means by which political parties could get their followers jobs and salaries paid by government funds. In early 2005, Basra's police chief General Hassan Suadi al-Saad (who had been appointed by Baghdad and was not linked to the Islamists) revealed that 50 per cent of his men owed their primary loyalty to militias and he trusted no more than a quarter of his force.[37]

An incident on 15 March 2005 highlighted the problems of Islamist intimidation and militia impunity. A group of Sadrist militiamen assembled to watch a spring picnic held in Andalus park by students from Basra University's engineering college. Local Sadrist clerics had warned the organizers to cancel the picnic but it went ahead anyway. In full view of the police, militiamen attacked a young female student with clubs, publicly shamed her by ripping off her clothing, and videotaped the action to use as propaganda. Two male students were shot as they attempted to intervene, and the girl later committed suicide. Outraged students held several protest demonstrations against the Islamist parties but they fizzled out after the Sadrists threatened to bomb them. In spite of their political rivalries, the Islamist parties who dominated the provincial council closed ranks. None of the militiamen were punished.[38]

The worst section of Basra's corrupt and highly politicised police force was a unit called Jamiat. It included the Police Intelligence Unit, the Internal Affairs Directorate, and the Major Crimes Unit at a single facility. Although Jamiat was thought to have been responsible for several political murders, the British left it alone until two British soldiers were seized and handed over to the unit. Sadrist militiamen had abducted the soldiers a day after British forces arrested two Sadrist clerics on suspicion of helping to plant roadside bombs. The British persuaded the Ministry of the Interior in Baghdad to order Jamiat to release the troops, but when Jamiat refused, the British sent a powerful force to storm the building and free the two soldiers. The attack led to clashes with hundreds of Sadrist militiamen and the deaths of four Iraqis, the firebombing of 13 British armoured vehicles, and the wounding of several soldiers.

Basra's governor, Muhammad al-Waeli from the Fadhila party, described Britain's presence as 'destabilising'. Closing ranks once again, the Islamist-controlled provincial council suspended cooperation with the British for several months. By early 2006, Basra was in a state of lawlessness. An internal staff report by the US embassy and the military command in Baghdad, called 'Provincial Stability Assessment' and dated 31 January, described Basra as one of six provinces whose condition was 'serious'. Basra was marked by a 'high level of militia activity including infiltration of local security forces', the report said. 'Smuggling and criminal activity continues unabated. Intimidation attacks and assassination are common.'[39]

Brigadier James Everard, commander of British forces in Basra, put it graphically a few months later when he told the *New York Times* in June 2006: 'We're into political porridge, that's what's changed. It's mafia-type politics down here.'[40] The murder rate had tripled since January, and secular professionals lived in fear.

Much of the violence in Basra revolved around oil. Basra's fields are the richest in Iraq and huge profits can be gained from fiddling the production figures and smuggling undeclared oil. Mowaffak al-Rubaie, Iraq's national security adviser, explained:

> If you don't understand what's happening there, follow the dollar sign … There is a 6,000-barrel-per-day difference between the level of production for export and the level of actual export. It goes into the pockets of these warlords, militias, organized crime, political parties.[41]

As Islamist criticism of the British occupation grew, attacks on British troops, which had been relatively infrequent in 2003 and 2004, increased sharply throughout 2005 and 2006. British officials said they detected growing use of a more lethal kind of roadside bomb. Known in the jargon as explosively formed projectiles (EFPs), they used charges that were put in a tube with a concave or steel liner on top. On detonation the liner becomes a weapon that travels with a velocity that gives it a high chance of going through armour-plating. The new technology reflected an increase in sophistication, although these EFPs could be made from commonly available pipe in a back-street workshop. They did not require industrial production.

US and British officials chose to blame Iran, claiming Iran had given them to the Lebanese guerrilla group Hizbullah, who had passed them on to Iraq's Shia militias. Using the standard label 'terrorist' to describe Hizbullah, official spokesmen sought to demonise the militias. Once again, they failed to see the link between the way Iraqis perceived the US/British occupation of Iraq and Israel's occupation of Lebanese and Palestinian land. The militias felt attacks on the British in Basra were as legitimate a form of resistance as

Hizbullah's resistance to Israeli tanks in south Lebanon. They did not recognise the description of Hizbullah as 'terrorist'.

The EFPs reduced British forces' mobility and forced them to lower their profile. They increasingly had to patrol in armoured vehicles rather than Land Rovers. Helicopters took up much of the burden of transporting people and goods between British bases. The futility of the British role gradually convinced senior British officers that their mission was hitting a brick wall. 'We are in a tribal society in Basra and we [the British army] are in effect one of these tribes,' Lt Col Simon Brown, commander of the 2nd Battalion, told Ghaith Abdul-Ahad, my *Guardian* colleague. 'As long as we are here the others will attack us because we are the most influential tribe. We cramp their style.'[42]

General Sir Richard Dannatt, the recently appointed head of the British army, shocked Downing Street in October 2006 by saying in an interview that Britain should

> get ourselves out sometime soon because our presence exacerbates the security problems … We are in a Muslim country and Muslims' views of foreigners in their country are quite clear. As a foreigner, you can be welcomed by being invited in a country, but we weren't invited ... by those in Iraq at the time. The military campaign we fought in 2003 effectively kicked the door in. Whatever consent we may have had in the first place, may have turned to tolerance and has largely turned to intolerance.[43]

Painful evidence from the ground supported the argument that the longer the British stayed, the more they would become the target of resistance. In 2005 their casualty figures doubled. In 2006 they went up by a third again. Military commanders pushed for a partial pull-back and the British withdrew from their main base in Amara in Maysan province that year – but they remained in the centre of Basra.

The military value of their presence looked increasingly negligible, yet Blair did not want to bring the troops out and thereby end Britain's role in the occupation. He was afraid this would look as though he was abandoning his friend in the White House. In effect, the troops became Downing Street's hostages.

That was certainly how many of them felt. After a trip to Basra, members of the House of Commons Defence Committee reported soldiers as telling them the only reason they were still in Iraq was 'because of our relations with the US'. One MP said their missions were pointless. He described the trips the troops made every night to bring supplies from the airport to the British garrison at Basra Palace in the city centre as 'suicide missions', since they were always attacked and often took serious or fatal casualties.[44] In the autumn of 2007 the British left Basra Palace but the new prime minister Gordon Brown was no more willing than Blair had been to end the occupation. He insisted that troops stay at the airport to continue training the Iraq army.

As the partial retreat began, independent analysts came to almost identical conclusions about the failure of Britain's second occupation of southern Iraq. Circumstances had changed since the 1920s. Britain was the junior partner in an occupation run by a more powerful ally. The Shia Islamist parties were stronger and better organised. But Britain's inability to win acceptance for British rule was as striking the second time round as it had been the first. So was its failure to bring in the 'effective, representative government' that its pre-war document 'Vision for Iraq' originally claimed as Britain's goal.[45]

According to Knights and Williams of the Washington Institute for Near East Policy:

> The overarching cause of policy failure in southern Iraq might be traced to an initial misapprehension of the nature of the population in southern Iraq. One image of the population of the deep south was that of a passive long-suffering community, leading to the expectation that it would remain patient and largely passive in the post-war period. In fact, deep factional and theological divisions were boiling beneath the surface.

> A second image of the local population was that of a relatively benign community that lacked military capability or anti-coalition intent. Once again, the reality was very different ... The south included a range of very violent and methodical political and criminal factions from the very earliest days of the occupation, and these factions did not hesitate to strike out at coalition forces whenever such forces threatened their interests.[46]

British commanders always argued that they used softer tactics than the Americans. In terms of prisoner handling, the difference was only relative. British troops were photographed using appalling methods on Iraqi detainees, including the use of a fork-lift truck to suspend a trussed captive from a height. British interrogators in several battalions put hoods over prisoners' heads for long periods, even though the technique had been banned in Northern Ireland after public outcry. On more than one occasion prisoners were forced to jump into the Shatt al-Arab waterway, causing at least two to drown.[47] Baha Mousa, a hotel receptionist in Basra, died after severe beating by troops from the Queen's Lancashire regiment.

Charges were brought in only a few cases, but deliberate obstruction led to insufficient evidence emerging about which individual soldiers had committed the crimes. This made it hard to produce convictions. In the case of Baha Mousa, a judge found that a group of soldiers had engaged in systematic torture and humiliation but none was charged because of an 'obvious closing of ranks'. Six soldiers were acquitted. One soldier admitted inhumanly treating civilians, a war crime under the International Criminal Court Act 2001. He was gaoled for one year.

Iraqis saw British abuses in the same light as they saw Abu Ghraib. Foreigners were assaulting Iraqi dignity and honour once again. There was similar outrage over the fact that soldiers had photographed their own atrocities, clearly to boast about their actions when they got home.

Where the British were softer than the Americans was in their political strategy. The British tried to avoid confrontation. They allowed the strongest political forces in the region, the Islamists, to have their way. Reidar Visser, a Norwegian Arabist and an expert on Basra, summarized the British record thus:

> Shortly after the onset of the occupation of Iraq in 2003, there was much fanfare about Britain's 'soft' approach to the policing of Basra, with a 'hearts and minds' focus ... Quite soon, however, it became clear that British soldiers gradually gave in to the advance of militia rule and were themselves less and less in evidence on the streets of Basra ... They left everyone in the south who was not affiliated with a militia disadvantaged and exposed in the political process – not least those vulnerable elements of Basra's population who refused to abide by neo-fundamentalist Islamic conformity.[48]

A senior Iraqi general in the interior ministry strongly criticised the British record four years after their arrival in Basra:

> The British came here as military tourists. They committed huge mistakes when they formed the security forces. They appointed militiamen as police officers and chose not to confront the militias. We have reached this point where the militias are a legitimate force in the street.[49]

193

The Washington analyst Anthony Cordesman commented in February 2007:

> The British long ago essentially ceded the two provinces they control – Basra and Maysan – to Shi'ite Islamist factions. They lost Basra in 2005 to rival Shi'ite extremist parties and essentially let most of the city become a no-go zone unless they conducted active operations. They pulled out of much of the southeast in 2006.

He described the British experience as defeat:

> The British soft approach has worked little better, if at all, than the American hard approach. The British were not defeated in a military sense, but lost in the political sense if 'victory' means securing the southeast for the central government and some form of national unity. Soft ethnic cleansing has been going on in Basra for more than two years, and the south has been the scene of the less violent form of civil war for control of political and economic space that is as important as the more openly violent struggles in Anbar and Baghdad.[50]

The International Crisis Group also used the word 'defeat'. Its researchers visited Basra to look at the final British effort to rout out militias and hand security over to newly vetted and stronger Iraqi security forces. Known as Operation Sinbad, it lasted from September 2006 to March 2007. Blair and Britain's Ministry of Defence touted it as a success, but the ICG team said that by April renewed political tensions once again threatened to de-stabilise the city:

> Relentless attacks against British forces in effect had driven them off the streets into increasingly secluded compounds. Basra's residents and militiamen view this not as an orderly withdrawal but rather as an ignominious defeat. Today the city is controlled by militias, seemingly more powerful and unconstrained than before.[51]

These independent analyses were accurate. The British experience in Basra and Maysan was a classic case of an occupation that was based on false premises and it failed to achieve the political goals that the government in London had set for it. The invasion was neither legal, necessary, nor wanted by most Iraqis. In removing Saddam's regime it opened the way for

Islamic parties that did not support the values of secular liberal democracy the invaders claimed they intended to introduce.

As the situation worsened and resistance grew, the British government rewrote its occupation aims, reducing them to a mission to train Iraqi forces. Even this relatively minor mission ran into trouble because of the prevalence of militias.

The British military's acceptance of the power of the local Islamists was at least prudent. Senior British officers were pragmatists rather than neoconservatives. They allowed the Islamist governors of Basra and Maysan provinces to run things in the way they thought fit. However much this policy disappointed the region's secular middle class, it caused less bloodshed than attempts to exclude the Islamists would have done.

Being wise after the event is not good enough, however. Outside experts had no difficulty in predicting that Saddam's downfall would produce a rise in Islamist power in Iraq as a whole, and particularly in the south. It remains extraordinary that the government's political and intelligence analysts did not see what was coming. If they had done a better job of warning ministers before the war, Blair's case for regime change would have been immeasurably weaker.

VIII

SECTARIAN CONFLICT: WHO'S TO BLAME?

If you look deep into our history, seven thousand years of history, we never ever had a single incident of unrest built on ethnicity or sect or religion.

Ghazi Ajil al-Yawer, November 2004[1]

We are turning Iraq into a sectarian state like Lebanon, where ministers have no value except as representatives of this or that sect.

Mustafa Alani, September 2003[2]

As Baghdad sank into sectarian violence in 2006, with Shia death squads storming into Sunni neighbourhoods to kill civilians and Sunni suicide bombers retaliating with car bomb attacks on crowded Shia street markets, Iraqis and foreigners reacted to the horror very differently.

Among Western politicians and in the media the prevailing view was that Iraqis were playing out 'ancient hatreds'. The only fact most outsiders knew about Iraq was that its population consisted of Sunnis, Shias, and Kurds. It was easy to jump to the notion that Saddam Hussein had 'kept the lid' on deeply seated tensions. As soon as the strongman was removed, conflict and blood-letting were bound to resume.

Most Iraqis took a contrasting line. 'We never used to know or care whether our neighbours or friends were Sunni or Shia,' they would tell Westerners. Iraqi Arabs and Iraqi Kurds have always been aware of their different traditions (they speak separate languages) but among the country's Arab majority national consciousness outweighed the sectarian issue of Sunni or

Shia. This was especially true among the educated urban middle class. They saw the rise of sectarianism and its turn to violence as entirely the work of outsiders.

Some blamed the Americans for provoking tensions in order to weaken and divide Iraq. Others blamed Al-Qaeda and its jihadi supporters who followed the extreme Salafi doctrine that sees all Shias as infidels. They came to Iraq to kill Shias for collaborating with the Americans to usurp the Sunnis' right to rule Iraq.

Which version was right? Was there truth on both sides? Can anyone disentangle the complex issues that had led Iraq to the verge of collapse and was producing the world's worst humanitarian disaster by 2007 (2 million refugees, another 2 million people displaced inside Iraq, and a rate of killing that was taking an average of a hundred lives a day)?[3]

The Sunni–Shia divide has existed for 14 centuries. It originated in Iraq with the murder of Imam Hussein in Kerbala in 680 CE. His last words, according to Shias, were, 'Death with dignity is better than a life of humiliation.' In spite of this bloody start, sectarianism has only been used as a political weapon during rare periods of Iraq's history. For most of the time it was not a source of hostility or violence but simply a cultural and social fact of life, and often a mark of class. Sunnis tended to be landlords, and therefore richer and more able to give their sons education.

Iraq's British colonial rulers favoured them largely for this reason. Signs of Sunni–Shia cooperation always alarmed the British, especially when it took on a nationalist hue. Describing the uprising of 1920 the historian Charles Tripp wrote: 'Gathering by turn at Sunni and Shia mosques, increasing numbers of Baghdadis attended, providing vivid symbolic proof of cooperation between members of the two sects in the cause of Iraqi independence.'[4] To counter this, Britain devised different techniques to split them, as discussed in Chapter IV.

Like Iraq's American occupiers two generations later, Britain's colonial secretary, Winston Churchill, had a poor understanding of the relevance of sects. He sent a request for guidance to one of his staff on 14 June 1921 about the man the British were installing as Iraq's king:

> Let me have a note in about three lines as to Faisal's religious character … Is he a Sunni with Shaih [sic] sympathies or a Shaih with Sunni sympathies, or how does he square it? … Which is the aristocratic high church and which is the low church? … I always get mixed up between these two.[5]

It was not until the overthrow of the monarchy in 1958 that Iraq saw a significant increase in the influence of Shias in politics. They migrated from the countryside in large numbers to Basra, Baghdad, and other cities. Some Shias began to do well in commerce, making intermarriage of Sunnis and Shias, at least among the middle class, relatively common. This began to undermine the pre-eminence of Sunnis in Iraq's economic and political elite.

Saddam's rule is often described as an attempt to reverse this by re-imposing Sunni Arab dominance over Iraq. This is an over-simplification, however. As he built up his personal power, usurping the machinery of the Baath party so as to favour his own tribe and family, his first victims were other Sunni Arabs. Later, he turned on the Kurds, expelling some 40,000 Kurdish Shias, known as Faili Kurds, to Iran.

In the 1950s and 1960s the main political vehicle for Shias was the Communist party. Its programme for social change appealed to the poor, and they were mainly Shia. However in the 1970s Saddam's persecution of the Communist party and other secular forces created a political vacuum which Shia Islamists began to fill. Anti-Saddam protests organised by the Dawa party during the religious festivals at Najaf and Kerbala in 1977 were brutally put down. Saddam used helicopters against them because many Shia soldiers deserted rather than attacking people of their own sect. Iranians are predominantly Shia, and the toppling of the Shah by Islamists in 1979 added to Saddam's anxiety about the potential for revolt among Iraqi Shias.

Many Shias had joined the Baath party for career reasons, since it was a requirement for advancement in most professions. Others went into the army. Supporters of the underground Dawa party were not banned by the party from taking jobs in the regime; they needed to feed their families and having them in the Baath party might help Dawa eventually.

When Saddam launched his war on Iran in 1980 he was motivated in part by a wish to stop radical Islamist influences from seeping across the border into south-eastern Iraq. The war also gave him the pretext to purge the officer corps of anyone who was or could be a potential Dawa supporter. Whether because of repression or from a sense of Iraqi patriotism, most Shias did not mutiny or surrender. They formed the bulk of the conscript army and held firm against the Iranian forces. When the Iranians counterattacked into Iraq after 1982, Iraq's Shias again contained and blocked them. Sectarianism had proven to be largely irrelevant politically.

It only seemed to emerge in a significant way after Saddam's defeat in Kuwait in 1991. The uprising in the largely Shia towns of the south-east as well as in Baghdad's Saddam City took on a sectarian tone, promoted by Dawa and exile loyalists of the opposition movement SCIRI, who crossed in large numbers from Iran. To turn the middle classes against the uprising, Saddam deliberately put out propaganda on state television and radio about Shia mobs rampaging out of control. He accused Shias of being *shu'ubiyya*, a medieval term for non-Arab outsiders, particularly Persians. The message was that Shias were behaving like foreigners and had become traitors to Iraq.

In the aftermath of the 1991 revolt and the weakening of the Baath party Saddam increasingly turned back to Iraq's tribal structure in order to keep his regime safe. He promoted some tribes and bought off others in both Shia and Sunni regions. He gave his regime an Islamic colouring by awarding favours to a few selected clerics and adding the words '*Allah akbar*' to the Iraqi national flag. His aim was to fragment Iraqi society and prevent opposition coalescing around groups with a potentially national appeal.

Iraq on the eve of Saddam's removal was well described by Sami Zubaida, an Iraqi-born sociologist:

> The years of wars and sanctions in the 1980s and up to the demise of the regime in 2003 witnessed the increased localisation and communalisation of Iraqi society ... Local society tends to be traditional, religious, and tribal. These forces were encouraged and fostered by the Saddam regime as means of social control when the reach of the Baath party contracted.[6]

Zubaida rejected the notion that Saddam had 'kept a lid' on ancient hatreds – the same simplistic analysis that was made about Tito and Yugoslavia to explain Balkan turmoil after Tito's death. On the contrary, by deliberately playing on differences Saddam created tensions that had not been there before. Zubaida argued:

> The present sorry state of Iraqi politics, dominated by religious authority and sectarian interests, is not the natural state of Iraqi society without authoritarian discipline. It is the product precisely of that authoritarian regime and the social forces that engendered it.[7]

While deliberately creating tensions, Saddam used his brutal security apparatus to contain and control them. His policy was one of 'divide and repress'. Removing those restraints might well produce an explosion of disorder and violence. This has happened at various times in Iraq's history. When British forces entered western Baghdad in 1941 and toppled the regime of Rashid Ali, for example, there was a sudden pogrom against the city's Jewish population. Close to two hundred were killed and many Jewish businesses were looted in what was known as the *farhud* (meaning taking things to excess). The British did not intervene until the pogrom was over. Similar violence followed the temporary collapse of Saddam's authority in 1991, and it was seen again with the widespread looting of public buildings after his fall in 2003. However, these short outbursts of violence did not mean that the class, ethnic, and sectarian differences within Iraqi society would necessarily turn to long-term violence or spark a civil war once dictatorial rule was gone. There was nothing inevitable about the sectarian murders that devastated Baghdad from 2005 onwards.

Saddam's shift towards manipulating tribal and sectarian issues in the 1990s was mirrored, in a milder but nonetheless significant way, within Iraq's exile politics. Until 1992 there were four trends aiming to overthrow Saddam: Islamic, Kurdish, pan-Arab nationalist, and secular democratic. The latter included liberals, independents, and the Communist party. At a conference in Beirut in March 1991 attempts were made to unite the forces by creating a Joint Action Committee (JAC). It was sparked by Saddam's defeat in Kuwait and the realisation that the USA had become the main international player in the anti-Saddam effort. Washington had supported Saddam against Iran in the 1980s but from 1991 onwards was committed to containing and undermining him. Various opposition groups felt they needed to make overtures to Washington.

In Vienna in June 1992 the opposition groups formed the Iraqi National Congress (INC). Ahmad Chalabi who ran the London office of the JAC became the INC's leader. A key issue among the exile groups was who could claim to have the best access to Washington. The pan-Arab nationalists and Communists lost influence because their contacts with the USA were minimal. Sunni exiles, while critical of Saddam, did not publicly call for his overthrow. The Iraqi Islamic party, which was almost entirely Sunni, had little influence because it was not well organised.

Iraqi opposition politics thus began to assume the shape they were to have when the Americans invaded Iraq in 2003. There were now three main currents – the Kurds, the Shia Islamists, and the secular liberals. Most Shia

Islamists took an ambiguous line towards Washington but a few, along with the Kurds and the liberals, were pro-American. Resentment of Chalabi's lack of consultation and his authoritarian style had reduced the INC to little more than a faction, rather than a genuine umbrella for the exile parties. However, this did not matter as the other groups formed their own direct links with Washington's various power-centres – the CIA, Pentagon, and State Department.

Once Saddam was removed, the field was open for these groups to return, each anxious to persuade the Americans that they commanded widespread support. The Kurds were in a special category after enjoying autonomy and freedom from Saddam's rule for the past 12 years. The two dominant Kurdish parties (each with a powerful clan-based militia) fought a civil war in the mid-1990s, but their leaders decided to present Washington with a united front in the new post-Saddam world. They realised that Kurdish politicians had to speak to the Americans with one voice if they were to maintain their region's autonomy and have the concept of federalism enshrined in a new Iraqi constitution. They also hoped to gain the oil-rich district of Kirkuk and other parts of northern Iraq, which they felt were historically theirs. For this they would need American help against Iraq's Arabs.

The headache for the Americans was how to deal with these Iraqi Arabs. The neoconservatives' initial plan had been to appoint a provisional government for Iraq, with Chalabi as its head. This was dropped shortly before the invasion. Although the idea still had some champions in Washington after Saddam fell, there was no obvious candidate to lead it. Chalabi's role in giving false intelligence about Saddam's weapons of mass destruction undermined his authority in Washington.[8]

The neoconservatives' next idea was to dust off the imperial model that the USA had used in post-war Japan. The way to impose their agenda would be for the USA to become Iraq's colonial master by appointing a powerful American governor. Through a series of decrees and a set of constitutional principles that the USA would draft, he and his team would turn Iraq into a liberal democracy with an open, privatised economy that would be friendly to foreign investors. In foreign policy Iraq would recognise Washington's global interests and allow the USA to build a set of major military bases.

As they arrived to take control of Iraq, most American policy makers knew as little about the fabric of its society as Churchill did in 1921. One official with the CPA commented after he left office:

> Senior CPA advisors and the political leadership in both Washington and Baghdad saw Iraq as an amalgam of three monolithic communities, and as long as you kept the Shiites and Kurds happy, success was guaranteed because they were not Baathists, formed the majority, and essentially had the same idea as liberal Americans ... This simplistic mindset explains most of the mistakes of US policy including the disbandment of the army and Baath party which they also saw in sectarian terms. Today we have the sectarian and ethnically based politics that the US always claimed existed, a self-fulfilling prophecy.[9]

So the USA exacerbated Iraq's sectarian differences, just as Saddam had done. Saddam did it deliberately. Were US actions also intentional, or only misguided? Many Iraqis thought Washington wanted to encourage a situation of low-level, perhaps outright, civil war in order to have a pretext for keeping its forces in Iraq as long as possible. The notion of neutral peacekeepers holding the ring between unruly groups of natives is, after all, one of the well-known tropes of empire.

This conspiracy theory became increasingly common in Iraq in 2006 and 2007 as the violence worsened. I heard it as early as 2004 from a young would-be recruit to the Iraqi army who was severely wounded when a car bomb went off near where he was standing in a line of applicants outside the Muthanna base in central Baghdad. 'The Americans did it,' he replied when I interviewed him in Yarmuk hospital less than a hour later. It seemed far-fetched, but I was not going to argue with a bandaged man in a hospital bed.

Other Iraqis thought the Americans' exaggeration of sectarian issues arose from incompetence and ignorance rather than from cunning and cynicism. Whatever the truth of US intentions, the result was a continuation of the growth in sectarian consciousness among Iraqis that had begun in Saddam's last decade.

The abolition of the army and the sacking of senior Baathists from any government job were certainly perceived by Sunnis as moves against them. Occupation officials and the Western media (which was played back into Iraq via Arab satellite stations and the Iraqi press) reinforced that impression. They constantly repeated the refrain that Sunnis were a minority in Iraq who had dominated the country for too long and it was time to give the Shias their chance. Ali Allawi, a secular Shia who served briefly as defence minister in 2004 and finance minister in 2005, acutely described the way Sunni Arabs perceived the new situation:

> All were united in their refusal to accept that the ground rules of Iraqi politics were about to be recast along sectarian identity … To them Iraq had always been an Arab country: sectarian differences were a throwback to the dark ages. Iraq was a unitary and centralised state and a powerful army was necessary to fend off foreign invaders, especially if they were Persians.[10]

The USA turned de-Baathification into a sectarian weapon. It was to be administered by a 'de-Baathification Council', controlled by Chalabi, who used it to remove potential rivals and build his credentials with the Shia religious establishment. Its deputy chair was Nouri al-Maliki, a fiercely sectarian Shia politician from the Dawa party who became prime minister in the first freely elected government in 2006. As the ICG pointed out in a February 2006 report on sectarianism, the Shia parties

> helped to sectarianise the process by giving Shiite Baath party members within their own community the opportunity to repent. The standard approach toward Sunni Arab members, however, was to exclude them from senior posts in government and the security forces.[11]

Instead of being used to 'de-Saddamise' Iraq, the de-Baathification process became one of 'de-Sunnification'.

The US process of choosing a governing council to work under the CPA also helped to reinforce the Sunnis' exclusion of power in the new US-run Iraq. It was operated along the lines of a quota system based on criteria that were not comprehensive. It could have been geographic and sectoral with seats for key cities, rural regions, the major tribes, trade unions, and professional associations. In fact, it was picked on ethnic, sectarian, and religious grounds, as though this provided a fair representation of Iraq.

Iraq's second largest city, Mosul, had no member on the new council, nor did the trade unions. Giving three places to women and other seats to Christian and other minority communities was progressive, but in other respects the composition of the council's 25-person membership was misguided. CPA officials did not mind. They argued that the five seats given to Sunnis fairly reflected the fact that Sunnis formed only 20 per cent of Iraq's population. But statements such as these only strengthened Sunni perceptions that Iraq was now going to be ruled on a sectarian basis. They felt they were being told they deserved their fall from grace and should not complain.

It did not help that two of the five Sunnis, Adnan Pachachi, a foreign minister from the pre-Saddam era, and Ghazi al-Yawer, a wealthy businessman, were long-time exiles. The only significant Sunni group that represented people who had stayed in Iraq under Saddam and now had a member on the governing council was the Iraqi Islamic party.

In defending their selections, occupation officials argued that it was hard to find Sunnis who represented anyone other than themselves. The Baath party had shut everyone else out of power during its 30-year monopoly of rule. However, this should have been a spur for the USA to choose former Baathists who had broken their links to Saddam and could speak for the large number of Baathists who welcomed his removal and had long felt he had betrayed the party's pan-Arabist and secular ideals.

Bremer praised the composition of the governing council for being 'for the first time in Iraq's history a balanced representative group of political leaders from across this country'.[12] But it drew criticism from Iraqis. 'We are turning Iraq into a sectarian state like Lebanon where ministers have no value except as representatives of this or that sect. It's very dangerous because you can't build a democratic stable state based on sectarianism,' Mustafa Alani, an Iraqi political scientist, commented.[13]

The occupation's next political blunder was to refuse to commit itself to a clear timetable for elections and an end to the occupation. Bremer's prevarication aroused the suspicions of Ayatollah Sistani and the senior Shia clerics, as Chapter IV explained. Less than three months after the occupation started the ayatollah called for elections and made it clear he would be satisfied with nothing else. Sistani feared the Americans might have a plan to put the Baathists or other Sunnis back in power. He saw elections as the best way to prevent this, since Shias' demographic majority would give them victory. The ayatollah's concerns about Bremer's alleged pro-Sunni bias were wildly misplaced, however. Bremer's de-Baathification decrees and his measures against the Iraqi army were directed against Sunnis and were intended to be seen as such.

The CPA found itself caught between Sunni anger and Shia suspicion. Two lessons should have been drawn. One was that once sectarianism is used as the basis for political decision-making it tends to grow in strength and malignancy. The second was that no occupation force can successfully navigate between competing sectarian claims. Only local people can.

The history of empires shows that as long as foreigners try to retain overall control each side will appeal to them for help against the other. If the foreigners tilt one way, the community that falls out of favour will blackmail or intimidate them to tilt the other way. An occupation quickly becomes a distorting factor. It impedes the natural progress of a society emerging from dictatorship and prevents 'normal' politics. Outsiders may try to 'hold the ring' for a time, but this only suppresses problems without resolving them. Both sides will sooner or later turn against the occupiers. The only solution is to end the occupation quickly and have the foreigners leave.

In Iraq, this was not to be. Bush and the neoconservatives intended to remain in Iraq for the long haul. As sectarian thinking developed in the Shia Islamist camp, partly in collusion with the CPA's deliberately anti-Sunni policies and partly as a defence mechanism against a potential change of American policy and a new betrayal (like 1991, when the Americans first urged the Shias to rise up and then abandoned them), it became inevitable that sectarianism would also grow among the Sunnis. They first directed their anger at the Americans, since they held the power. Later, the Sunnis turned against the Shias too.

Before the invasion many analysts had warned that it would turn Iraq into a magnet for terrorism. This was the view of CIA professionals, although George Tenet, the CIA director, never passed it on to the White House. 'The CIA repeatedly warned Tenet of the inevitable disaster an Iraq war would cause – spreading bin Ladenism, spurring a bloody Sunni–Shiite war and lethally destabilizing the region,' Michael Scheuer, the first head of the CIA's Bin Laden unit, commented later.[14] On another occasion, Scheuer put it more colloquially: 'If Osama was a Christian, the invasion of Iraq would have been the Christmas present he long desired.'[15] In other words, having US troops in an Arab country would serve Al-Qaeda's purposes by giving them a wonderful new issue on which to campaign to find recruits. Osama bin Laden would relish the challenge. He felt he had defeated the Soviet Union in Afghanistan. Now he would aim for a second triumph by driving the Great Satan out of Iraq.

In earlier chapters I have explained how Al-Qaeda in Iraq (it was also called Al-Qaeda in Mesopotamia) did not spark the anti-occupation insurgency. The movement's jihadis from around the Arab world were not very quick on the scene in Iraq. Their first attack took place on 7 August 2003, four months after Saddam was toppled. A truck bomb was detonated outside the Jordanian embassy in Baghdad, the first time a vehicle packed with explosives had been used in Iraq. By then, the Iraqi nationalist insurgency had been under way for at least three months with primitive booby-traps directed at US convoys and patrols, the so-called IEDs. These were planted by Iraqis.

Under questioning, US military officials always admitted that foreign fighters comprised a small minority in the insurgency. Even at the height of the killing in early 2007 the new US defense secretary, Robert Gates, told the House of Representatives' Armed Services Committee: 'There are some foreign fighters but they are not the principal source of the problem.'[16]

When the anti-occupation insurgency developed in Sunni areas, Western officials initially explained it in simplistic terms as being motivated entirely by disgruntled Baathists who resented the loss of their privileges. In CPA-speak they were dubbed 'FREs' – Former Regime Elements. While some senior Baathists and former army officers who were Sunnis did form part of the resistance, they had differing motives. Only a few wanted to restore Saddam to power. The others hoped for a renewed Baathism without Saddam's narrow, clan-based dictatorship. Neither group was the dominant force in the insurgency.

The key trend was a combination of nationalism and Islamism. Most resistance groups had Islamic names such as the Islamic Resistance Movement in Iraq, the Islamic Army in Iraq, and the Mujahideen's Army. Even the Baathists within the resistance took on an Islamist colouring after realising they had to use Islamist slogans to gain support. They called their armed wing the Army of Muhammad (*Jaish Muhammad*). Some former Baathists joined the Islamists out of conviction. They were disappointed that Saddam had given orders not to resist the US capture of Baghdad and had run away. 'In the days after the invasion the TV stations were full of army officers saying Saddam had betrayed Iraq. Many became Islamists or Sadrists because Sadr was seen as an authentic Iraqi voice,' said Sami Ramadani, a London-based Iraqi analyst.[17]

Many Sunni Islamists had suffered under Saddam. They had no interest in seeing him restored to power. They opposed the American occupation on nationalist and religious grounds, and because it was seen as handing Iraq to the Shias. Some of them joined the armed resistance, or gave it financial and logistical support. Islamism had grown among Iraq's Sunni Arabs in the last decade of Saddam's rule, just as it had among the Shias.

The CIA and the administration's other analysts ought to have known this. They should have warned Bush that an occupying army would run into a combination of nationalist resentment and Islamist fervour. This was not going to be Germany and Japan.

Financed and promoted by supporters in Saudi Arabia, the dominant trend among Iraq's Sunnis in 2003 was the purist movement known as Salafism. It produced clerics who were more active politically than traditional imams. While Shias took their lead from ayatollahs, Iraqi Sunnis had no such organised and pyramid-shaped structure. There were no leaders or hierarchies and each imam was more or less autonomous. By the time Saddam fell, however, the Salafi imams were on the rise, helping to produce a moral and religious revival in Sunni Arab communities. The Salafis were contemptuous of Shias, believing them not to be true Muslims. Their increasing authority helped to boost sectarian thinking.

So the ground was already fertile for sectarianism before Al-Qaeda's foot soldiers and organisers arrived in Iraq in the summer of 2003 from Saudi Arabia, Algeria, Yemen, and other parts of the Arab world. They undoubtedly gave it a further boost since they were also Salafis. But, just as Al-Qaeda did not launch the nationalist resistance, it would be wrong to see the advent of Al-Qaeda in Iraq as the trigger for the sectarian violence that exploded through Baghdad and Iraq's other mixed communities in 2006. The slide towards sectarianism was started by Saddam, and further helped by the Americans in the first months of the occupation.

As Sunni anger grew, not all Sunni clerics favoured violent action against Shias. The Association of Muslim Scholars (AMS), which became an open champion of resistance to the occupation, made contact with Shia leaders like Sadr early on. They hoped to forge a common resistance front against the Americans.

The AMS refused to have dealings with the CPA or any other institution linked to it. Its leader, Harith al-Dhari, was a graduate of Cairo's respected Al-Azhar religious university. Under threat from Saddam's regime, Dhari had been forced to flee Iraq in the late 1990s and only returned in 2003. He and his colleague, Mohammed Ayash al-Kubaisi, published a set of articles that proclaimed the 'jurisprudence of resistance' (*fiqh al muqawamma*). This said people not only had the right to resist invaders but that it was every individual's duty to resist. Resistance, they said, was on a par with a Muslim's other obligations such as fasting and prayer. The AMS saw the Shias as allies in this cause.

In an interview in March 2004, in a small side room at the AMS head-quarters in the Umm al-Qura mosque where men in long *dishdashas* were busy photocopying statements and leaflets, Sheikh Sabah Nouri al-Qaisi, a founder-member and spokesman for the 16-member council, explained its purpose. It was set up to find a united political voice for the three main strands of Sunni thought: the Sufi, the Salafi, and the Muslim Brotherhood, he said.

Unlike Dhari, Sheikh al-Qaisi was a Salafi. 'Under Saddam you got an immediate death sentence for being a Salafi. We had to propagate our ideas secretly,' he told me. He made no attempt to disguise his support for armed resistance against the Americans:

> The occupation is the number one, and most dangerous, issue for Iraq and for the world. It's not really right to call it an occupation. It's a war against Islam, a crusade against the Muslim world. Any honest revolutionary resistance has to have two methods. One is military, the other is to explain what is going on.

He made it clear he welcomed foreign jihadis coming to Iraq, although he opposed anti-Shia activity:

> It's the right of every Muslim to join in defending Iraq. We call on every Muslim in our beautiful country to remove this black cloud over us. We call on all honest Iraqis to gather round this just and patriotic programme, based on the unity of society and the rejection of sectarianism.

When Al-Qaeda in Iraq literally exploded on to the scene in August 2003 with the attacks on the Jordanian embassy and the UN, its actions were typically massive and designed to create publicity as well as terror. The aim was to frighten foreign institutions and governments from working with the occupation. The car bomb that killed Ayatollah Baqir al-Hakim in Najaf on

29 August also seemed to be primarily an anti-occupation move, since his organisation, SCIRI, had just agreed to join Bremer's governing council.

Whether or not it was also intended as a warning to Shias, the assassination was perceived as such. Over the next few months more than a dozen Sunni imams were assassinated, mainly in Baghdad. As with all such murders, the police never arrested any suspects. Scores of other Iraqi community leaders and prominent professionals, mostly Sunnis, including over 300 academics, as well as doctors and engineers, were assassinated within the first year of the occupation. Were they killed in a settling of old scores because some had been Baathists? Was it an Al-Qaeda-in-Iraq policy of destroying Iraq's intellectual elite so as to make Iraq ungovernable? Was it sectarian-based revenge by Shias? No one knew.

The first car bomb attacks on unarmed civilians began in early 2004. More than 200 Shias were killed on 2 March during the festival of Ashoura as bombs ripped through crowds in the holy city of Kerbala and at the main Shia shrine in Baghdad in the northern suburb of Kadhimiya. Body parts and strips of flesh were scattered all over the blood-stained streets. The vast number of deaths, the biggest on a single day, as well as the symbolic impact of attacking unarmed pilgrims during a religious festival, shocked Iraqis.

Grand Ayatollah Ali al-Sistani, Iraq's leading Shia, immediately called for calm and restraint. Other Shia clerics followed suit. At mass funerals the day after the bombing Ayatollah Hadi al-Muddaresi warned, 'There are parties and groups that are willing to push Iraq towards civil war, but the material to make it happen isn't there … We as Shias refuse to be drawn into such a conflict.'

In Baghdad, in an impressive display of solidarity and unity, Sunni and Shia clerics jointly led mourning processions. The largely Sunni district of Adhamiya and the largely Shia area of Kadhimiya are separated by the Tigris but a huge column of Sunnis from Adhamiya marched across the bridge to join the Shia funerals.

Western analysts started to talk of civil war, but Iraqis were still denying that sectarianism was of any relevance. The subject was taboo. I found that out during a series of interviews in Sunni and Shia areas at the time. In Nassiriya one young militant I talked to was Salman Sharif Duaffar, an intense 35-year-old who had studied engineering at university and now represented a small Islamic political party, the 15th of Shabaan movement.

Duaffar was famous for leading a hit squad that fired a volley of shots at Uday, Saddam's sadistic playboy son, in Baghdad in 1996. The gang fled the scene successfully, and Duaffar escaped to Iran. It took another 18 months for the regime to discover anything about the hit squad, and then only by chance when one of its members was arrested in Baghdad on different suspicions. Under torture he confessed to having taken part in the failed assassination attempt and named his colleagues. Retribution was swift. Duaffar's father and seven brothers were taken to Abu Ghraib and killed. Their house was demolished.

'Our movement began as Shia but we have many Sunni members. History has taught us that nothing has happened between the Sunnis and the Shias in the past,' Duaffar said proudly. 'I'm sure there won't be sectarian clashes in the future. The Sunnis and the Shias know the enemy want to provoke clashes, but we are containing the danger successfully.' Duaffar was one of many political leaders who worked hard to prevent retaliation in the hours after the bombings at Kerbala and Kadhimiya. He assumed they were probably the work of Sunni militants from abroad or from the Salafis .

In March 2004 in Fallujah, which the Americans saw as a 'Sunni bastion' and a hotbed of militant Islam, Abed Ruzuqi, a retired employee in the agriculture department, was keen to tell me that the town had a well-integrated Shia minority and there were no sectarian problems. As his brothers offered us rice and chicken at a shaded table in his front garden, he described an American attack a few nights earlier which, the Americans said, was a response to grenades being fired at a US patrol.

Ruzuqi heard a helicopter in the night sky, with its lights doused as usual. Suddenly a minivan across the road went up in flames. After the chopper moved off, neighbours rushed out with buckets of water to put the fire out. When a helicopter engine was heard again, the neighbours fled. Ruzuqi's elderly brother-in-law, Muwaiyed Abdul Munim, was too slow. As he neared his front gate he was struck by shrapnel from a rocket that crashed into the road. Severely wounded in the abdomen, his family took him to hospital, where he died. 'The Americans say they are fighting terrorism, but it's they who bring terror by using bombs and rockets on innocent people,' Ruzuqi said. His son was a policeman and, like many Iraqis, he denounced the killing of police, even as he praised the resistance to US troops.

Interspersed with his anger with the Americans, Ruzuqi explained Falluja's solidarity with Shias. 'About 5 per cent of the people here are Shias. We socialise with them. They intermarry. At first they came to the town as day labourers but now they have small shops and businesses. They're bringing their whole families. House prices are going up,' he remarked in the familiar manner of suburbanites anywhere.

He boasted of how, after the bombings at the Shia shrines in Kerbala and Kadhimiya, imams used Fallujah's many minarets to put out loud-speaker messages urging people to donate blood. 'More than 1,000 people went to the main hospital here to give blood. I was one of them,' Ruzuqi said.

In Baquba, a mixed Sunni-Shia town about 50 miles north of Baghdad, I was almost set upon by students of the technical institute when I asked about sectarianism in April 2004. A protest demonstration had just taken place against the American onslaught on Fallujah and in support of the uprising in Sadr City by the radical Shia cleric, Moqtada al-Sadr. I asked whether both Sunni and Shia students took part. 'We are not Sunni or Shia. We are Muslims,' one student shouted. Others called me a Zionist. 'Why do you focus on whether people are Sunni or Shia?', asked an older man who turned out to be a faculty member, as he tried to calm the crowd of enraged students who had started to jostle me. As he led me to safety I tried to explain I wasn't 'focusing' on the issue. It was just one of a range of subjects I wanted to understand.

The students' irritation with me was well founded. Intermarriage between Sunnis and Shias was common, particularly among better-educated people, and many Iraqis refused to define themselves in sectarian terms. A survey in January 2004 by the Iraq Centre for Research and Strategic Studies, one of Baghdad's best opinion pollsters, asked people which of the following expressions 'suits you well': Sunni Muslim, Shia Muslim, or Just Muslim. The biggest category, 39.9 per cent, chose the last option.[18]

As the number of assassinations of Sunni imams gradually increased, Sunni leaders were as reluctant to blame Iraqi Shias as Shias had been to blame Iraqi Sunnis for the bombs at Kerbala and Kadhimiya or the assassination of Ayatollah Hakim. Sabah al-Qaisi, the AMS spokesman, accused 'Iranian agents' of being behind the Kerbala and Kadhimiya bombings. Their motive, he suggested, was to prevent Iraq emerging as a stable and united state. He saw the murders of Sunni imams as a kind of slow-motion version of the bombings in Kerbala, with the same aim of trying to provoke revenge and civil war. When I spoke to him in Baghdad in April 2004, he told me:

Shias have special holy days which mean a great deal to them, and they gather in large crowds. Sunnis don't have big occasions so they go for individual targets ... They hope they'll provoke us by killing our leaders, and get an immediate reaction, but we will not act unreasonably.

The imams' killers were trained in Iran and took their orders from Iranian security agents, he insisted. When I asked how he knew, his response was somewhat chilling:

I started an inquiry and arrested a man who admitted he was an agent for a local militia which has relations with Iran. He confessed to killing several of our Sunni imams. We didn't give him to the police, but transferred him to his family.

My interpreter explained later that this last phrase meant they killed the man.

To find victims of the spate of killings at Sunni mosques we drove to a low-income area of western Baghdad, a dusty suburb of wide streets with a mixed Sunni and Shia population. At the Hamed Findi al-Kubaisi mosque Sunni clerics took us to a side building in the front yard. One wall was covered in shelves with Qur'anic and other religious texts. The opposite wall on either side of the window was a grisly sight. Bits of black hair were stuck to the paint amid sinister brown stains of dried blood. 'We kept this to show people,' explained Abu Abdullah, whose job it was to make the call to prayer.

A mosque guard had been sitting in the room one evening when a grenade was thrown from the street, the sheikh explained. He and the other guards rushed out of the mosque and saw a BMW that was similar to one they had spotted four days earlier when their imam, Ali Hassan, was walking to the mosque for evening prayers. About eight shots were fired from the car, killing the imam.

Abu Abdullah was sure the murders were either the work of Iran, the USA, or Israel. 'The attacks are done by Iraqis who come from Iran, or by Iranians,' he said. His other theory was that Americans and Israelis were responsible. 'It could be Iraqi mercenaries paid by America or Israel. Since the Americans got here, they've been working to create a spark for a sectarian conflict. They will not succeed,' he said. As evidence, he cited the fact that US troops had come to the mosque a few hours before their imam was killed. They invited him to their headquarters to meet the local US commander. Photographs of the meeting were taken. 'I believe this was done to give pictures to the killers to help them identify their target,' Abu Abdullah said. Whatever the validity of his claims, the significant point was that he refused to blame local Shias for the spate of murders: 'It was not done by Shias. Inshallah, we will not fight each other.'

This phrase had become a mantra, repeated by every Iraqi politician at senior or local level, whenever the issue of civil war was raised. They included Sheikh Ghazi Ajil al-Yawer, a rich businessman who headed the Shammar, one of Iraq's largest tribes with more than 2 million members. He was appointed by the Americans to serve on Bremer's governing council in July 2003 and became Iraq's interim president a year later.

An imposing, portly figure in beautifully laundered white robes, he had an impeccable command of English. Two months before the Americans selected him as Iraq's president, I visited him in his well-protected Baghdad villa. 'We have Sunni and Shias in our tribe,' Sheikh Ghazi explained expansively:

> We stretch along most of western Iraq from the Turkish–Syrian border down to Saudi Arabia. We had a clash with the Wahhabis when they started. We migrated north of Euphrates in the eighteenth century. The people who stayed south became Shias.

He was born in Mosul, and counted himself a Sunni, although 'half the time I vote with the Shia in the governing council. I don't like to be put in a corner.' As a child, his parents regularly took him to the Shia holy cities of Kerbala and Najaf for festivals, and his best school friend was a Chaldaean Christian. 'I'm a believer and I do my religious duties every day. But I'm really secular. I never think about things in a religious way. You never find a Bedouin who goes to religious extremes,' he laughed engagingly.

The Americans had just conceded there would have to be elections to a constituent assembly – though not until January 2005. Sheikh Ghazi was worried that Shia parties would outbid each other to get support in the Shia community by taking anti-Sunni positions, either openly or in a disguised way by emphasising social justice and the need to redress the economic wrongs of the past. Shias formed most of Iraq's underclass and would understand what was meant.

At the time of our conversation, the sheikh insisted that sectarianism was only being raised by foreigners:

Someone is trying to invent a sectarian problem in Iraq. It's mostly outsiders … But there is trouble with the politicians here. People in the street are ten times more responsible than politicians. The politicians say 'I'm a Sunni'. People say 'I'm an Iraqi'.

Sheikh Ghazi was not the only prominent Iraqi who saw the danger of sectarianism and sought to forestall it. Iyad Allawi, who was selected by the Americans to head the interim government that superseded the governing council in June 2004, firmly opposed sectarianism. He presented himself as a secular figure with national appeal. However, rather than promoting national reconciliation or reaching out to Sunnis as prime minister, Allawi made it his priority to defeat the occupation's opponents. In August 2004 he encouraged the Americans to launch an assault on the holy city of Najaf to destroy Sadr's Mahdi army. In November he approved the second US onslaught on Fallujah, code-named Operation Phantom Fury.

The two episodes were turning points. The Americans failed to disarm the Mahdi army and from then on it was impossible for Sadr to do it for them by voluntarily disbanding his militia. He was bound to retain it as an anti-occupation force as well as a weapon in the struggle with the other main Islamic militia, SCIRI's Badr organisation.

On the Sunni side it was equally hard for politicians to maintain credibility as Arabs and as nationalists if they worked with the Americans. They were bound to be treated with suspicion, if not contempt, by other Sunnis. The attack on Fallujah left hundreds dead, destroyed more than half the town, ruined the electricity and water systems, and turned more than 350,000 people into refugees. Sunnis across Iraq were enraged. It was hardly surprising that most Sunni politicians refused to put up candidates for the January 2005 elections. They argued that free elections could not take place until foreign troops withdrew from Iraq's cities.

A rare attempt not only to denounce sectarianism but to create a united front to fight it was made by a group that called itself the National Foundation Congress. It was put together in May 2004 by some 450 Iraqis who met at Baghdad's Babylon Hotel shortly after the Kerbala and Kadhimiya bombings. They included pan-Arab Nasserists, leftists, and Baathists from the era before Saddam turned the party into a personal fiefdom, as well as representatives of the AMS. No Sadrists attended but a representative joined later. There were other Shias, both Islamist and secular, as well as Kurds and Christians. The Congress made two calls – for an early end to the occupation and for an end to sectarianism. It argued that the latter could not happen without the former.

To meet the congress's general secretary I went to Kadhimiya in July 2004. Less than 50 yards from the shrine where hundreds of pilgrims had been attacked in March, steps led up to a small gatehouse and then down into the courtyard of a Shia religious school. After removing my shoes I was ushered into a mercifully cool room with deep carpets and even deeper armchairs. Sheikh Jawad al-Khalisi and four guests rose in friendly greeting. While many Iraqi clerics exude a sanctimonious, mildly impatient air with foreigners despite their elaborate expressions of welcome, al-Khalisi had a look of genuine attentiveness. He listened and discussed rather than declaimed.

His grandfather, Mahdi al-Khalisi, was a distinguished ayatollah who led the Shia opposition to the British occupation in 1923. Arrested and deported, he took refuge in Iran. This pedigree of resistance was matched by Iraq's other proud nationalists and Islamists, Moqtada al-Sadr and Harith al-Dhari; they also had parents and grandparents who had fought occupation. I found it a useful reminder of Iraq's long history of occupation as well as of the importance of honour in Iraqi families. Each generation feels conscious of the nationalist legacy it has to protect.

Although Khalisi did not reject armed resistance, his main point was that peaceful politics were not yet exhausted. The media's focus on violence and Allawi's stress on 'defeating the insurgency' gave the impression that the Americans' opponents only used force. This also implied that people who supported peace supported the occupation. The National Foundation Congress wanted national reconciliation but believed this could only happen once the Americans announced a timetable for withdrawal. Congress members would not take part in the US-supported national conference that the US embassy was trying to organise as a kind of surrogate legislature before the January elections. 'We see no benefit in institutions designed to implement American plans. If the conference were to set a timetable for a US troop pullout, it would be worth it. But in the context of the occupation the conference is powerless and we don't want to disappoint our supporters,' Khalisi said.

Wamidh Nadhmi, a veteran Arab nationalist and political science professor, stressed the National Foundation Congress's role as a bridge between Iraq's communities and a potential barrier against a collapse into sectarianism. He argued:

> National unity cannot grow in a country that emphasises sectarian divisions or expects ethnic strife ... There has to be reconciliation between Sunnis and Shias. We're not interested in religion as such but we feel that by bridging the gaps the ground will be better prepared for a national struggle.

The real division in Iraq, he argued, was not between Arabs and Kurds, Sunni and Shia or secular and religious but between 'the pro-occupation and anti-occupation camps'. In his view:

> the pro-occupation people are either completely affiliated to the US and Britain, in effect puppets, or they saw no way to overthrow Saddam without occupation. Let's agree not to indulge in slander but discuss the issue openly. Unfortunately, the pro-occupation people tend not to distinguish between resistance and terrorism or between anti-occupation civil society and those who use violence. They call us all Saddam remnants, reactionaries, revenge-seekers, mercenaries, misguided, or foreigners.

By the autumn of 2004 attacks on Iraqi police and army recruitment centres were increasing in frequency. Car bombs in street markets and other places where civilians gathered were creating a climate of desperation. There were an average of 23 such incidents a month between June and September (a toll which was to increase three-fold in the next two years).[19] Killing Iraqi police and other officials who collaborated with the occupation army was one thing. Detonating bombs among crowds of civilians was another. Who decided these tactics were legitimate? Were the bombs the work of Al-Qaeda in Iraq alone? Were they also planted by the Iraqi resistance?

No one knew for sure. Groups like the National Foundation Congress denounced both types of attack. 'The car bombs are intended to isolate the resistance from Iraqi people. I have some doubts about who is carrying them out,' Khalisi told me. The AMS, which had close links to the resistance, rejected random acts of violence against civilians, though it was vaguer about the legitimacy of bombing Iraqi police and army recruits.

The attacks on police or civilians did not for the most part have sectarian motives, at least in 2004 and 2005. Spectacular outrages like the bombs set off by Al-Qaeda militants at Kerbala and Kadhimiya in April were clearly aimed at Shias, but the constant drip-drip of smaller attacks in various parts of Iraq seemed to have a wider purpose. They were meant to destabilise the new US-appointed government and create a sense that neither the Americans nor their close Iraqi allies could provide security for people. This type of terrorism had motives that were anti-occupation rather than anti-Shia.

Nevertheless, in small communities the violence could take on a sectarian tone. This was starkly illustrated by the killing of a group of Shias from Abbasiyat, a village south of Baghdad, who had signed up to join the Iraqi National Guard in November 2004. Police and army recruits tended to be Shias. This was not seen as 'collaboration' by Shias, even by nationalist followers of Moqtada al-Sadr. He was happy for them to join the police and army since he wanted his men to be trained and paid. They could also provide a valuable future reserve since his main militia rival, the Badr organisation loyal to SCIRI, was infiltrating its supporters into both forces in large numbers. By contrast, any young Sunni who thought of joining the police or army would come under family and peer-group pressure, if not direct threat, not to do so.

The slaughter of young recruits at Abbasiyat hit the local Shia community hard. As Alissa J. Rubin put it in a powerful report in the *Los Angeles Times*: 'Every one of Abbasiyat's ten homes lost a son ... A month after the attack, the sounds of women wailing still rose from the courtyards of the brick and mud homes.'[20] Twelve men from the village had driven in a minibus to Baghdad to sign up for the Iraqi National Guard. On the way back at Latifiya, a largely Sunni town on the main road, they ran into a traffic jam where men dressed as Iraqi police pulled them over. They were told they were suspected of carrying explosives, according to the driver, who survived. The young men denied it but one of them, perhaps fatally, blurted out, 'We are your brothers. We are all in the Iraqi National Guard and are protecting this country.' Like most vans owned by Shias, theirs had pictures of Imam Ali, the sect's founder, on the dashboard, making their sectarian identity obvious.

The police led the minivan off the road. Two cars full of gunmen then forced it to drive into the desert to a small Shia mosque. There the men were beaten, disfigured, and ordered to curse the Shia saints, according to a survivor. Then they were shot, each about a dozen times. Before leaving the corpses in the mosque, the killers daubed graffiti on the walls: 'Shia apes, idol-worshippers' and 'No more Shias after today'.

When relatives approached the site several days later, armed men were waiting, perhaps to claim more victims. Only with the help of US troops and the police chief in the large town of Hillah did they manage to have the armed men arrested and retrieve the bodies. The bereaved families, all members of the Dohan clan, were convinced their sons' murderers were from the Janabi tribe, a nearby Sunni group.

In the days after the tragedy the Dohans met representatives of Ayatollah Sistani and SCIRI to seek permission to take revenge. In spite of the families' anger, the clerics refused to authorise a vendetta. However, they saw the problem was serious and growing. More than 75 Iraqi police and guardsmen had been killed in the region in a three-month period. The clerics backed a proposal for a meeting between the chiefs of the Middle Euphrates tribes, where a letter was written to Prime Minister Allawi calling for action in response to 'the killings in Latifiya that targeted Shias. We can't keep silent about them. There must be a solution for this big problem, and if there is no solution, the tribes will take action themselves.'[21]

Sheikh Ali Dohan, the clan chief, was still consumed with anger a month after losing his son in the incident. He would not stop recommending young Shias to join the army. He told the *Los Angeles Times*:

> We feel afraid but what choice do we have? We have to defend our country, and if we gave up sending our sons and others give up sending their sons the country will not work ... The Janabis started the violence. They must be crushed. The criminals must be beheaded. This will deter those who are thinking of doing the same things. It's the same as with Saddam. He was so brutal to stay in power and whoever is less than brutal will not succeed.[22]

In microcosm, the Abbasiyat slaughter highlighted two looming new dangers. First, sectarian killings were prompting a clamour for revenge, and second, Iraq's new security forces were increasingly becoming part of the problem. The more they became a preserve of Arab Shias (and Kurds), the more likely it was that Arab Sunnis would see them as a sectarian weapon in what they already perceived was a nationwide, US-supported, anti-Sunni campaign.

Sectarianism was also deepening at the political level nationally. Although many Iraqi politicians made statements denouncing it, it had become the dominant factor in people's electoral choices. The Bush administration called the January 2005 poll a triumph of freedom because it was the first contested vote Iraqis had been allowed for decades. But it was deeply flawed by the fact that most voters cast their ballots on sectarian or ethnic lines. The Shia Islamist list took 48 per cent of the vote, and the Kurdish list 26 per cent. Allawi's secular list, the only major non-sectarian grouping, took only 14 per cent. Lists headed by secular former exiles Ghazi al-Yawer and Adnan Pachachi got a derisory 1.78 and 0.28 per cent respectively. The Islamic party took 0.25 per cent. Sunnis boycotted in droves, with a turnout of only 4,000 in Anbar province, the epicentre of US counter-insurgency operations where Fallujah and Ramadi are located.[23]

By now the sectarian genie was truly out of the bottle. National politics were dominated by sectarian thinking. The army and police were turning into sectarian structures. Sectarian murders were growing in number and frequency.

Three trends were to exacerbate the problem from 2005 onwards. First, the new Iraqi constitution that was drafted under US guidance during the summer gave provinces the right to band together to form federal districts and claim autonomy from Baghdad. The move was proposed by SCIRI's Abdel Aziz al-Hakim. Although it did not have the support of other in-fluential Shias including the Sadrists, it was enthusiastically backed by the Kurds. Other members of the Shia alliance gradually came round behind it. Sunnis saw this clause in the constitution as yet another move to undermine them since it raised the spectre of allowing the areas with the country's oil reserves, which had predominantly Kurdish or Shia populations, to move away from central government control. From then on most politics in the Iraqi parliament and government were coloured by sectarian identities and loyalties.

The second disastrous sectarian trend was the rise of Shia death squads within the Iraqi police and security forces. They targeted Sunnis almost ex-clusively. Although no aims were spelt out, one motivation seemed to be re-venge for Saddam's crimes, a kind of bloody version of de-Baathification in which all Sunnis were treated as guilty. The other goal was to send Sunnis a warning that any attempt to re-assert their power would be pre-empted. One Shia death squad, a commando unit known as the Wolf Brigade, had already started by October 2004. It was founded, ironically, by a former general in Saddam's army who went by the name Abu Walid. A Shia, his unit was com-posed of roughly 2,000 fighters. Most were young Shias from poor families in Sadr City. They dressed in olive uniforms and red berets with the logo of a wolf. Backed by the Iraqi army and US military the brigade achieved notoriety after launching a series of brutal counterinsurgency operations in Mosul. Their fame was further boosted by the success of *Terrorism in the Hands of Justice*, a primetime show on US-funded Al-Iraqiya television that showed live footage of the commandos interrogating insurgents.

The use of this type of special unit intensified when the Shia-dominated government that emerged from the January elections took power in March 2005. It appointed Bayan Jabr, a hard-line senior commander of SCIRI's Badr brigades, to be the interior minister. Reports soon circulated that the Wolf Brigade and other special commando and police units were brutalising and killing Sunnis. Jabr was alleged to have sacked most Sunni officers in the police, while recruiting hundreds of former Badr brigade members.

When the bodies of 15 Sunnis, including leading clerics, were found on empty wasteground in different parts of Baghdad less than a month after Jabr was appointed, calls were made for his resignation. 'This is state terrorism by the interior ministry,' Harith al-Dhari told mourners at a communal funeral at the Umm al-Qura mosque. 'We will take revenge on the Brigade of Shame,' hundreds of demonstrators shouted. The cry was similar to the anguished demands for revenge from the villagers of Abbasiyat after their sons were killed for joining the National Guard. The only difference was that in the Baghdad case the vengeance-seekers were Sunnis and in Abbasiyat they were Shias.

By now the Americans were beginning to get worried. Fear of civil war did not seem to be their main concern, nor was it the unfolding human catastrophe. Washington had decided that it must restore a measure of power to Sunnis in the hope this could weaken the relentless growth in Sunni resistance to the occupation. Zalmay Khalilzad, the US ambassador to Afghanistan, who had been the special US envoy to the Iraqi exile opposition in the run-up to the invasion, was posted to Baghdad in June to become the new US overlord. His mission was to tilt back to the Sunnis after Washington's earlier tilt towards the Shia.

In the aftermath of the elections US officials had been scornful of the Sunni boycott, implying the Sunnis had only themselves to blame for having no power in Iraq's transitional national assembly and the committee drafting the constitution. Washington failed to understand the depth of Sunni anger over the attack on Fallujah and the hundreds of Sunnis killed in counter-insurgency operations, as well as the thousands held in US and Iraqi prisons. On arrival in Baghdad Khalilzad continued this cool tradition. He acknowledged no US responsibility for Sunni feelings. If anyone was guilty of alienating Sunnis, he implied, it was Shia zealots who were taking the sectarian issue too far.

Inadequate though this approach was, the practical effect of the US shift of line was quickly felt. Within days of Khalilzad's installation in the US embassy, 15 Sunnis were proposed as extra members for the committee drafting the constitution. The new appointees came too late to be able to obtain significant changes on the issue of federalism and oil revenues, but Khalilzad persuaded Shia and Kurdish leaders to announce that the next assembly, which would be elected in December, would set up a new committee to revise the constitution. Armed with this nominal concession, the new US envoy convinced the main Sunni politicians that the door was still open for their community to have a share in power. Nothing was yet written in stone. Reluctantly, they agreed not to boycott the referendum on the constitution in October, or the subsequent elections.

The issue of sectarian violence, particularly the continual murder of Sunnis, had moved high up the Sunni politicians' agenda. Bodies were turning up on wasteland almost every night, often with appalling marks of torture inflicted before they were killed. These included, among other things, holes in arm- and leg-bones made by electric drills.

The downward spiral of sectarianism was taking a new turn. Cases of Balkan-style ethnic cleansing had started to occur. In the suburb of Ur in north-eastern Baghdad, Sunnis and Shias had lived peacefully as neighbours for decades. However, in the spring of 2005 several tit-for-tat murders took place. Insurgents drove car bombs into Shia restaurants and mosques; Sunni clerics and worshippers were assassinated.

Shias formed roughly 80 per cent of Ur's population. Now beleaguered, the Sunni minority began to leave Ur to look for safety in parts of Baghdad where Sunnis predominated. Abu Diyar, one of the refugees, said he initially trimmed his beard so as to try to pass as a Shia. Later, he gave up and moved. 'The Shias feel that for 35 years they were victims. Saddam put them down. Now they have power and are taking revenge. They think the solution is to kill Sunnis', he said.[24]

Sectarian 'cleansing' in Ur was a relatively slow process. There was no mass flight by refugees. Individual families gradually lost confidence, packed their bags, and slipped away. In other mixed Sunni–Shia districts the pressure on minorities was rushed and brutal, aided and abetted by government forces. In Salman Pak, for example, a majority Sunni town about 20 miles south of Baghdad, a Shia paramilitary commando unit called the Karrar brigade suddenly set up a headquarters. From here, gunmen in uniform went into Sunni neighbourhoods and detained thousands of young men, often on the basis of nothing more than their Sunni-sounding names.[25]

The Americans felt they had to take action. The existence of death squads and the brutal treatment meted out to Sunnis by the Iraqi police was known to everyone. It shocked members of the Iraqi government itself.

In December 2005 I twice went to see Aida Ussayran, the deputy human rights minister, a brave secular Shia who had left Saddam's Iraq for exile in London. Back in Baghdad after 2003 she found the situation almost as hazardous as before. We both had to be extremely cautious. She was discussing government abuses with a reporter; I was at risk from kidnappers. Her ministry was not in the fortified Green Zone, and no one could be sure whether the guards at the gatehouse or officials in the ministry would not reveal that a foreign visitor was in the building. By this stage I had taken to wearing a moustache and an Iraqi-style sports jacket, tie, and dark trousers in the pretence that I was my translator's father. I would stand back as he went ahead to show the receptionist his credentials with a nod over his shoulder towards me. It worked, and I was not asked to identify myself.

Ussayran showed me reports by investigators who had gone into special prisons accompanied by senior US officers. They found appalling abuses. In one case in the suburb of Jadriyah, 173 men were found in an underground bunker. More than a hundred showed signs of beatings and burn marks from lit cigarettes.

Ironically, I had visited the bunker in the first days after the invasion with two other reporters. Attached to a house once used by Saddam's wife, we thought it might have been a store for chemical weapons or a bomb-proof shelter. Steps led down to a heavy metal door, which we wedged open for fear it might swing shut and be impossible to open from the inside. There were no windows and mobile phones could not function. Inside, we found several rooms with bunkbeds and a cavernous hall with sets of curtains along the wall to give the impression that they covered windows. When you drew them aside there was only reinforced concrete. The place clearly could make a useful prison and torture centre, which is exactly what the interior ministry turned it into.

In a second raid, Iraqi and US investigators found more than 600 men and boys in old stables once used by Saddam's son, Uday. This torture centre was run by the Wolf Brigade. A DVD, made available to me later by Salah al-Mutlaq, a leading Sunni politician, showed prisoners standing or sitting in a large room with not enough sleeping space for everyone. One by one detainees came forward, showing welts across their backs, fingernails pulled out, cigarette burns on their shoulders, and severe head wounds, in one case with a bloodstained section of brain exposed. 'Many victims were teenagers, some as young as 15,' Aida Ussayran said.

As the scandal broke, Khalilzad took the unusual step of calling for Bayan Jabr's replacement as interior minister when the next government was formed. The US envoy realised that the Americans had to show the Sunnis they were taking the issue of Shia abuses seriously, both as a way of keeping Sunni politicians in the election contest and in order to try to prevent a new wave of revenge-seeking by angry Sunnis.

In addition to the move towards federalism under the new Iraqi constitution and the rise of the death squads, the third trend that led to sectarian conflict was the shift of Al-Qaeda in Iraq away from attacking Americans and towards targeting Shias, a brutal tactic that enraged Iraqis, including many Sunni nationalists and resistance groups. After initially attacking high-profile foreign targets like the Jordanian embassy and the UN headquarters, Al-Qaeda's jihadis increasingly put their lethal focus on Shia civilians. The number of Shia victims became so high that in October 2005 US intelligence published a letter allegedly written in July by Ayman al-Zawahiri, Osama bin Laden's deputy, in which he criticised the use of car bombs on Shia civilians. Addressed to Abu Musab al-Zarqawi, the Jordanian militant who headed Al-Qaeda in Iraq, the letter described the struggle in Iraq as an 'historic battle against the greatest of criminals and apostates in the heart of the Islamic world'.[26]

Much of its content was typical of previous Al-Qaeda statements. Muslim lands had been invaded by infidels. The rulers who welcomed the invaders were apostate Muslims. Chief among the infidels were the US occupiers of the Land of the Two Holy Mosques (Saudi Arabia) and the Zionist occupiers of the Holy Sanctuary (Jerusalem). The recent invasions of Afghanistan and Iraq added to the historic humiliation suffered by Muslims. A defensive jihad was needed against the Zionists/Crusaders until they were expelled from the Islamic world. An Islamic state should first be established in Iraq's Sunni areas and then be extended to the rest of the region.

The letter's novel element was its warning to Zarqawi that jihad depends on 'public support from the Muslim masses'. It said the Taliban had failed to retain power in Afghanistan because they forgot that mujahedin have to ensure victory after expelling the infidels and not just while they are fighting to expel them. This point is so vital, the letter stated, that doctrinal differences among the Sunni clergy between Salafis and others have to be temporarily overlooked.

Equally important was the need to be careful about the attitudes of Shias. The letter said Sunnis were justifiably outraged by 'the treason of the Shias and their collusion with the Americans to occupy Iraq in exchange for the Shias assuming power'. It attacked Iran's Shia regime for cooperating with the Americans in the invasion of Afghanistan. It accused Shiism of falsehood and being 'a danger to Islam'.

In spite of all this, the letter told Zarqawi: 'Many of your Muslim admirers among the common folk are wondering about your attacks on the Shia'. It mentioned attacks on Shia mosques and shrines and ordinary Shias, and asked sharply, 'Can the mujahedin kill all of the Shias in Iraq? Has any Islamic state in history ever tried that?' It suggested that by opening a second front against the Shias the mujahedin were making things easier for the Americans.

Some Western analysts treated the letter as a US forgery, designed with a variety of possible aims: to create splits within the resistance, to bring the Shias even more fully to the American side, and to discredit Zarqawi by highlighting Al-Qaeda's responsibility for the car bomb attacks. Whether genuine or not, the letter correctly stated the Salafi view of Shias as dangerous for Islam. It also reflected a debate that was undeniably happening. Disagreements between Al-Qaeda and Iraqi nationalists surfaced frequently in the next two years. When the Americans finally located Zarqawi in June 2006 and killed him with an air strike, it was as a result of a tip-off from within the insurgency.

If the letter was genuine and reached Zarqawi, he ignored its main thrust. Attacks on Shia civilians increased in the second half of 2005, sparking predictable calls for revenge against Sunnis. The most provocative anti-Shia atrocity occurred shortly after dawn on 22 February 2006. Around a dozen men in paramilitary uniforms entered the al-Askariya shrine in Samarra about 60 miles north of Baghdad. They handcuffed four guards before placing a bomb in the shrine's golden dome, causing most of it to collapse. Although no one was killed, the attack caused massive outrage among Shias. It was one thing to assassinate Shia ayatollahs, but to destroy a sacred building seemed to touch a raw nerve. Al-Askariya is one of four major Shia shrines in Iraq and the burial place of two of the 12 imams revered by Shias. No one took responsibility for the atrocity, but Iraqi officials pointed the finger of suspicion at Al-Qaeda in Iraq.

Some Shia leaders said the Americans had to accept a share of the blame for not protecting the building and for contributing to anti-Shia prejudice. According to Abdel Aziz al-Hakim, Khalilzad's commments about interior ministry death squads had provoked the bombing. Moqtada al-Sadr said the new Iraq parliament should pass a motion asking occupation forces to leave Iraq since it was clear their presence was leading to more harm than good.

Both men called on fellow Shias to show restraint, but to no avail. There was an explosion of rage in the streets that same day. Thousands of Shias came out to protest. In Basra, crowds destroyed two Sunni mosques and attacked the offices of the Iraqi Islamic party, the main Sunni Arab party. In Baghdad, armed men drove into Sunni areas shooting at mosques and attacking Sunni Arabs. At least 138 people were killed on a single day, most of them Sunnis.

Previous atrocities had also produced outbursts of anger, but they had always subsided within hours. The Samarra bombing was different. It was as though a dam had broken. A great wave of sectarian cleansing poured through, with armed gangs from each community wreaking vengeance. Discipline within the militias, such as it was, collapsed. Sunnis reported that as well as the Shia-dominated police, Mahdi army militants in their usual black clothes were taking part in the revenge-seeking. Over the next few months the rate of killing averaged a hundred a day. More than a million people fled their homes and moved to areas of Iraq where their own sect was in the majority, or left the country for Syria and Jordan. The less well-off moved to the Kurdish region in the north.

Sunni suburbs of Baghdad set up barricades and organised vigilante groups based at their mosques. Using the minarets as watch-towers, they had round-the-clock alerts. The killing became so widespread that some Sunni residents of Baghdad started to see US troops as protectors. One mosque-defender in the Sunni suburb of Yarmuk told me he and his neighbours had orders to fire immediately if they saw Iraqi police vehicles approaching; if an American patrol arrived, they should leave it alone. The tit-for-tat murders prompted Khalilzad to make a dramatic statement: 'More Iraqis are dying from the militia violence than from the terrorists,' he declared during a visit to a Baghdad youth club.[27]

The sectarian tension that Al-Qaeda in Iraq had deliberately provoked by its campaign against Shias widened the gap between the nationalist anti-American resistance in Sunni communities and Al-Qaeda. 'Our people have come to hate Al-Qaeda, which gives the impression to the outside world that the resistance in Iraq are terrorists. We are against indiscriminate killing. Fighting should be concentrated only on the enemy,' said Abd al-Rahman al-Zubeidy, the political spokesman of Ansar al-Sunna, an Iraqi resistance group which combined nationalism with Salafi ideology.[28]

His group and six other nationalist and Islamist Sunni groups signed up to a common anti-sectarian and anti-Al-Qaeda platform in 2007, which opposed attacks on civilians and called for negotiations with the Americans on a full US withdrawal, followed by elections.

It took courage to criticise Al-Qaeda and its local activists. Groups affiliated with Al-Qaeda had no compunction in assassinating Sunni imams and others who challenged them. 'They have plenty of money to bribe people and they are absolutely ruthless. They will put severed heads on lamp-posts,' a resident of the Sunni Baghdad suburb of Ghazalia told me. In desperation some tribal sheikhs in Fallujah and Ramadi even started to see Al-Qaeda in Iraq as greater enemies than the occupation – at least for the moment. In 2007 they agreed to take money and arms from the Iraqi army and the Americans in a campaign to drive Al-Qaeda back.

The alliance between the Americans and tribal leaders in the largely Sunni province of Anbar led to a fall in attacks on the Americans, as people focused on combating Al-Qaeda. The US commander Gen David Petraeus touted this as the major result of the 'surge' of extra US troops that Bush sent to Iraq in the spring of 2007. But there was no guarantee that the trend would last or that the marriage of convenience would be permanent.

The movement against Al-Qaeda was described as the Anbar Awakening and the tribes who worked with the Americans called themselves the Salvation Council. Harith al-Dhari, the leader of the Association of Muslim Scholars, dismissed them in an interview with me in Amman in October 2007. (He was living in exile after the interior minister issued an arrest

warrant in November 2006 alleging that al-Dhari's support for armed resistance was trying to spread division and strife between the Iraqi people). He
told me:

> There are very few of them. They don't represent all the tribes or people of
> Anbar … The situation in Anbar is very bad, and many are out of work and
> impoverished. Some will work with anyone who pays them, whether it is
> Al-Qaeda or the US army. I agree that the number of attacks on US forces in
> Anbar has gone down, but in a few months' time it may go up again. The US
> is building its hopes on a small trend. Ordinary people in Anbar don't trust
> either Al-Qaeda or the Salvation Council.

His remarks chimed, coincidentally, with a poll conducted in Anbar in
mid-August for the BBC and ABC news. It found Anbar was still Iraq's
strongest bastion of hostile anti-US opinion. While criticising Al-Qaeda's
attacks on civilians, every Anbar respondent supported attacks on US
forces. Seventy per cent wanted the US to leave Iraq immediately.[29]

Sheikh Majed Abed al-Sulaiman, who runs the Jordan-based Board of
Tribes and Notables of Iraq, was a friend of the Salvation Council's founders.
He saw the alliance between Anbar tribes and the Americans as a painful
necessity:

> What other alternative do we have? The Americans have the power, the con-
> trol, the technology. We have to work with them until we get out of this situ-
> ation. Then we have to see … In World War Two they asked Roosevelt why
> he worked with the Soviet communists. If my interests force me to work with
> the devil, he replied, I will cross the bridge with the devil hand-in-hand.[30]

In summary, no single group can be blamed for Iraq's devastating slide
towards sectarian war. Saddam started the rot. The Americans then played
a significant part by emphasising sectarian issues in their post-war policies.
Iraqi Shia politicians and the death squads that were run by their militias
compounded the problem and gave it a lethal dimension.

Last came Al-Qaeda and the foreign Arab jihadis they mobilised,
as well as the Iraqi Sunnis who agreed to work with them. They were
not numerous but the spectacular atrocities they mounted as well as the
vicious cruelty they showed to critics gave them a disproportionate impact.

As the chaos mounted, the collapse of the US neoconservatives' project could not have been highlighted more starkly. Their ambitious imperial

aspiration to create a stable and democratic Iraq, run by secular politicians friendly to Washington, lay in tatters. The Islamist forces that had already started to gather strength under Saddam had become the dominant powers in a country fragmenting into sectarian enclaves, where Iraqis of whatever class or tribe lived in fear.

The daily insecurity exceeded in awfulness anything which Iraqis of any generation had ever known before. Most felt the primary blame for the mayhem lay with the foreigners who had chosen to occupy their country without thinking ahead to what was likely to follow.

IX

THE FARCE OF SOVEREIGNTY

The Americans say they don't intervene, but they have intervened deep. They gave us a detailed proposal, almost a full version of a constitution.

Mahmoud Othman, 2005[1]

The American commander would only have to say, 'OK, we're out of here' and the Iraqis would back down.

Senior US official, 2004[2]

Twice a week a US military transport plane lifted off from Amman in Jordan and landed on the 'American side' of Baghdad's international airport. This was the Baghdad shuttle. No visas required. No need to show a passport to any Iraqi official. For embassy staff, contractors, and other civilians working for the occupation it was the perfect beeline into the 'other Iraq', the network of vast US-controlled compounds where Iraq's real power resided.

If you had access to a helicopter, it could whisk you from Baghdad airport to the Green Zone in ten minutes. The swooping zig-zag trip only a few metres above the city's minarets was far from risk-free but it was not as dangerous as the overland alternative, a 30-minute ride in an armour-plated US bus (called a Rhino) on a road where suicide bombers were frequently in action. On this trip you could not avoid spotting a few Iraqis at close quarters, although in your sealed vehicle you would no more be required to notify any locals of your arrival in their country than the helicopter passengers.

These high-handed immigration arrangements applied even more stark-ly to VIPs. US congressmen and senators, the secretaries of state and defense and other cabinet ministers, and of course the vice-president and president of the USA would land in Baghdad without even the formality of an invita-tion. In no other country of the world are foreign leaders able to show up at whim. In Iraq, they could.

Many of these VIPs would proceed to lecture their 'hosts' on how to run the country. In the best imperial manner they would recommend who to sack from the Cabinet, and who to appoint. They would insist on certain laws being passed or demand changes in the constitution.

They would even tell elected Iraqi leaders to resign, as I witnessed on 3 April 2006. The scene was Iraqi Prime Minister Ibrahim al-Jaafari's office deep in the Green Zone. A fleet of bullet-proofed Chevrolet Suburban SUVs with tinted windows was parked in the drive. American security guards in reflective dark glasses and baseball caps patrolled the building's entrance, with their forefingers clamped on the triggers of submachine guns. There was no sign of any Iraqi security personnel.

Inside, almost like a hostage, al-Jaafari was being harangued by Condo-leezza Rice and her British counterpart, Jack Straw. The two had decided on the trip just one day earlier, exasperated by the Iraqi prime minister's refusal to heed a steady flow of hints from the US ambassador that it was time to go. All kinds of arguments were trotted out. Iraq needed a leader who could unify the country. The government must clamp down on Shia militias. The Cabinet had to be led by a man who could command support across the spectrum, including from Kurds and Sunni Arabs.

Jaafari did not listen, or at least he did not obey. Not even a phone call from Bush in the White House had done the trick. Now he was being given his marching orders by Rice and Straw in person.

Their brutal mission got off to a bad start. A rare torrential storm burst over Baghdad just after they landed, making it too risky to take helicopters to the Green Zone. Forced to travel like low-level officials in a Suburban, they got stuck in a Baghdad traffic jam caused by an Iraqi army checkpoint. It was a unique opportunity for Rice and Straw to sample the fear of car bombs felt by Iraqis every day.

Why Washington did not like Jaafari was never entirely clear. The head of the Dawa party and a family doctor who spent many years of exile in Lon-don, Jaafari had served as prime minister for just over a year. It was true that he was a dull, humourless man without charisma who tended to lecture his visitors. It was also true that his government's record was patchy. But he had usually done what the Americans wanted, and it was hard to see how any Iraqi government could make much impact in the midst of an insurgency and growing sectarian tensions. In any case, as head of a coalition dominated by Shia Islamist parties, Jaafari had little freedom of manoeuvre.

Accustomed to a presidential system, the Americans hankered for a 'strong leader' who would take tough decisions. Ignorant of any culture other than his own, Bush is reported to have shouted during the 'crisis' over Jaafari: 'Where's George Washington? Where's Thomas Jefferson? Where's John Adams, for crying out loud?'[3] But giving a single leader overwhelming powers is not how parliamentary politics usually work, especially in a system where the majority party is itself a coalition. In Iraq cabinet posts were not even in the patronage of the prime minister, as in Britain. They were shared out after bargaining between factions. Jaafari had only won the contest to be the candidate for prime minister by the smallest of margins – 64 votes to 63. This made it likely that, if he did resign, his successor would also be from the Dawa party, since any other choice would disturb the balance that had been painstakingly reached when the Shia coalition first carved up the government jobs.

The Bush administration's hostility to Jaafari was based mainly on frustration. It was one more sign of the 'Iraq without Iraqis' syndrome. Security in Iraq was manifestly not improving, so let's blame the chaos on the Iraqis. What better target than the man who is nominally in charge?

The other reason for US anger was that Jaafari's winning score of 64 votes within the Shia coalition depended on MPs loyal to Moqtada al-Sadr. Sadr had long been an American bugbear because he was the one Iraqi leader they had not been able to co-opt or isolate. He also irritated Washington because he and his MPs regularly called for a timetable for the USA to leave Iraq.

Dislike of Jaafari was not limited to the Americans. It was shared by Sunni Arab leaders and the Kurdish parties. The Kurds preferred SCIRI to Dawa, because of the SCIRI leader Abdel Aziz al-Hakim's enthusiasm for federalism with strong powers for the regions. They hoped the next prime minister would be a SCIRI man, preferably Adel Abdel Mahdi, who had studied economics in France after leaving Baghdad College, a high school run by American Jesuits that was widely regarded as the best in Baghdad.

His schoolmates included Iyad Allawi and Ahmad Chalabi. Washington also favoured Mahdi because of his support for neoliberal economics and an open-door policy of generous concessions for foreign oil companies. As for the Sunnis, they did not like Jaafari because he had done nothing to curb the Shia militias who were terrorising Sunni neighbourhoods.

While Rice and Straw were urging Jaafari to step down, I was in a side room with the prime minister's press secretary and other officials. Jaafari had decided to turn to the *Guardian* to get his point of view across, perhaps as a snub to the Americans or because he knew the paper regularly criticised the British government. I was promised an interview before I knew of the super-secret Rice/Straw trip. As news of it broke, I rang Jaafari's press secretary expecting to be told that the interview was off. 'Only delayed,' she told me, which was why I was now waiting in the prime minister's office.

The meeting with Rice and Straw was a tense affair, and when it ended I could see through the open door into the hall as the two Western visitors swept out angrily. They went off to lunch with Mahdi, a snub of which they knew Jaafari would soon learn. The prime minister showed his own annoyance by not bothering to accompany his uninvited guests to the door of the building. After a ten-minute pause he was still so upset that he decided he could not do the interview. It was rearranged for the following day.

This time I was asked to come to the prime minister's official residence, a typically tasteless sandstone Saddam-era palace in the Green Zone, surrounded on three sides by an artificial lake. It was still light outside but the heavy velvet curtains were drawn, adding to the sense of a bunker-within-a-bunker.

Looking stern and unsmiling as he fingered yellow-brown worry beads, Jaafari struck a defiant note. He would not step down in spite of the pleas from Rice and Straw, he told me. 'I heard their points of view even though I disagree with them,' he declared. Using the argument that the USA and Britain had toppled Saddam in order to bring democracy, he turned it against them by recalling that he had won the vote within the Shia block to be the next prime minister. 'There is a decision that was reached by a democratic mechanism and I stand with it ... We have to protect democracy in Iraq and it is democracy which should decide who leads Iraq,' he said.

Tampering with democracy was risky, he went on. 'People will react if they see the rules of democracy being disobeyed. Every politician and every friend of Iraq should not want people to be frustrated. Everyone should stick to democratic mechanisms no matter whether they disagree with the person,' he added pointedly.

The State Department had announced a major policy shift a few days earlier. Ambassador Khalilzad was instructed to open talks with Iranian officials on security in Iraq. (The decision was reversed a few weeks later, and then reversed back again in early 2007.) As though wanting to signal his sense of independence, Jaafari proudly told me that the historic talks with Iran should not go over Iraq's head. 'When the two countries are talking about Iraq, Iraq must be a member of those talks,' he said. 'Definitely. Of course. It's in Iraq's interest, and in the interests of the other two countries that an Iraq representative be there, as long as the subject is Iraq.'

It was powerful, though perhaps rather desperate stuff. Like every other mainstream Iraqi politician, he knew the rules of the game. The Americans could not be opposed for ever. They had the money and the troops, and could always pretend to threaten to withdraw one or both.

Three weeks later Jaafari resigned. Nouri al-Maliki, his replacement, was a colleague from the Dawa party and another Islamist, as was predicted. If anything, his background was less satisfactory to the Americans than Jaafari's since he had spent the Saddam years in Syria and Iran rather than the West. As time went on, the Americans became as frustrated with him as they had been with Jaafari. Maliki ran a pro-Shia regime, refused to make concessions to the Sunnis, and used the language of national reconciliation without doing anything to give it substance.

When Maliki's appointment was announced, US intelligence knew little about him, so Rice flew back to Baghdad to check him out. This time she came with Rumsfeld. They wanted to discover Maliki's gut feelings about the crucial issue of US troop withdrawals. The danger that an Iraqi government might take the plunge and ask for an end to the occupation was always Washington's biggest anxiety.

Sitting stiffly with his American visitors, Maliki told them of his plans to handle sectarian tensions and improve public services, including electricity. So far, so good. He talked of retraining and improving the police. Then he mentioned a security plan with the ambiguous name 'Take Back Baghdad'. It was not clear if he meant from the insurgents or from the Americans. Rumsfeld decided to test him by hinting at the need to discuss cutting back on the number of US patrols in Baghdad. 'It's way too early to be talking about that,' Maliki replied to the Americans' relief.[4]

Keeping US troops in Iraq long-term was a key part of the neoconservatives' agenda. It was not important whether American forces were involved in a combat capacity or merely remained in garrisons on a reserve footing. As students and practitioners of empire the neoconservatives were well aware of the link between military power and political control. As long as the USA had troops on the ground that the Iraqi government believed it needed, the USA would be able to use them as leverage for defining the main lines of Iraq government policy. It might not mean you could micromanage every last Iraqi decision, but you would have a veto on anything with which you disagreed fundamentally.

This was the trick that underlay the transfer of sovereignty from the CPA to an Iraqi government in June 2004. Two problems had to be solved. The first was economic. How could an Iraqi government be made to follow the neoconservatives' prescriptions for privatising the economy, abolishing food rations and other subsidies, getting rid of state control of the oil sector, and giving foreign oil companies the freedom to make lucrative profits from it?

During his time as unchallenged US overlord, Bremer issued a series of decrees governing the Iraqi economy. Order 39 allowed foreigners to take up to 100 per cent of the shares of any Iraqi business and set up new businesses with no Iraqi share. There would be complete freedom to repatriate profits. Order 49 cut corporation tax from 40 per cent to 15 per cent, while companies working with the CPA would pay no tax at all. Order 12 lifted all import tariffs, thereby removing the advantage Iraqi producers had over foreign ones.

To ensure these decrees continued in force Bremer enshrined them in a 'Transitional Administrative Law' (TAL), mentioned in Chapter IV, a prototype constitution drafted by US lawyers six months before the CPA came to an end. The TAL cleverly did not mention the economy. It said only that Bremer's orders would remain in effect until rescinded or amended by an Iraqi legislature – in effect until December 2005 when the first four-year parliament would be chosen. It was not easy to get the Iraqi governing council to accept the TAL but the disputes centred exclusively on clauses dealing with political questions, including the role of Islam, arrangements for federalism, and the mechanism for ratifying a permanent constitution. The Iraqis overlooked the section extending Bremer's economic decrees.

The second sovereignty issue for the Americans was how to guarantee the future of the military occupation once the Iraqis had their own government. Bremer described Article 59 in the TAL which handled this problem as 'in effect our "security agreement" providing the legal rationale for our post-sovereignty troop presence'. 'For us,' he said, 'it was the brightest of red lines'.[5]

Article 59 referred to Iraq's newly formed armed forces 'as a principal partner in the multi-national force operating in Iraq under unified command'. The use of the word 'principal' was an oxymoron, since the stipulation of a unified command meant the Iraqi army would be a junior partner under US orders. If that was not sufficiently clear, Bremer spelt it out unambiguously in an order in March: 'All trained elements of the Iraqi armed forces shall at all times be under the operational control of the commander of coalition forces for the purpose of conducting combined operations,' it said.[6]

The USA still had to square this on the international stage, preferably through a UN Security Council resolution. Once again the main champion of a dignified arrangement for Iraq was France. French officials said they wanted

to give the Iraqi people credible assurances that the presence of foreign troops is temporary and limited in time, in order to clarify the political horizon of the Iraqi people and assure them that the coming transition period will end as soon as possible.[7]

The Americans argued the case with the French and, as usual, got most of what they wanted. UN Resolution 1546, jointly sponsored by the USA and Britain, said that by 30 June 2004 'the occupation will end and the Coalition Provisional Authority will cease to exist and Iraq will re-assert its full sovereignty'. However, 'the multinational forces' would have the authority to take all necessary measures to contribute to Iraq's stability and security. There would be a security 'partnership' and coordination between these forces and the Iraqi government.

The limitations of these promises were spelt out in a letter describing the role of the multinational force sent by Colin Powell, the US secretary of state, to the president of the UN Security Council. The US commander of the multinational force was required only to 'inform' and 'consult' the Iraqi government. The two sides would work to reach agreement on sensitive offensive operations, but nothing was said about what would happen in the event of disagreement. In other words, the Iraqis had no veto over

US actions, a fact which had become painfully obvious two months earlier when a few members of Iraq's governing council objected to the US assault on Fallujah.

The resolution put a time-limit on the mandate of the foreign forces, saying it would 'expire' on completion of the political process for electing a government (i.e. soon after December 2005). But this posed no great problem for the Americans since they assumed they could come back to the UN before that date and get a new resolution to renew the mandate.

It was expected the Americans would sign a 'status of forces agreement' (SOFA) with the Iraqi government. These are standard arrangements that Washington has with the dozens of countries where it bases US troops. They cover a broad range of issues such as taxes, compensation for claims, the exit and entry rights of forces, and, most importantly, criminal and civil jurisdiction over foreign forces. The last category can be highly controversial, as the experience of South Korea and Japan has shown. US troops raped local women but escaped prosecution in local courts.

Bremer had already given US troops total immunity from proceedings in any criminal or civil Iraqi court under CPA Order 17 in 2003. This also applied to foreign officials and the vast army of private contractors, many of whom carried weapons. As the transfer of sovereignty approached, Bremer simply issued a regulation to extend Order 17. It said the order would remain in force until the coalition forces finally left Iraq, unless it was rescinded or amended by later legislation.

With everything in place, legally and politically, for an open-ended occupation, Washington saw no urgency in signing a SOFA. It already had what it needed. For its part, the Iraqi government was also not keen to have one. Iraqi ministers made occasional noises about the need to get the Americans to conform to Iraqi law and respect Iraq's border controls rather than flitting in and out at will. But they shied away from agreeing to a document whose central clauses would legitimise US immunity. As a result Iraq remained in a category of its own among countries with US bases. There is still no SOFA almost five years after the invasion.

The best argument for the USA to use in justifying maintaining troops in Iraq was of course the armed insurgency. As long as the emphasis was kept on dealing with it militarily rather than finding a political solution, the USA could always claim American troops were needed in Iraq to train Iraq's own security forces. The USA could not leave until Iraqis were ready to take over

– although the definition of 'ready' was infinitely flexible. The criteria kept varying. Sometimes the progress of the programme was measured in numbers of men recruited and trained. Sometimes it was calculated in terms of combat capability. It was axiomatic at all times that the Iraqis would be less well equipped than US forces, with worse communications systems, less modern weaponry, and less experience. The Americans could always argue plausibly that it was not yet safe to hand total control over security to the Iraqis.

High-profile media events were held to mark the transfer of responsibility for security in various provinces from the USA to the Iraqis. However, in every case the Americans or the British remained as a back-up to provide air support, logistical assistance, and on occasion the use of their own troops. The British government called it 'overwatch'. It was exactly the same system as 'Vietnamisation' during the Vietnam war. Local forces would take an increasing share of front-line combat as well as static guard duty and manning checkpoints, but the foreigners remained in ultimate charge.

Their military superiority gave the Americans political control at almost every level of Iraqi government. This was highlighted in almost comical fashion during a security meeting I attended in the northern city Mosul in November 2006 in the heavily guarded mansion used by the governor of Nineveh province. I reached the city from Irbil in Kurdistan in a convoy of seven cars, each with two armed guards inside. The vehicles were beaten-up BMWs, Mercedes, and Toyotas, deliberately inconspicuous saloons so as not to attract attention from potential attackers. Khasro Goran, the deputy governor, a Kurdish politician who lived in Irbil for safety, was in the third car. The convoy's lead car made radio contact with Iraqi army guards to allow us to speed into the governor's compound over a bridge across the Tigris that was reserved for military vehicles. It was one sign of how hazardous life had become in a city where tensions between the two main communities, Kurds and Sunni Arabs, was producing a wave of ethnically based murders as well as frequent attacks on police stations and political parties' headquarters.

Governor Duraid Kashmoula, a Sunni Arab, invited me to join the regular security meeting he was about to hold with the top American commander and his team. I was asked to wait while he went into the conference room to check with Col Steve Townsend of the 3/2 Stryker Brigade Combat Team from the US army's Second Infantry Division. Ushered into the meeting a moment later, I shook hands with the colonel, who looked uncomfortable.

It was highly unusual to have a reporter at a security discussion, but the colonel must have felt that as the governor was the host, it would be rude to refuse his request. Round One in the sovereignty battle had gone to the Iraqis.

We sat down and Col Townsend opened the meeting by saying it was fine for me to write about general issues but not to report any sensitive details of security deployments if they came up. Did I agree? I nodded. He then distributed pieces of paper in English and Arabic, which outlined the main points for discussion. The meeting was in the governor's mansion but the Americans controlled the agenda, I noted. Round Two to the Americans.

Colonel Townsend moved quickly to matters of substance. 'Do you agree that security can be colour-coded green?', he asked. There was an awkward pause. The governor, the deputy governor, and the police chief looked at each other, then stared at the paper that the Americans had handed out.

Six items were listed for discussion, with coloured circles beside each one. Electricity: half yellow, half amber. Fuel supplies: red. Anti-government activities at Mosul university: yellow. Activities of the judiciary: yellow and amber. Reconstruction and development funding: yellow. The only circle marked green was security.

I recalled our arrival at the building in a specially disguised convoy. I had seen the armoured vehicles and Humvees that had brought the Americans. I remembered the concrete blast walls, the coils of razor wire, and the dozens of Iraqi troops at the entrance, as well as the portrait on the wall of the governor's office. It showed the governor's eldest son, killed by unknown gunmen some months earlier.

'Well, it's true the terrorists cannot stand up to the police on the street during patrols,' the governor began his reply to the colonel's question, somewhat evasively. Hinting that all might not be perfect on the security front, he then asked for two new measures: extra fortification for police posts on two key roads and the rescinding of an order for an Iraqi army battalion in Mosul to be sent to Baghdad.

Khasro Goran, the Kurdish deputy governor, decided not to beat about the bush. He said bluntly:

> I don't agree that security is green and people feel safe. Not one day goes by without someone being killed in Mosul … The terrorists are a hidden force. They go out in civilian clothes and threaten contractors with death if they

240

start work on reconstruction projects. They kill interpreters. They hand out flyers at the mosques, calling for support for Al-Qaeda and the Baathists. On Thursday when I was visiting people they told me 15 families had been told to leave town. A well-known singer was shot in the street this week.

In Mosul, unlike Baghdad, car bombs and suicide attacks were relatively rare, but as the deputy governor made clear, a more complex war was under way, a combination of ethnic cleansing and preparations for an armed uprising. He went on:

Of course the army can do raids, but what we have here is a cat and mouse game ... We have 18,000 police now and orders to recruit 3,000 more. It would be good to have them as secret agents, in the mosques and at the university. There are 40,000 students and it's easy to recruit terrorists there.

To combat the resistance, unorthodox methods were necessary, he suggested. 'The Baath party had spies in every classroom. We don't want to be like the Baathists and violate human rights but we need intelligence. If we had intel, we could kill the terrorists in their houses.'

We broke for lunch in a side room but the Iraqis were in no mood for small talk. As we ate, they hammered on about security. The police chief, General Wathiq Mohammed al-Hamdani, said the university was 'infested with terrorists'. Over a dozen professors had been identified as sympathisers, but it was hard to sack them because the minister of higher education was a Sunni from the Iraqi Islamic party. He complained that judges were afraid to give convicted terrorists long sentences. New judges were being sent up from Baghdad, in the hope that as outsiders with no family in Mosul they would feel free to be tough.

The deputy governor described how one of his bodyguards suffered a severe cut on his finger and was taken to hospital. Soon after his release, men appeared at his home. His brother opened the door. 'Where's the one with the finger?', they demanded, before pushing in, seizing the bodyguard, and taking him away. His headless body was discovered the next day. 'Someone at the hospital got his address and betrayed him to the terrorists,' the deputy governor told the Americans.

Back in the conference room, the police chief's mobile phone rang. His conversation was agitated, and discussion stopped while everyone listened. The American interpreter whispered to the colonel. After finishing his call, the police chief explained dramatically: 'A distant cousin of mine is linked to the terrorists. The police have just raided his house. One policeman was killed in an exchange of fire, another is injured. One terrorist was killed.'

The phone call provided a fitting climax to the security discussion. Colonel Townsend said he had listened carefully to the points raised and would adjust the colour rating. 'We'll change the coding to yellow,' he said. Round Three of the sovereignty battle to the Iraqis. The Americans had been persuaded to think again. But, I wondered, would the Americans really change policy in line with the new colour in the circle?

The other items on the agenda were hardly more cheerful: shortages of electricity, petrol being siphoned out of the nearby Beiji refinery by fleets of black-market tankers, money for the police academy running out at the end of the year. The governor called for a special guard force to be recruited for the Beiji refinery – 'they can't be local people because they're all thieves'.

With his agenda complete, Col Townsend asked if the Iraqis had other points to raise. The governor complained that the Americans had poured concrete over a small roadside garden where insurgents had planted a bomb a few days earlier. He acknowledged there was a security issue but local people had not wanted to lose the garden. 'You should have told us before you covered it over,' he said. The colonel apologised but said the Americans had discussed it in advance with lower-level Iraqi officials.

The governor brought up a second grievance, this time about an incident he had seen on local television. People were shown bringing problems to an Iraqi complaints commission, but it was an American who was writing everything down. Wasn't this a matter for Iraqis, the governor wanted to know? 'Yes, you're right. The Americans should only observe and advise,' the colonel said. Trivial though the governor's points were, they reinforced an impression of an American presence that was micro-managing and failing to consult.

When the meeting ended, the US colonel embraced the three Iraqis. His officers picked up their M-4 rifles and they all piled back into their armoured vehicles. The Iraqis sank back into their armchairs for a brief post-mortem. They wondered how their guests could have coloured the security circle green. Was it cynical, so that the Americans could claim that progress in Iraq was greater than it was? Deputy governor Khasro Goran plumped for a less malign explanation. 'Americans can sometimes be naive,' he commented. 'At least they now call it yellow. They're moving in the right direction.'

He delivered his remarks in a weary, almost resigned way. As a member of the Kurdish political elite, he supported the US invasion but even he felt the cultural gulf between Iraqis and the American military mindset: realism versus professionally conditioned optimism, pragmatism versus ideology, seeing the complexity of things versus denial.

Sovereignty came up again in a dispute that erupted in April 2007 during the 'surge' of extra US troops to Baghdad. A statement from the Multi-National Division's public affairs office announced that a wall was being built round Adhamiya, a largely Sunni district in the north-west of the Iraqi capital, as well as two other Sunni areas in Baghdad. It was described as 'one of the centrepieces of a new strategy'.

The collapse in security had made it almost impossible for journalists to move about in Baghdad, so news of the wall had gone unreported. Local people who spotted the first concrete blocks being erected had not understood the planned extent of it. When the army's press statement appeared, however, it provoked a storm. Three days later reporters were sent another article from the Multi-National Division's public affairs office. It carried the amazing headline, 'Baghdad's gated communities explained'. Was this some bizarre joke?

The press release quoted Baghdad's deputy commanding general, Brig Gen John F. Campbell, as saying that several neighbourhoods were to get special security barriers like the Green Zone:

> The intent is not to divide the city along sectarian lines. The intent is to provide a more secured neighbourhood for people ... We've selected communities that have seen an increase in violence, a heightened violence, and we're protecting some of those communities with walls.[8]

Furious crowds gathered in protest near the district's main mosque, Abu Hanifa. Just as they had done in the first weeks of the occupation they marched through the streets of Adhamiya with banners saying 'No Shias, No Sunnis, Islamic Unity'. Iraq's Prime Minister Nouri al-Maliki, who was on a visit to Cairo, reacted in outrage. He said the building of the wall would stop. Other Iraqi politicians were equally angry. The Iraqi Islamic party as well as Moqtada al-Sadr's organisation both announced they were against dividing Baghdad by sect. 'The Sadr movement considers building a wall around Adhamiya as a way to lay siege to the Iraqi people and separate them into cantons. It is like the Berlin Wall that divided Germany,' said a statement from the Sadr organisation.[9]

Local residents compared the wall to the barriers put up by the Israeli army on the West Bank. Others complained of the use of residents' fingerprints and other biometric information that US and Iraqi security forces took from people in order to determine who could or could not come in. They feared their neighbourhood would become a giant prison on the pattern of Fallujah.

As the row continued, Major General William Caldwell, the top US military spokesman, denied there was any new strategy. The wall was just a temporary tactic, he promised. 'Obviously we will respect the wishes of the government and the prime minister,' the new American ambassador to Iraq, Ryan Crocker, told a press conference.[10]

Who would get the upper hand – the Iraqi prime minister or the Americans? It was a good test of sovereignty. Sameer al-Abeidi, the sheikh of the Abu Hanifa mosque, put the issue clearly. Welcoming Maliki's call for construction of the wall to stop, he said, 'We shake hands with the government in such stands and hope the occupation forces would not abort these stands.' However, on Maliki's return to Baghdad they did exactly that. A day or two later officials in the prime minister's office said Maliki's opposition to the wall had been provoked by media reporting that he now felt was exaggerated. Construction would continue.[11]

The biggest and most sensitive issue for any country is its independence. In the Middle East, in particular, it is a marker of a country's dignity and its people's honour. The constitution is one of the key symbols of sovereignty. Yet the USA interfered in both.

The process of drafting Iraq's new constitution in the summer of 2005 was largely controlled by American officials, acting under the leadership of the highly interventionist ambassador Zalmay Khalilzad. The Reuters news agency reported him as being a 'ubiquitous presence' during the discussions on the draft.

The embassy felt no embarrassment about proposing its own draft on the most contentious points. 'The Americans say they don't intervene, but they have intervened deep. They gave us a detailed proposal, almost a full version of a constitution,' as Mahmoud Othman, a Kurdish member of the constitution committee, put it.[12]

Even Bush weighed into the process. To reinforce Khalilzad's recommendations, he rang Abdel Aziz al-Hakim, the SCIRI leader, to discuss the constitution. When Shia and Kurdish leaders announced they had agreed on a final text, Khalilzad was standing there beside them. The *New York Times* reported he had worked 'furiously through the night to broker a deal'.[13] He endorsed it as 'right for Iraq at the present time'.[14]

Because of the constant US interference some members of Iraq's constitutional committee felt they had been reduced to bystanders. One Shia member complained: 'We haven't played much of a role in drafting the constitution. We feel that we have been neglected. We have not been consulted on important issues'.[15] A Sunni negotiator grumbled: 'This constitution was cooked up in an American kitchen, not an Iraqi one'.[16]

Imperial relationships are complex. Orders cannot be shouted. They have to be conveyed diplomatically so that the weaker party can give the appearance of consent while both sides preserve the fiction of sovereignty. At times, if it feels its pride or image are threatened, the weaker party may even disagree in public.

This was the case as tensions rose between Bush and Maliki in early 2007. Ever since Maliki took office after the Americans pushed Jaafari out, Khalilzad had been struggling to get the new prime minister to agree to a series of policies intended to reduce Sunni suspicions. Public opinion in the USA was growing increasingly impatient. US casualties were rising. The insurgency showed no sign of being defeated. Sectarian violence was taking a phenomenal toll of Iraqi lives.

The American public mood was well captured in December 2006 by a bipartisan commission under James Baker and Lee Hamilton that was set up by the US Congress. Asked to make recommendations for US policy, they laid out the terms of future American engagement with the Iraqi government in the bluntest terms: Obey us or we leave.[17] They recommended that

> the United States should lay out an agenda for continued support to help Iraq achieve milestones, as well as underscoring the consequences if Iraq does not act. It should be unambiguous that continued US political, military, and economic support for Iraq depends on the Iraq government's demonstrating political will and making substantial progress towards the achievement of milestones on national reconciliation, security, and governance.[18]

Privately, senior US officials had given the same message before, but this was the first time it was put publicly by such an eminent group. Baker, Hamilton, and the rest of their team were not members of the Bush administration so they felt they could speak clearly. In the past senior Americans had not dared to be so blunt, partly for fear that the Iraqis might take them at their word and ask them to leave.

Now the crisis in Iraq was so dire that the Americans felt they could take the risk. The Iraqi prime minister was as beleaguered and isolated in the Green Zone as the American ambassador. There was no way Maliki would dare to call for US troops to go.

Bush's first response to the Baker-Hamilton Report was cool, but in a nationally televised speech in January 2007, in which he also announced a 'surge' of 30,000 extra US troops to Iraq, he endorsed the 'obey-us-or-we-leave' line. Taking up a series of promises made by Maliki, Bush turned them into 'benchmarks' (rather than Baker's 'milestones'). Continuing US support would depend on their implementation, he said. 'I've made it clear to the prime minister and Iraq's other leaders that America's commitment is not open-ended. If the Iraqi government does not follow through on its promises, it will lose the support of the American people,' Bush warned.

The benchmarks consisted of a new law to share oil revenues fairly throughout Iraq, a softening of the de-Baathification laws, amendments to the constitution, and for more money from Iraq's budget to go towards reconstruction. The trouble with the benchmarks, as some senators and congresspeople saw it, was that they were vague. The USA appeared to be threatening a pull-out but without a mechanism for judging if and when the benchmarks had been reached. The Democratic majority in the US Congress tried to correct that by linking the amount of funds that the US could spend in Iraq to periodic reports by the White House on Iraqi compliance.

The dispute continued throughout 2007, both in Washington and Baghdad. In the USA the struggle was between an increasingly recalcitrant Congress and a president who was determined to bequeath the Iraq mess to his successor rather than admit defeat. In Baghdad the battle was between the Americans and the Iraqi government. The USA tried everything, from giving signals that it was looking for a replacement for Maliki that would involve a new coalition led by Iyad Allawi to direct threats that the USA would withdraw its support. In June it even sent Admiral William Fallon, the top American military commander in the Middle East, to sit down with Maliki. According to normal protocol a senior military officer would not discuss politics with a foreign prime minister. On this occasion, there were no such inhibitions. To make sure the message would go public, Fallon and

Crocker invited a *New York Times* correspondent to attend the meeting. The admiral 'warned Iraq's prime minister that the Iraqi government needs to make tangible political progress by next month to counter the growing tide of opposition to the war in Congress,' the paper reported. 'You have the power,' Fallon said. 'You should take the initiative.'[19]

Even more strangely, at least at first sight, Fallon raised the oil law. This had long been one of Washington's top issues since the law was drafted with US advisers' help and gave very generous terms over Iraq's lucrative but un-developed reserves to foreign oil companies. They were more favourable to foreign companies than any concessions given by other states in the region, including Kuwait, Saudi Arabia, and United Arab Emirates. Fallon asked Maliki whether the law would be passed within the next month.

The Fallon meeting was only the latest in a long series of US pressure tactics. Taken as a whole, they illustrated the farce of sovereignty. An Iraqi government that was meant to be in charge of its own country was in hock to a military occupation. It was too frightened to ask for it to end and too sectarian in its outlook to make a political deal with the resistance or with its parliamentary opponents, yet too proud to do things in the way or at the pace the Americans wanted.

The dilemmas will remain until Iraq regains its independence. An Iraqi government that the USA is propping up will never have the strength to ask it to leave, even as many of its members make private arrangements to abandon Iraq and seek refuge abroad. Some have dual passports from their time in exile under Saddam. Others are seeking visas for their families and themselves.

A US decision to withdraw its troops is the only way to cut the knot.

CONCLUSION

The first and the biggest American error was the idea of going for an occupation.

Kanan Makiya, March 2007[1]

It's not difficult to defeat Saddam, but that is not victory.

Taher al-Masri, April 2003[2]

This book has not been about blood but I hope it is not a bloodless book. No one who has spent time in Iraq in recent years or watched its tragedy deepen in every TV bulletin can fail to be moved by the appalling horror of what has become the greatest humanitarian catastrophe in the world.

I have made too many Iraqi friends, and seen too much of the pain they still endure, not to share their anger and despair. It is this that impelled me to go beyond daily journalism and write this book.

But I wanted to stay cool. I felt it was better to explain rather than describe. Why did the occupation fail? Could it have 'worked', or was it bound to be a disaster? Why did resistance develop? Who bears the blame for the carnage, initially only between the occupiers and insurgents, and later among Iraqis themselves?

My central argument has been that Washington's war planners, from the president and his closest advisers to the neoconservative academics who spurred them on, took no account of the nature of Iraqi society or Iraq's history, or indeed the deep well of Arab resentment throughout the region that would doom a Western occupation.

They had the wrong template. Most thought it would be like the successful American occupations of Germany and Japan in 1945, which met no resistance and went on peacefully for years. Some took their analogies from post-Communist Central and Eastern Europe. They saw Saddam's Iraq as a one-party state with a state-controlled economy like Poland or Bulgaria. The solution seemed formulaic: remove the dictator, ban his party, and open the door to private enterprise, and you then begin the 'transition' to a Western-style democracy and free market economics. The only opposition would come from a few ideologues and Saddamists.

The fact that Iraq was in the Middle East seemed to escape Washington's notice. The Bush administration did not understand that Arabs feel great sensitivity to assaults on their honour, dignity, and independence, especially by Westerners. Most occupations fail. In the Middle East they fail absolutely. If analogies were relevant when Washington's war planners prepared their attack on Iraq, it was Israel and Palestine that should have been the template, not Germany or Japan. Sending US and British troops to occupy an Arab country in the twenty-first century was bound to be as difficult as it has been for Israeli troops to occupy the West Bank for the last 40 years. In Palestine the issue is land. In Iraq the USA wanted control. In both cases the struggle is perceived in the Muslim world as a Western army assault on Arabs.

At another level, of course, the fact that Iraq is in the Middle East is the central reason why it was invaded. Had Saddam been presiding over an island in the South Pacific, he would have been ignored. Washington chose Iraq, not only in order to remove an independent anti-Israeli ruler but also to secure access to the country's oil reserves and to send a message of dominance across the region. The USA intended to create a new client in the northern part of the Middle East by turning Iraq into a secular, liberal, free-market, and US-friendly bastion and in so doing warning the anti-Western leaders of its neighbours, Syria and Iran, that their time was also coming to an end.

It was a highly risky endeavour. Arabs resent the contempt for their culture and religion that they see in the Western media and regularly meet in their encounters with Westerners. They have long memories of the West's political and military intervention in their region, and deep suspicions of Western motives. The two states with the longest records of such intervention are the very countries that invaded Iraq in 2003. Britain occupied and ran Iraq for four decades in the first half of the last century. The USA took over Britain's dominant role in the Middle East in the century's second half, starting with support for the coup that put Saddam's Baath party in power in 1963. Both countries were closely involved in the Zionist project – Britain in the creation of Israel, and the USA as Israel's main sustainer since 1967. To expect Iraqis to view Britain and the USA as altruistic liberators flew in the face of common sense.

That did not mean Iraqis were not glad to see the fall of Saddam. The vast majority of Iraqis were delighted to be without him and his regime. Throughout this book I have quoted from interviews with Iraqis which explain their complex mixture of attitudes to Saddam's departure and to the arrival of foreigners. Only a few expressed gratitude to the invaders. An important minority determined early on to resist the Americans and the British. Most Iraqis adopted a wait-and-see position, however, hoping the USA and Britain would rapidly fix their country's sanctions-affected infrastructure and improve their basic services. They were ready to tolerate an occupation provided it was short and sweet.

Two sets of factors turned many of these fence-sitters into opponents, leading them to condone or help the resistance. The first was Washington's refusal to set a time limit on the occupation and its blatant and humiliating domination of the various Iraqi governments it put in charge. This fulfilled the prophecy perceived by many Iraqis when the invasion started: that this is an imperial project designed to dominate our country and take our oil. The Bush administration's central blunder was not – as is so often alleged – the disbanding of the Iraqi army and the banning of the Baath party, or the decision not to send more troops to stop the looting and police the occupation more efficiently from the day Saddam was ousted. It was the American failure to announce an early timetable for leaving Iraq.

Bush and his advisers never took that on board. First, they assumed it would be easy to run the country. Then, when it turned out to be more difficult than expected, they turned the issue into a macho exercise in 'staying the course' and 'not surrendering to terrorism'. Andrew Card, Bush's first White House chief of staff, recognised the failure as he stepped down in the spring of 2006, three years after the occupation began. 'Alternative courses of action were never considered ... there had been some informal blue-sky discussions at times along the lines of "What could we do differently?" But there had been no formal sessions to consider alternatives to staying in Iraq,' he recalled.[3]

With hindsight, one American war-hawk regretted the failure to hand power to Iraqis early on. Richard Perle, the former chairman of the Defence Policy Board, told CNN in April 2007 that: 'The biggest mistake was not turning political authority over to the Iraqis immediately when Baghdad fell.'[4] In an earlier interview in 2007 for a British play by Richard Norton-Taylor entitled 'Called To Account', which examined whether Blair committed the crime of aggression, Perle said, 'I believed we would turn things over to the Iraqis more or less immediately. I am not sure the insurgency would have evolved out of that situation. I think we screwed it up.'[5]

As the blame game intensifies in Washington, this line of argument is likely to gain ground. Some neoconservatives always wanted to put an Iraqi favourite like Ahmad Chalabi in charge of Iraq as soon as Saddam was removed. Others toyed with the idea of nominating a provisional government but had no clear idea who should lead it. The Future of Iraq project, which was run by Iraqi exiles under State Department supervision, proposed setting up a 'sovereignty council' of three to five senior Iraqis within two weeks of Saddam's fall.

The idea that a quick transfer of power to hand-picked Iraqis would have worked may become the new conventional wisdom within the US policy-making elite. Blame for the occupation's failure will then be put on those who decided to set up Bremer's apparatus, the CPA.

This book has argued that the delay in transferring sovereignty was indeed a major blunder. However, it also argues that sovereignty had to be genuine and this could only be so if there were a full American troop withdrawal. Transferring sovereignty to Iraqis while retaining a massive troop presence and constantly exerting leverage on the Iraqi government undermined the country's independence and humiliated Iraqis at every level. Giving power to Iraqis had to involve more than nominating a provisional government or a sovereignty council. It required that there be no occupation. In his British interview, for example, Perle only took the argument halfway. He declined to say the invasion was a mistake, or that US troops should have left quickly. Similarly, the Future of Iraq project proposed that the US should keep its forces in Iraq for between five and ten years.

The second set of factors to turn Iraqis against the occupation arose from the way US forces operated. They created resistance by their own excesses. Kicking down doors at night, arresting men in front of their families, putting hoods and handcuffs on them, smashing furniture, and detaining thousands of innocent people and abusing them in prison struck at Iraqis' sense of dignity and gave them the impression that every Iraqi was considered an enemy. Trigger-happy US behaviour at checkpoints and the use of air strikes on villages killed hundreds of Iraqis and added to their anger. People felt their honour was being targeted, and they looked for revenge. Tens of thousands of Iraqis who were initially neutral were turned against the Americans and became supporters of the insurgency. The Abu Ghraib scandal was only the tip of an Islamophobic and racist pyramid of repression and humiliation that gradually affected almost every Iraqi.

The rising tide of Iraqi anger fuelled the growth of armed resistance in the Sunni heartlands and from Shia militias in Baghdad and Basra. The number of attacks on US and other foreign troops rose remorselessly. Between April and June 2004 they amounted to around 350 per week; by the period between February and May 2007 they had more than doubled to 750 per week.[6] American troops were dying at an average rate of three a day.

This growing animosity was a key factor in the increasing strength of Iraq's Islamists who played a leading role in dooming the American project. In the last decade of Saddam's rule experts on Iraq had already seen that Islamism was growing as a political force. Once he was toppled, Islamists were likely to fill the vacuum left by the removal of his regime. This is exactly what happened. The neoconservatives' pre-invasion hopes that Iraq could become a secular liberal society were always unrealistic. Saddam's heirs would not be the secular professionals and dissident former Baathists who had gone into exile in the West. They would be the Islamists who had taken refuge in Iran or were biding their time underground inside Iraq.

The growth of Islamism was a phenomenon in both the Iraqi Arab communities, Shia and Sunni alike. It was not inevitable that it would lead to sectarianism, however. Indeed, religious leaders on both sides fought hard to resist sectarian tensions when they first appeared. Sectarianism developed for a multiplicity of reasons, not least the clumsy policies of the CPA and the US embassy. Al-Qaeda in Iraq also played a major role by successfully provoking sectarian tensions through the use of violence and car bombs with the aim of making the country ungovernable.

As Iraq's carnage continued, the many Iraqis who had argued against an invasion could feel vindicated, though it did not help them in their current agony. They had warned that it would produce resistance and might lead to sectarian conflict and civil war. They worried that Iraq would become a magnet for Al-Qaeda's terrorists. They feared Washington's true intention was to take control of their country and its oil, and that US troops would therefore stay long after Saddam was toppled. Western opponents of the war, including the millions who demonstrated in New York, London, and many other European cities on the eve of the invasion, could also take little comfort from the disaster. They argued that the war was neither legal nor necessary. Saddam was not a threat to neighbouring states, his weapons of mass destruction had been dismantled or were unusable, and there was no compelling new reason for taking action against him on human rights grounds.

A White House fact sheet, published on 4 April 2003,[7] recalled that the greatest killing under Saddam took place in the 1980s when up to 100,000 Kurds were massacred during the so-called Anfal campaign. Another 100,000 people, mainly Shias, may have died in the 1991 uprising. These are huge numbers, but the available evidence suggests that Saddam's dictatorship was less harsh on Iraqis in 2003 than it had been a decade earlier. The 'humanitarian' case for foreign intervention in Iraq was therefore less urgent or convincing than it had been in the 1980s when Saddam was an ally of the West against Iran.

As for the damage done to human rights since Saddam's downfall, accounts of the excess mortality among Iraqis since April 2003 – for example, the surveys published in the medical journal the *Lancet*, which produce a figure of 655,000 'extra' deaths up to July 2006, of which 601,000 were caused by violence[8] – suggest that more people have been killed in Iraq during the occupation than during the 32 years of Saddam's rule. Even the Iraq Body Count, which uses a statistically more conservative methodology and tabulates deaths confirmed by at least two sources, produces a death toll of civilians killed by violence that averages around 16,000 annually over the first four years of the occupation. The annual rate of killing exceeded Saddam's. In the first two years, more than a third of these civilian deaths were directly attributable to occupation forces.[9]

Bush and Blair refused to come to terms with these facts. In his resignation speech on 10 May 2007 Blair declined to admit that the occupation was the direct cause of any killing. He blamed Iraq's problems on something called 'blowback', as though it was an unpredictable natural disaster, a hurricane or a tsunami: 'Removing Saddam and his sons from power, as with removing the Taliban, was over with relative ease. But the blowback since, from global terrorism and the elements that support it, has been fierce and unrelenting and costly.'[10]

Blair went to war claiming it was a moral crusade. He saw Saddam as 'uniquely evil', as I reported in Chapter I. That, in his view, was enough to justify the effort to remove him. Blair showed no interest in what adverse consequences there might be, and paid no attention to those who tried to warn him. As he left office, his moral certainties remained staggeringly intact. He did not see that anti-Western Islamism had grown stronger in Iraq because of the occupation. He had no feel for Iraqi pride or the nationalism that underlay much of the Iraqi resistance. He refused to accept publicly that, as with Vietnam in the 1960s and 1970s, the struggle was not a clash of ideologies but a defensive war by local people against foreign invaders. In that epoch the distorting lens portrayed the enemy as faceless agents of 'international communism'. A generation later the enemy was described, equally falsely, as 'global terrorism'.

In the face of all the criticism Blair's plea was sincerity. 'Believe one thing if nothing else,' he told a group of Labour party loyalists as he announced his departure date, 'I did what I thought was right for our country.'[11] A politician's responsibility to weigh options seriously, evaluate the pros and cons, listen to experts, and think long and hard about possible consequences – everything was swept aside by moral certainty and Blair's view that Britain must stand beside the USA whenever choices of war or peace are on the agenda. Sincerity that takes no account of consequences is normally described as recklessness.

Bush's motivation was similar. His Iraq policy rested on a combination of faith, mendacity, and imperial arrogance. He too put Iraq in the context of the war on terror, even though he had been told there was no evidence to link Saddam to Al-Qaeda or the 9/11 attacks. After Saddam's fall he described Iraq as the front line in the war on terror, using the argument that it was better to fight the terrorists abroad than let them reach the USA. The fact that his policies created more terrorists and that Iraq never was the front line before 2003 was ignored. Nor did he admit to the grim truth that the number of Americans who died in the unnecessary war he launched on Iraq had gone well above the number killed on 9/11.

As pressure mounted in the USA for a withdrawal from Iraq, a new argument emerged for remaining there. The USA had a moral duty to stay, it was claimed, because it must accept some responsibility for the mess. This argument – You broke it, so now fix it – was heard, paradoxically, from some people who had opposed the invasion as well as from people who supported it. It was an odd line, since if being in Iraq was the original mistake there was no evidence that staying longer would make things better rather than compounding the original mistake. Far better for the USA to discharge its responsibilities through paying financial compensation for the mess it had created and giving money for Iraq's reconstruction.

With the chaos in Iraq deepening the Bush administration began to look for ways of 'internationalising' the issue. Bringing Iraq's neighbours fully into discussions about Iraq's future security was one element. This made good sense, but the key condition, which was put by Iran and Syria, was that a US troop withdrawal or at least the announcement of a timetable for a withdrawal must be part of the equation. Otherwise, they feared they would be lured into a trap in which they would approve the prolongation of an open-ended US occupation in return for nebulous benefits.

Meanwhile, public opinion in Iraq continued to call for the USA to leave. A poll commissioned by the State Department and leaked to the *Washington Post* in September 2006 found a strong majority of Iraqis calling for US forces to withdraw from the country immediately, saying their swift departure would make Iraq more secure and decrease sectarian violence. In Baghdad, nearly three-quarters of residents polled said they would feel safer if US forces left Iraq.[12]

Another survey, made in the same period by the Program on International Policy Attitudes at the University of Maryland, found 71 per cent of Iraqis wanted the Iraqi government to ask foreign forces to depart within a year. By large margins, though, Iraqis believed the US government would refuse the request, with 77 per cent of those polled saying the USA intended to keep permanent military bases in the country.[13]

Among US troops in Iraq – the group of Americans who best understood the challenges the US army was facing and the futility of the war – support for the war had already collapsed by early 2006. A Zogby poll found that 72 per cent of troops in Iraq thought US forces should get out of the country within a year. Only 23 per cent accepted the White House and Iraqi government line that they should stay 'as long as they are needed'. In other words, the overwhelming majority rejected the 'conditions-based approach' under which US troops would only leave as and when Iraqi security forces were ready to take over. The troops questioned were not novices. Three-quarters had served multiple tours in Iraq.[14]

Even at this late stage, nearly five years after the invasion, the announcement of readiness to withdraw all US troops within a matter of months would give a vital boost to Iraq's processes of national reconciliation. It would also end Washington's delusional focus on victory. Before the invasion the issue was couched as victory over Saddam. After the invasion it became victory over the insurgency, the same false yardstick underlying Bush's 'surge' in 2007.

The emphasis needs to be put back on intelligent politics. Getting international guarantees of regional support for Iraq's stability and territorial integrity is important. But the key negotiations have to be internal. The Vietnam War only began to wind down when the USA backed its declarations of a willingness to withdraw with the start of negotiations with the Vietnamese nationalists – the government of North Vietnam and its supporters in the south. In Iraq, too, there has to be an inclusive process that brings about talks between the Sunni resistance, the Shia militias, the parties in parliament, and the USA. This can only work when Iraqis see there really is light at the end of the occupation tunnel. Only then will the resistance make a deal with the USA to refrain from attacks on US troops as they pull out.

There has to be agreement on a complete withdrawal. Statements by Robert Gates, the defense secretary, in May 2007 that the USA intended to keep a 'long and enduring presence' in Iraq by pulling back to the vast bases it has established across Iraq in contrast to Vietnam where 'we just left lock, stock, and barrel', confirmed to many Iraqis that Washington still harboured imperial ambitions to control the country and its oil.[15]

The Bush administration and its Democratic party challengers must repudiate those plans. Nor is it enough to 'hand over' to Iraqi security forces as US troops withdraw from any provinces that seem calm. Politics have to play the primary role in reducing insecurity. A local mechanism, run by Iraqis, needs to be set up in each province for engaging the political, tribal, religious, civic, and resistance leaders and forming 'unity administrations'. Holding immediate provincial elections is not the best solution under the 'winner-takes-all' system that the occupying authorities constructed for Iraq. This has been a problem, particularly in predominantly Shia areas where parties with militias have fought for power.

The Bush administration fears an American withdrawal will be perceived as an American defeat. Some senior Democrats fear the same thing, which explains why they are cautious about attaching binding restrictions on bills that fund the war. Most of the leading Democratic party contenders have blurred their earlier calls for a withdrawal of US troops, and now talk of keeping a reduced number there for a long time. This sounds little different from the Gates plan. Both parties should recognise that the defeat has already happened. It cannot be disguised. The USA has not lost a military battle but after almost five costly years it has failed to win, and will go on failing to win, what has become an increasingly bloody war of attrition. In the asymmetrical warfare of guerrillas against a conventional army the loss of any prospect of victory counts as defeat, especially when the invaders' political objectives have ceased to be attainable. Sending more Americans to die in Iraq will not change that painful reality. Nor will it suddenly produce a miracle where five years of war have failed. Only a negotiated withdrawal can bring an orderly and relatively casualty-free departure.

Defeat was inevitable once the USA decided to stay in Iraq after April 2003. The goals that Bush and Blair set for themselves in Iraq – democracy, stability, security – may be reached one day. For the sake of the millions of Iraqis who have lost loved ones under the occupation, or who have been forced to flee abroad, one must hope so. But these goals can only be achieved by Iraqis. They cannot be imposed through the barrel of a foreign gun.

Epilogue

Barack Obama's election victory in November 2008 has been greeted with delight by almost every Arab political grouping in Iraq and throughout the Middle East. Here is a man who offers the hope of a fresh start for US relations with the region and an end to the arrogance of the previous administration. He accepts that under George W. Bush the USA has lost power, prestige and influence, and a new policy direction is needed. How will he go about that? What can or should be done?

In Iraq Arabs know Obama as an advocate for withdrawing US troops and as a man who had opposed the 2003 invasion in part because he respected Iraq's sovereignty. Only among Kurds – the community that overwhelmingly supported the original US invasion – is there some anxiety, it seems. Many see the USA as a bulwark against Arab dominance in the region and are reluctant to see this influence diminished.

During the long campaign for the White House Iraq's Prime Minister Nouri al-Maliki had given Obama a major boost by using an interview with the German magazine *Der Spiegel* to endorse the Democratic candidate's pledge to take all combat troops out of Iraq by the summer of 2010. Maliki's remarks broke the convention that foreign leaders abstain from intervening in US elections. They also signalled growing irritation among Iraq's new elite with the Bush administration's persistent refusal to name a date for the exit of US forces from Iraq. Washington's standard formula that any withdrawal had to be 'conditions-based' and not linked to an 'artificial timetable' was running up against the Iraqi public's impatience and suspicion about US intentions.

For a long time the Iraqi leadership resisted this nationalist pressure, but by 2008 it too was affected. Tense negotiations were underway with Washington over a status of forces agreement that would authorise a temporary continuation of the US presence in Iraq in place of the annual UN Security Council mandate which defined Iraq as a threat to international peace and security – a phrase seen by Iraqis, rightly, as out-of-date and insulting. The Iraqi government insisted on a clear date for the departure of all troops and a ban on any permanent US bases on Iraqi territory. It wanted an end to the immunity of US troops from crimes committed in Iraq. It also sought a veto over all US ground and air operations and a pledge that Iraq would not be used as a springboard for attacks on its neighbours, in particular Iran and Syria.

The Iraqi government's new confidence in dealing with Washington was remarkable. Some analysts put it down to Iranian influence. Iraq's leadership was dominated by parties like Dawa and SCIRI (later renamed ISCI, the Islamic Supreme Council of Iraq), whose leadership had spent years in exile in Tehran. Iran's close relations with the Iraqi government were highlighted in 2008 by a visit to Baghdad by the controversial Iranian president, Mahmoud Ahmadinejad – no Iranian president had even been to the Iraqi capital before – and return trips by Maliki and President Talabani. Significantly, Ahmadinejad's trip was announced in advance, unlike those made by Bush, Cheney, and other senior American figures, who always came in secret, like thieves in the night.

Iran was certainly the single biggest victor of the war. Its close links to the new Iraqi government reveal how much Tehran had benefited from the US invasion. Nevertheless, it is important not to exaggerate Iran's influence in Iraq. The relationship between the two countries contains elements of rivalry and competition, and there is no reason to think the two capitals will always see eye-to-eye. Indeed, the emergence of a strong Shia-led state in Iraq would remove Iran's uniqueness in the region. In the eyes of the Shia communities in Bahrain, Kuwait and Saudi Arabia, which have always been marginalised or repressed, Iraq as an Arab state is a preferable champion once its sovereignty and stability are restored.

Iranians are ambivalent about a US withdrawal from Iraq. Tehran had welcomed the toppling of Saddam, the man who launched a horrendous war on them in 1980. That conflict (including the resulting half a million casualties) was the defining life experience for many Iranians who had reached leadership positions by 2003, including Ahmadinejad, who was based on the northern sector of the front. However, once Saddam was gone Tehran was not unhappy to see the US occupation become bogged down since this made it harder for the USA to put pressure on Iran, let alone contemplate a direct attack. But instability was a two-edged sword. What Iranians feared most in Iraq after the US invasion was that chaos could lead to the Baathists returning to power. Hossein Adeli, who had earlier served as Iran's ambassador in London, put it to me in Tehran in October 2008 in concise terms:

> In general Iran is against any foreign bases but if US bases provide stability and security for Iraq they could be a benefit to us all in Iran. But we don't want the US to manipulate the situation in Iraq in favour of Baathists or Arab regimes which were supportive of Saddam Hussein.[1]

Public statements from Iranian leaders criticising the status of forces agreement quickly changed after Obama's victory. They realised the Iraqi government had achieved a surprisingly good deal, and their own aim of opening the door to dialogue with the new US president could be undermined by continuing to oppose the USA's pact with Iraq. In short, Maliki's demand for a firm withdrawal date, the retreat of US combat troops to barracks by mid-2009, and no permanent US bases was motivated by internal Iraqi dynamics rather than Iranian pressure. Maliki had to take account of the views of the large section of the Shia community who supported Moqtada al-Sadr, the radical Shia leader who was a firm opponent of US bases and could bring tens of thousands of anti-American demonstrators on to the streets. Maliki wanted to project himself as the real nationalist, the man who had achieved an end to a humiliating occupation. It was noticeable that the pact with the US was titled as an 'agreement on the withdrawal of US forces'.

Maliki's confrontation with the Americans over their troop presence also stemmed from confidence that Al-Qaeda in Iraq had been defeated and that Sunni power in Iraq had been contained. Al-Qaeda's collapse in Anbar and the mainly Sunni suburbs of western Baghdad was the great story of 2007 and 2008. The number of sectarian abductions and murders had declined sharply. This resulted mainly from two factors: a unilateral ceasefire in the summer of 2007 announced by Moqtada al-Sadr, who ordered his militias to cease revenge attacks on Sunnis and stop fighting the Americans, and the activities of Sunni tribal leaders, who set up militias run by local Salvation Councils or Awakening Councils (al-Sahwa). The Bush administration claimed the 'surge' of an extra 30,000 US troops as the main reason for the reduction in violent deaths. While US troops played a role by building concrete walls in Baghdad and mounting extra patrols in some Baghdad neighbourhoods, the main causes of improved security were decisions taken by Iraqis. The emergence of al-Sahwa preceded the surge by several months. Fed up with Al-Qaeda's Salafi ideology that treated Shia as heretics – a doctrine that was alien to most Iraqi Sunnis – as well as with Al-Qaeda's efforts to recruit Iraqis and provoke civil war, Sunni tribal leaders banded together to resist them. The US commander in Iraq, General David Petraeus, saw the trend and chose to take advantage of it. He offered al-Sahwa money and guns, which they were willing to take in spite of the risk of the reprisals they might face once the Americans leave Iraq. Al-Qaeda leaders were foreign invaders just as much as the Americans, and in 2006 and 2007 Al-Qaeda seemed to be the greater evil.

Sheikh Mustafa Kamil Hamed, a leader of the powerful al-Jibouri tribe who controlled about 3,500 men in al-Doura (an area of farms and small towns east of Baghdad), provides a dramatic example of the zigzagging loyalties of many in the Awakening movement. Sporting a machine-pistol and a leather belt of bullets across his white *jalabiya*, this former resistance leader showed me proudly a medal from Bush when I visited his headquarters in September 2008. The Americans had by-passed Doura on their way towards capturing Baghdad in April 2003 and the sheikh boasted of how the local resistance had kept them from patrolling there for over a year. But in 2005 Al-Qaeda arrived, kidnapping government employees, taking hostages, putting up fake checkpoints, and killing Shias. He explained:

> Al-Qaeda pushed us hard to work with them. They even killed my brother's two sons. We said to them, 'If you've come to resist the US occupation, Iraq is an open field. You're free to do what you want but don't come here and kill our people.'[2]

Gradually he and his tribal colleagues decided to band together and resist Al-Qaeda. The trend was replicated in other Sunni areas. Doura was soon criss-crossed with al-Sahwa and Iraqi army checkpoints. Displaced Shia families started to come home, although the mood was not completely calm. There was considerable tension over the future of the sheikh's fighters. The USA had struck a deal with Maliki to include some 20,000 of al-Sahwa's 100,000 men into Iraq's security forces so as to dilute the power of Shia commanders in the army and give al-Sahwa a new focus. The other 80,000 were supposed to go onto the government's payroll while getting help in finding civilian jobs. The process went slower than al-Sahwa leaders wanted, but they kept their anger in check.

While Anbar and Baghdad saw a marked improvement in security, Al-Qaeda continued to play a devastating role in the mixed Sunni/Shia province of Diyala, north of Baghdad, where neither sect had the upper hand. In isolated rural communities Al-Qaeda's foreign leaders recruited Iraqis by playing on suspicions of Iran, which were strong in many Sunni minds. Al-Qaeda also remained strong in Mosul, playing here on Arab suspicions of Kurds. The city and the surrounding province of Nineveh had a large Kurdish minority, which sought to split several districts away and join to Kurdistan. Kurdish leaders persuaded the Americans not to encourage the emergence of al-Sahwa in Mosul for fear it would become a strong Sunni militia that might confront the Kurds rather than Al-Qaeda. In the resulting vacuum Al-Qaeda was able to project itself to Sunnis as the only force in the Arab community with the means of resisting Kurdish nationalism.

In spite of these difficulties Maliki felt supremely confident by the time of Obama's victory. He had worked with Sunnis to defeat Al-Qaeda in central Iraq. He had forced the Americans to accept a date for taking US troops off the streets of Iraqi cities by mid-2009 and for giving a firm date for withdrawing all remaining troops from the country. He had presided over Moqtada's gradual retreat from armed revolt.

The young Shia cleric has shown himself to be an adept tactician, veering between confrontation and compromise and never staking too much. In 2004 his militias twice launched attacks on the Americans but his unilateral ceasefire in 2007 reduced sectarian tension and contributed to the fall in tit-for-tat killing. In March 2008 when Iraqi forces launched an anti-militia drive in Basra he pulled his troops back after a week even though they had scored initial success. In part he was unsure whether they could hold their ground as Iraqi reinforcements raced to Basra, but Tehran also played a role. The Iranians were not keen to see armed clashes between two Shia forces, but if compelled to choose between the moderate Maliki and the headstrong populist Moqtada, they preferred Maliki. They helped to broker a truce in Basra under which Moqtada's militia would leave the streets to the army but retain their weapons intact.

The sense of calm and normalisation that began to spread across Iraq during Obama's emergence in 2008 as a credible contender for the White House supported the analysis of those both in and outside Iraq who had long called for the US to announce a timetable for withdrawal. The Bush administration as well as John McCain, Obama's Republican opponent, made blood-curdling predictions of chaos and all-out civil war in Iraq if US troops were forced to pull out by a fixed date. The opposite argument was that violence would subside and Iraqis would start to come together politically once they knew they would soon be in charge of their country at last. Armed resistance to the Americans would also abate since there would be little point in fighting US troops that were already moving to the exit. Five years after disbanding it, Washington's policy of restoring the Iraqi army was also bearing fruit. Although Sunnis worried that some units had sectarian instincts, the army was back in action as a source of national pride. Iraqi politicians were questioning why Americans should stay in charge any longer.

At the grassroots level political reconciliation still has a long way to go. After the carnage of 2006 and 2007 close to four million Iraqis were made homeless, either abroad or within Iraq. Controlling feelings of revenge will be hard. Newcomers have moved into empty houses and Baghdad's mixed Sunni/Shia districts will take time to restore. But politicians and religious leaders who have kept quiet for two years are willing to take a lead in calling for communal peace again. A case in point is the reopening of the Bridge of the Imams in northern Baghdad in November 2008. It closed in August 2005 after a lethal stampede as hundreds of Shia pilgrims were walking over it towards a shrine. Rumours of a suicide bomber caused panic and nearly a thousand people died, some by drowning as they fell into the river, with others being crushed underfoot. The bridge across the Tigris links largely Sunni Adhamiya and largely Shia Kadhimiya. Just three years later both Sunni and Shia clerics attended the reopening ceremony, proclaiming it a symbol of a new spirit of unity. Ahmed Abdek Ghafour al-Samarraie, head of the Sunni Endowment that supervises Sunni mosques, said Iraqis were united in one body and if any part fell sick, all other parts would fall sick too.

As Obama takes office, it is clear that Iraq and the rest of the Middle East have changed immeasurably in the six years since the invasion. So too have the power and prestige of the USA. The new president faces a daunting agenda as he tries to overcome the Bush legacy and find a new US position. In Iraq the Bush administration has suffered political defeat on at least four fronts.

Operation Iraqi Freedom, Bush's goal of creating a liberal pro-Western democracy in post-Saddam Iraq that would be a beacon for the rest of the

Middle East, lies in ruins. The first two years of the occupation provoked an insurgency in Iraq's Sunni and Shia areas. In other countries Washington's programme for encouraging free and fair elections was abandoned after the Muslim Brotherhood did well in Egypt in 2005 and their Palestinian counterparts, Hamas, won elections in the West Bank and Gaza shortly afterwards. Arabs saw that Bush's policy was not based on principle: calling for freedom was fine against regimes that defied the West, like Saddam's Iraq and the Islamic Republic of Iran, but it was muted when it came to Saudi Arabia, Jordan, or Egypt.

Bush had hoped to use Saddam's overthrow as a dramatic projection of US power in the region and a blow against Al-Qaeda. It had the opposite effect, however. A new generation of Al-Qaeda volunteers rushed to Iraq, where they had not been before, with the aim of killing Americans and undermining the occupation. While they suffered a major setback after the Iraqi al-Sahwa movement came out against them in central Iraq, they did enough damage to keep the US bogged down in a long and costly quagmire and to take the gloss off the initial three-week invasion that defeated Saddam. The Iraqi national resistance also took a heavy toll on US forces, particularly in the occupation's first year before Al-Qaeda arrived. By 2008, although they had not lost any set-piece battles, US military forces had failed to pacify the country in spite of the loss of some 4,300 men and women, and the permanent maiming of tens of thousands more.

Washington's success in quickly toppling the dictator created its own problems. Iraqis found it hard to understand how a superpower could be so slow and inept at restoring electricity and clean water supplies once the war was over. Every act of sabotage by insurgents added to the image of the US occupiers as incompetent. Far from projecting a picture of overwhelming power, the occupation confirmed an image of US ignorance and arrogance in the minds of most Arabs. The gap in opinion widened between Arab rulers and the Arab street. While the leaders of Egypt, Jordan, Saudi Arabia and the Gulf States did not dare to criticise Washington's invasion, opinion polls showed that their people opposed it, not primarily out of support for Saddam but because of the wound to Arab pride caused by the invasion of a sovereign Arab country. Photographs of Saddam's bungled execution and his taunting by Shia guards added to Saddam's status in some Arab minds as victim and hero. The scandal of Abu Ghraib was a further political defeat for Bush. Like millions in the rest of the world, Arabs were shocked by the way

US guards had sexually humiliated prisoners and the later revelation that torture was part of official US policy in the 'war on terror'.

The fourth defeat for Bush was the collapse of his hopes of turning Iraq into an Arab bastion of secularism and modernisation. The men who filled the post-Saddam vacuum were political Islamists, by definition suspicious of Western values. Chalabi, Allawi, and the other secular and pro-Western Iraqis favoured by Bush's advisers were pushed aside. The leaders who became dominant in the Shia community under the occupation all had good links with Iran. The USA had no real admirers except among the Kurds. Iraq's Sunni and Shia leaders made tactical alliances with Washington but genuine support for the USA was always weak. Thanks to its massive military and financial presence the USA did manage to wield considerable influence among the Iraqi elite but it won few friends.

How can Obama repair the damage, not just in Iraq but throughout the Middle East? The central task is to extract US forces from Iraq with dignity. There were major uncertainties in the positions he announced during the election campaign. He talked of keeping 'residual forces' in Iraq for an unspecified number of years. Their mission would be to hunt Al-Qaeda militants, train the Iraqi army and protect the vast US embassy in which Bush planned to have a staff of 3,000. Officials on Obama's team said the 'residual force' could number as many as 50,000 troops.

The withdrawal agreement Maliki signed with the Americans a few days after Obama's victory makes it possible for the USA to retain forces for all three of Obama's missions but only after the negotiation of new arrangements. Obama will lose much of the credit he won for his opposition to the Iraq war if he becomes entangled in a messy argument with Iraqis over the terms of the agreement. The Iraqi government managed to get Bush to accept the principle of a timetable for a final exit with no 'residual forces' or permanent bases. They rejected Gates's notion of a 'long and enduring presence' or the analogy of Japan and South Korea where the USA has retained bases for decades. They can expect no less from Obama.

In Obama's favour, it must be said that comparisons with the US defeat in Vietnam hold little water. South Vietnam was in the throes of a civil war between nationalist forces supported by the communist North and a narrow elite propped up by Washington, heavily dependent on US military aid. After eight years and the loss of 58,000 US soldiers' lives Washington had bought time, but no victory. The puppet government in Saigon desperately wanted the USA to stay. Washington's peace deal with the North in 1973 offered the USA, in Henry Kissinger's cynical words, a 'decent interval' to remove its troops before the inevitable collapse of the South. Washington had refused to accept a coalition government in the South. As a result the North and its southern allies prepared for a new round of war, and when South Vietnamese forces broke up in disarray in the face of their advance in the spring of 1975, it was a clear defeat for Washington. Pictures of the last US helicopter leaving from the roof of the US embassy in Saigon sealed the image of ignominious defeat.

Obama will not suffer a similar embarrassment. Iraq's civil war was never on the scale of that in Vietnam. Iraq's Arab politicians united in managing to negotiate a US withdrawal with the outgoing Bush administration. Resistance to the occupation became a successful national project and there was no group shouting betrayal or pleading for a long-term US presence. There were differences of view about the timing, with some Iraqi politicians wanting a date earlier than the 31 December 2011 deadline specified in the agreement with Washington. But the principle of a complete pull-out was widely accepted. Even the Kurds went along with the withdrawal agreement.

Humiliation for the loss of US influence in Iraq and the collapse of plans for long-term bases rests with Bush alone. Obama is not tarred by it. Nor is it likely that in the remaining months of their presence US forces will suffer a major military setback, thereby causing Obama a significant problem. Al-Qaeda is on the defensive and most of Iraq's nationalist insurgents have hidden their arms after achieving the US retreat they sought.

Questions about Iraq's medium-term stability remain. Most Sunni leaders seem to have reconciled themselves to having a Shia-led government for the foreseeable future. They see their task not as trying to overthrow it but as pressing for it to be inclusive, fair, and non-sectarian. The risk of a new outburst of Sunni versus Shia violence cannot be discounted, however, even though most Iraqis are tired of the blood-letting. If the Shia-led government frustrates legitimate Sunni demands for a fair share of government jobs and reconstruction money, there could be a return to violence.

In early 2009 the greater threat is that Arabs and Kurds might come to blows. Tensions are growing over the oil-rich region of Kirkuk and the various districts of Nineveh province around Mosul which the Kurds claim as historically theirs. Iraq's federal constitution planted several mines that could explode during negotiations between Baghdad and the Kurdistan regional government over sharing taxes, oil revenues, and other wealth. A violent flare-up over Kirkuk could precipitate moves by the Kurds to secede, leading to the country's collapse into a Kurdish north and an Arab south. While happy at Obama's victory, many Iraqi Arabs are angry at his vice-president, Joseph Biden, for sponsoring a US Senate resolution that advocated splitting Iraq into three ethnic or sectarian regions. The idea is anathema to Sunnis, who would be left with none of Iraq's oil, and to most Shia, with the exception of some members of ISCI. They would rather run the whole of Iraq than be left with the south-east. As Iraq's low-intensity civil war subsided in 2008, Biden seemed out of tune in believing that Iraq's future as a unitary state was doomed. The forces of centralisation were regaining the upper hand.

Apocalyptic scenarios are easily drawn. Pessimistic forecasts tend to be described as realism, while those who make the opposite case often stand accused of naivety. In policy-making circles the default option is that worse is more probable than better. Iraq suggests this may be wrong. Whatever apprehension there may be in some quarters, the evidence of 2008 is that life has improved for Iraqis as they begin to assume the USA is finally leaving.

Bush's defeat in Iraq was not confined to Iraq itself; US power has declined throughout the region. Iran feels a new sense of confidence and is breaking out of the isolation the USA sought to impose. Ahmadinejad was received in Turkey in 2008 as the first Iranian president to go there for decades. He also visited Saudi Arabia. In the dying months of the Bush administration Cheney toured the Gulf, attempting to fan the flames of suspicion about a resurgent Iran with nuclear ambitions and a Shia 'arc of crisis', a phrase first used by King Abdullah of Jordan. But whatever their concerns about Iran, none of the Gulf states favoured a US or an Israeli attack on the country.

The crucial questions as Obama takes over are whether the promised US/Iranian dialogue will lead to results and whether Iran will be integrated into the region's security arrangements. Iran already takes part in meetings held by Iraq and its neighbours every six months. Recognition that a US withdrawal from Iraq is a looming reality offers the chance for these meetings to produce a new framework for cooperation. Iraq's success in getting the USA to agree to leave delighted Shias everywhere. For the first time Shias are in charge of the government of two of the region's biggest oil producers, Iraq and Iran (three, if you count Azerbaijan). At 145 million they number half the Middle East's population. The conventional view that they are a minority has to be adjusted.

Ahmadinejad's visit to Istanbul contained important symbolism for Turkey. It highlighted a shift of power in the relationship between Turkey and the USA that many analysts have previously overlooked. On the eve of the Iraq war in 2003 the only Middle Eastern head of state who had ever made an official visit to Turkey was the Saudi King, back in 1966. An old US ally, Turkey always left everything to Washington. By 2009 leaders of six Arab countries, including Iraq, Kuwait and Syria, had visited the country, while trade with its neighbours has gone up from 8 to 30 per cent. The shift is a deliberate strategy by Turkey's moderate Islamist government to demonstrate its importance to the European Union, which it is trying to join. But the moves are also meant to reinforce Turkey's growing independence from the USA – a trend which first took dramatic form in 2003 when the Turkish parliament refused to let US troops transit the country on their way to invade Iraq.

As US power wanes, Syria too feels safer in spite of continuing threats from Washington over Syrian links to Hamas and Hizbullah. It has opened diplomatic relations with the pro-Western government in Lebanon and started indirect talks with Israel for a peace treaty. When the USA launched a helicopter strike from Iraq in October 2008 on a compound in Syria close to the Iraqi border, analysts were puzzled. The ostensible purpose was to kill insurgents crossing into Iraq. But insurgents had been moving between Syria and Iraq for years, so Washington's timing was queried. Was it trying to signal to Israel not to deal with Syria? The raid only served to highlight Washington's isolation from the new trends in the region. In another sign of its emerging sovereignty the Iraqi government sharply condemned the raid, reaffirming its insistence that the US withdrawal agreement that was on the point of completion must ban the use of Iraqi territory for attacks on its neighbours.

The central issue for the Middle East is still the conflict over Palestine. While many in Europe and the USA view the invasion of Iraq as a diversion or link it to the 'war on terror', most Arabs see a close connection between the two conflicts. They are convinced that Washington made Saddam a target, whether he had weapons of mass destruction or not, because of his defiance of US policy and his perceived threat to Israel. Washington's claims that Saddam was connected to Al-Qaeda are treated as a cover story. Arabs see the invasion and occupation of Iraq as a display of arrogance comparable to Israel's invasion and occupation of Palestinian territory; a Western army was once again seizing Arab land, sending shock waves of indignation throughout the Middle East. In Arab eyes the invasion highlights the West's double standards. Washington said it had to take action against Saddam because of his human rights violations, yet it did nothing about Israel's destruction of Palestinian homes and the violent confiscation of their land. Similarly, during the Israeli bombing of Beirut and the incursion into south Lebanon in July 2006 which took hundreds of civilian lives, the USA failed to join most of the rest of the world in pressing Israel to accept a ceasefire.

Hizbullah's success in emerging from the 33-day war in Lebanon with most cadres and much of its weaponry intact has helped to counter the risk of a widening schism between Sunnis and Shia throughout the region. Except in Lebanon itself, where many Sunnis feel under threat from the more numerous Shia community, Arab Sunnis admired what was seen as Hizbullah's victory in resisting Israel and forcing it to retreat, a feat not managed by Palestinians. Hassan Nasrallah, the movement's leader, made a point of not highlighting a Shia role in Israel's defeat. He talked of the region in class terms, as Moqtada al-Sadr does in Iraq, praising the poverty-stricken masses rather than the rich elite. He lauded Islamists who stood up for Arab rights in contrast to secular leaders who became intoxicated with the West, the so-called 'Westoxicators', a term also used by intellectuals in Iran under the Shah.

A key test for Obama is whether he can resist falling into the trap of trying to promote Sunni-versus-Shia tension. As the grandson of a Kenyan Muslim (after whom he was given his middle name Hussein) and the stepson of an Indonesian, he is widely perceived in the Muslim world as having greater sensitivity to Islamic culture and traditions than any previous American president as well as a better grasp of how clients of the US empire feel. Most US presidents seem unaware that their country's foreign policy is viewed in a negative light, as the latest unwelcome episode in a long string of Western colonial interventions in the Middle East. For Obama to talk of Sunni/Shia antagonism, let alone to try to exacerbate it, would be to ruin his reputation. In his book *Dreams from my Father* Obama relates how his mother 'taught me to disdain the blend of ignorance and arrogance that too often characterised Americans abroad'.[3] Nevertheless, some radical Arabs greeted Obama's election with the claim that he was just another 'ugly

American' regardless of his background and skin colour. He will have to prove them wrong by not forgetting the lessons he learnt from his mother about US behaviour.

Deeds speak louder than words, and the main issue for Obama, apart from honouring the agreement to withdraw from Iraq, will be to put his energy behind the search for Israeli–Palestinian peace. The first requirement is to recreate Palestinian unity so that Palestinians can negotiate with Israel from a firm political position. Conflict between Hamas and Fatah only serves the interests of Israeli hardliners who want to forestall peace talks by trotting out a new version of the mantra they used when Yasser Arafat was alive: 'We have no partner for peace'. To help to foster Palestinian unity the USA will have to end its boycott of Hamas. The movement was fairly elected in 2006 to govern the Palestinian territories and the West's policy of demonising Hamas and refusing to deal with it until it fulfils various conditions has run into the sand. Regrettably when Candidate Obama visited the Israeli border town of Sderot in July 2008 he not only failed to balance it with visits to places where Palestinians are oppressed, he failed to say that Sderot was more than a place under threat of terror. It was a model for the case that ceasefires are negotiable, and evidence that they are the first vital step towards any serious peace agreement. The cross-border ceasefire over Sderot was agreed between Israel and Hamas through Egyptian mediation without Hamas having to fulfil the three conditions. Renouncing violence and recognising Israel's right to exist will be formalised at the end of the peace negotiations, not at the beginning. Otherwise there is little incentive for Israel to make a deal.

In 2009 the prospects for peace are dimmer than they were in January 2001 when the Taba talks collapsed, thanks to the hundreds of thousands of new Israeli settlers in the West Bank, the land-grab caused by the building of Israel's 'apartheid' wall, and the virtual surrounding of Jerusalem. But the Taba framework for a two-state solution is still the most realistic formula that anyone has devised. Obama does not need to spend months sending an envoy to and from the region to craft a new package, or travelling there himself. The missing link is political will.

Israel still depends on US aid, just as the Palestinians do (or would, if the siege of Gaza was lifted and humanitarian and reconstruction money could enter unimpeded). Obama needs to be even-handed. He should announce a reduction in financial support to Israel until peace talks with the

Palestinians resume and show genuine progress. As part of a two-state solution he should also promise an aid package, supported by other donor
countries, which would compensate Israeli settlers as they pull back to areas
within the 1967 borders and would compensate Palestinian refugees for giving up their right to return to pre-1967 Israel. If the peace deal includes, as
it should, measures for some Palestinian refugees to go back to family land
within the 1967 borders under what is likely to be a small annual quota, this
too will need international financing. Previous US presidents wasted time
by talking the language of impartiality in advocating a two-state solution
while not acting in an impartial manner. Obama has the chance to change
that. He has to act fairly, and not just talk fairly.

The stakes are high. Bush's disastrous adventure in Iraq is drawing to a
close. It spelt misery and death for millions of Iraqis and accelerated the decline of US power throughout the region. The former cannot be undone but
the latter can be reversed – to a degree. The US dominance of the 1980s and
1990s will not return. But a president who can deliver a just peace between
Israel and the Palestinians will get a massive infusion of credit for himself
and for the USA as a whole. Arabs have had enough of US military might.
A display of soft power that brings results will go much further in winning
Middle Eastern hearts and minds.

Notes

Introduction

1 Speech from Tony Blair at the Foreign Office conference, 7 January 2003. Transcript available at *www.pm.gov.uk/output/Page1765.asp*.

2 See James A. Baker, III and Lee H. Hamilton (Co-Chairs) with Lawrence S. Eagleburger, Vernon E. Jordan, Jr., Edwin Meese III, Sandra Day O'Connor, Leon E. Panetta, William J. Perry, Charles S. Robb, and Alan K. Simpson, *The Iraq Study Group Report: The Way Forward – A New Approach* (New York: Vintage Books, 2006).

I Iraq Without Iraqis

1 Noah Feldman, *What We Owe Iraq: War and the Ethics of Nation Building* (Princeton, NJ: Princeton University Press, 2004), p.32.

2 Ibid., p.1.

3 James A. Baker, III and Lee H. Hamilton (Co-Chairs) with Lawrence S. Eagleburger, Vernon E. Jordan, Jr., Edwin Meese III, Sandra Day O'Connor, Leon E. Panetta, William J. Perry, Charles S. Robb, and Alan K. Simpson, *The Iraq Study Group Report: The Way Forward – A New Approach* (New York: Vintage Books, 2006), p.92.

4 Ahmad Chalabi in a brief intervention at a press conference of the Interim Governing Council at the convention centre in Baghdad, 13 July 2003.

5 Tim Pritchard, *Ambush Alley* (New York: Ballantine Books, 2005), p.234.

6 Senate Intelligence Committee, 'Report of the Senate Intelligence Committee on prewar intelligence assessments about postwar Iraq' (Washington, DC, 25 May 2007), available at *http://intelligence.senate.gov/prewar.pdf*.

7 Ibid., p.57, quoting from National Intelligence Council, 'Principal challenges in post-Saddam Iraq' (Washington, DC, January 2003).

8   Ibid.

9   Ibid, p.65.

10 Ibid., p.57, quoting from National Intelligence Council, 'Regional consequences of regime change in Iraq' (Washington, DC, January 2003).

11 Ibid., p.57, quoting from National Intelligence Council: 'Principal challenges'.

12 George Joffe in interview with the author, February 2007.

13 Ibid.

14 Alan George, Raymond Whitaker, and Andy McSmith, 'Inside story: the countdown to war', *Independent on Sunday*, 17 October 2004.

15 Charles Tripp in interview with the author, February 2007.

16 George Packer, 'Betrayed: the Iraqis who trusted America the most', *New Yorker*, 26 March 2007, pp.53–73.

17 Ibid.

18 Bob Woodward, *State of Denial* (New York: Simon and Schuster, 2006), p.252, quoting former House Speaker, Newt Gingrich.

19 David L. Philips, *Losing Iraq: Inside the Post-War Reconstruction Fiasco* (Boulder, CO: Westview Press, 2005), p.158.

20 Rory Stewart, *Occupational Hazards* (London: Picador, 2006), p.24.

II ARAB ANGUISH

1   Adnan Abu Odeh in interview with the author, April 2003.

2   Quoted in Albert Hourani, *Arabic Thought in the Liberal Age* (London: Oxford University Press, 1962), p.157. Hourani cites Wilfred Blunt, *Gordon at Khartoum* (London: S. Swift and Co., 1911).

3   Reuters, 18 March 2004, BBC report available at *http://news.bbc.co.uk/2/hi/middle_east/3525164.stm*.

4   Ali Ahmad Sa'id, 'Identity and questions of modernity', in *Questions of Nationalism on the Eve of a Third Millennium – Essays in Honour of Antoun Maqdisi* (Beirut: Dar al-Nahar, 1998), p.53.

5   Amin Maalouf, *The Crusades Through Arab Eyes* (London: Al-Saqi Books, 1984), pp.264–6.

6   Ibid, pp.265–6.

7   Charles Malik, 'The Near East – the search for truth', *Foreign Affairs*, 30 (January 1952), cited in Sylvia G. Haim, *Arab Nationalism: An Anthology* (Berkeley: University of California Press, 1962), p.222.

8   Edward Said, *Power, Politics, and Culture: Interviews with Edward Said* (London: Bloomsbury, 2005), p.382.

9   Ibid., p.388.

10 Hasan al-Banna, *Five Tracts of Hasan al-Banna* (Cairo: Muslim Brotherhood, 1930s).

11 See Michel Aflaq, 'Let us unify the leadership of the Arab struggle', in *Choice of Texts from the Baath Party Founder's Thought* (Arab Baath Socialist Party, 1977).

12 Sayyid Qutb, *Social Justice in Islam* (Kualar Lumpur: English translation by Islamic Publications International, 2000), p.19.

13 Ibid., pp.19–20.

14 Sayyid Qutb, *Dirasaat Islamiyya* (Cairo: Dar al-Shuruq, 1950s), p.162.

15 Khaled Hroub in a speech at the conference 'Academic Perspectives on the Middle East', German Embassy, London, 14 March 2007.

16 The report is available at *www.undp.org/arabstates/ahdr2002.shtml* and can be downloaded upon payment of a fee.

17 Ghassan Salame, *American Policy for the Arabs* (Beirut: Markaz Dirasat al-Wahda al-Arabiyya, 1982), p.7.

18 Mohammed Heikal, *Illusions of Triumph: An Arab View of the Gulf War* (London: Fontana, 1993), pp.428, 304–8.

19 Ibid., p.428.

20 Marc Lynch, *Voices of the New Arab Public: Iraq, Al-Jazeeera, and Middle East Politics Today* (New York: Columbia University Press, 2006), p.11.

21 Ibid., p.84.

22 Quoted in ibid., p.29.

23 Ibid., p.23.

24 Kanan Makiya, *Cruelty and Silence* (London: Jonathan Cape, 1993).

25 Fouad Ajami, *The Dream Palace of the Arabs* (Pantheon: New York, 1998).

26 Zogby International public opinion survey, April 2002, available at *www.zogby.com/news/ReadNews.dbm?ID=564*.

27 Ipsos-Stat, National Opinion Poll Survey, British Broadcasting Coporation, Jordan, 28 February 2003, cited in Lynch: *Voices of the New Arab Public*, p.14.

28 Zogby International public opinion survey, cited in Lynch: *Voices of the New Arab Public*, p.14.

29 Quotation from the Hearing of the House of Representatives International Relations Committee, 18 April 2002, quoted in Lynch: *Voices of the New Arab Public*, p.20.

30   Martin Indyk in interview with Marc Lynch, cited in Lynch: *Voices of the New Arab Public*, p.20.

31   Interview with the author, London, March 2007.

32   Lynch: *Voices of the New Arab Public*, p.206.

III CREATING RESISTANCE: THE SUNNIS

1   In interview with the author, April 2003.

2   Human Rights Watch, *Violent Response: The US Army in al-Falluja* (New York: Human Rights Watch, June 2003). This report contains a good summary of what happened in Fallujah in April 2003 and the background to the events.

3   Patrick J. McDonnell and Terry McDermott, 'Mystery blast highlights US military's dilemma: an unresolved, deadly incident at a mosque points up the difficulty of managing Iraq', *Los Angeles Times*, 13 July 2003.

4   Ibid.

5   Ibid.

6   Ibid.

7   Ibid.

8   Ahmed S. Hashim, a colonel in the US army, worked with US troops in Iraq between November 2003 and September 2005 and his writings show insight on the matter. He wrote a useful short essay on the insurgency, 'Iraq's chaos: why the insurgency won't go away', in the October/November 2004 issue of the *Boston Review*. He is also the author of *Insurgency and Counter-Insurgency in Iraq* (Ithaca: Cornell University Press, 2006).

9   Bob Woodward, *State of Denial* (New York: Simon and Schuster, 2006), p.116.

10   Ibid., p.133.

11   Christopher Segar in interview with the author, London, 8 March 2007.

12   Thomas E. Ricks, 'US adopts aggressive tactics on Iraqi fighters: intensified offensive leads to detentions, intelligence', *Washington Post*, 28 July 2003.

13   This information came from Dr Sala Hussein al-Ali and is reported in Associated Press news reports of 6 April 2004.

14   Associated Press, 7 April 2004.

15   Dr Scilla Elworthy, *Learning from Fallujah: Lessons Identified 2003–2005* (London: Oxford Research Group, 2005), p.12.

16   The siege is well described in Elworthy: *Learning from Fallujah*.

17   Iraq Centre for Research and Strategic Studies, 'The results of the public opinion poll in Iraq, field research: May 2004'. See *www.iraq-crss.org*.

18   Woodward: *State of Denial*, p.261.

IV CREATING RESISTANCE: THE SHIAS

1   Ali Allawi, *The Occupation of Iraq: Winning the War, Losing the Peace* (New Haven, CT: Yale University Press, 2007), p.12. Allawi was defence minister and finance minister in the interim Iraqi government, appointed in June 2004. His book is the most comprehensive narrative of the occupation by a senior Iraqi. However, unlike similar accounts of US mistakes written by senior Americans who worked for the Coalition Provisional Authority, Allawi recalls no anecdotes or conversations. Self-effacing to a fault, he only mentions his own role obliquely, preferring to deal with the occupation as a detached historian and political scientist.

2   Interview with the author, Basra, January 2005.

3   Charles Tripp, 'Militias, vigilantes, death squads', essay in the *London Review of Books*, 25 January 2007.

4   Denis Halliday in a speech made on 5 November 1998 at Harvard University.

5   Madeleine Albright, quoted in John Pilger, 'Squeezed to death', *Guardian*, 4 March 2000.

6   Charles Tripp, *A History of Iraq* (Cambridge: Cambridge University Press, 2000), p.39.

7   Ibid., p.44.

8   See William Polk, *Understanding Iraq* (London: I.B.Tauris, 2006), p.73. Polk's book is one of the most readable histories of Iraq yet available, which the author himself describes as a 'whistle stop from ancient Babylon to occupied Baghdad'.

9   Ibid., p.74.

10 Reader Bullard, *The Camels Must Go* (London: Faber and Faber, 1961), p.100.

11 Ibid., p.120.

12 Tripp: *A History of Iraq*, p.48.

13 Western diplomat in interview with the author, Tehran, March 2002.

14 Larry Diamond, *Squandered Victory: The American Occupation and the Bungled Effort to Bring Democracy to Iraq* (New York: Times Books, 2005), p.35.

15 Allawi: *The Occupation of Iraq*, p.11.

16 Ibid.

17 Bob Woodward, *State of Denial* (New York: Simon and Schuster, 2006), p.264.

18 Toby Dodge, *Inventing Iraq* (New York: Columbia University Press, 2003), p.68.

19 Ibid., p.68.

20 L. Paul Bremer, *My Year in Iraq* (New York: Simon and Schuster, 2006), p.129.

21 Diamond: *Squandered Victory*, p.227, 215.

22 See International Crisis Group, 'Iraq's Muqtada al-Sadr: spoiler or stabiliser?', Middle East Report No. 55, 11 July 2006, p.312. This report, largely written by Nicolas Pelham, is one of the best-researched analyses of the Sadr phenomenon.

23 Ibid., p.4.

24 Ibid., p.6.

25 Diamond: *Squandered Victory*, p.82.

26 Ibid., p.198.

V Leave in Time or Get Bogged Down

1 Conrad C. Crane and W. Andrew Terrill, 'Reconstructing Iraq: insights, challenges, and missions for military forces in a post-conflict situation' (Carlisle Barracks, PA: US Army War College, February 2003).

2 Cited in L. Paul Bremer, *My Year in Iraq* (New York: Simon and Schuster, 2006), p.360.

3 Bob Woodward, *State of Denial* (New York: Simon and Schuster, 2006), p.91.

4 Ibid., p.131.

5 Ibid., p.162.

6 Michael Gordon, 'Prewar planning for Iraq painted very rosy future', *New York Times*, 16 February 2007.

7 Woodward: *State of Denial*, p.163.

8 Ibid., p.185–6.

9 Secretary of Defense Donald H. Rumsfeld, '11th Annual Salute to Freedom', Intrepid Sea-Air-Space Museum, New York, 14 February 2003, available at *www.defenselink.mil/speeches/speech.aspx?speechid=337*.

10 See James A. Baker, III and Lee H. Hamilton (Co-Chairs) with Lawrence S. Eagleburger, Vernon E. Jordan, Jr., Edwin Meese III, Sandra Day O'Connor, Leon E. Panetta, William J. Perry, Charles S. Robb, and Alan K. Simpson, *The Iraq Study Group Report: The Way Forward – A New Approach* (New York: Vintage Books, 2006), p.37.

11 Bremer: *My Year in Iraq*, p.12.

12 Larry Diamond, *Squandered Victory: The American Occupation and the Bungled Effort to Bring Democracy to Iraq* (New York: Times Books, 2005), p.250.

13 Ibid.

14 Bremer: *My Year in Iraq*, pp.359–60.

15 Interview with the author, Baghdad, April 2004.

16 Samir al-Khalil [Kanan Makiya], *Republic of Fear: The Inside Story of Saddam's Iraq* (New York: Pantheon Books, 1989).

17 Edward Wong, 'Critic of Hussein grapples with horrors of post-invasion Iraq', Saturday Profile in the *New York Times*, 24 March 2007.

18 Crane and Terrill: 'Reconstructing Iraq'.

19 Sergio Vieira de Mello in interview with the author, UN headquarters in the Canal Hotel, Baghdad, July 2003.

20 See 'Report of the Secretary-General Pursuant to Paragraph 24 of Security Council Resolution 1483 (2003), July 17 2003', available at *www.un.org/documents/repsc.htm* as s/2003/715, p.3, para. 11.

21 Ibid., p.19, para. 4.

22 Interview with the author, Coalition Provisional Authority Headquarters, Baghdad, 7 July 2003.

23 Interview with the author at UN headquarters in the Canal Hotel, Baghdad, 27 July 2003.

24 Bremer: *My Year in Iraq*, p.82.

25 Ibid., p.79.

26 Interview with the author, French embassy, London, 14 March 2007.

27 Edward Mortimer, Kofi Annan's former speech writer, conversation in Oxford on 15 March 2007.

28 Interview with the author, London, 9 March 2007.

29 Edward Mortimer, 'Iraq's future lies beyond conquest', *Financial Times*, 22 August 2003.

30 Interview with the author, Najaf, July 2003.

31 Interview with the author, Baghdad, July 2003.

32 Iraq Centre for Research and Strategic Studies, September 2003 poll, see *www.iraq-crss.org*.

33 See Toby Dodge, 'The causes of US failure in Iraq', *Survival* (journal of the International Institute of Strategic Studies), London, Spring 2007, pp.85–106.

34 Ibid., p.9.

35 Ibid., p.10.

36 Woodward: *State of Denial*, p.188.

37 Ibid., p.197.

38 Diamond: *Squandered Victory*, p.39.

39 Bremer: *My Year in Iraq*, p.137.

40 Woodward: *State of Denial*, p.269.

41 Bremer: *My Year in Iraq*, p.205.

42 Ibid.

43 Diamond: *Squandered Victory*, p.240–1.

44 Woodward: *State of Denial*, p.325.

VI CREATING RESISTANCE: HUMILIATION AND DEATH

1 Saad al-Mahdawi, in interview with author, Muqdadiya, 20 March 2004.

2 Haifa Zangana, Iraqi exile writer imprisoned by Saddam Hussein, commenting in the *Guardian*, 12 April 2007.

3 Charles Heatly (CPA spokesman) in interview with the author, Baghdad, 29 July 2003.

4 Jeffrey Gettleman, 'US detains Iraqis, and families plead for news', *New York Times*, 7 March 2004.

5 Ibid.

6 See Amnesty International, 'Iraq: memorandum on concerns relating to law and order', 23 July 2003, paragraph 4.4, available at *http://web.amnesty.org/library/Index/ENGMDE141572003*.

7 *New York Times*, 1 June 2004. The full report is available at *http://download. repubblica.it/pdf/rapporto_crocerossa.pdf*.

8 Charles Heatly (CPA spokesman) in interview with the author, Baghdad, 29 July 2003.

9 Ellen Knickmeyer, 'Iraqi townspeople describe slaying of 24 civilians by marines in Nov. 19 incident', *Washington Post*, 27 May 2006.

10 See 'A dossier of civilian casualties 2003–2005', available at *www.iraqbodycount. org/analysis/reference/*. Published by Iraq Body Count in association with Oxford Research Group, the report is based on comprehensive analysis of over 10,000 media reports published between March 2003 and March 2005.

11 Ibid.

12 Ibid.

13 David Cracknell, 'British fears on US tactics are leaked', *Sunday Times*, London, 23 May 2004.

14 Iraq Body Count: 'A dossier of civilian casualties 2003–2005'.

15 Steven R. Weisman and Jeffrey Gettleman, 'An unexpected visit by Powell to Baghdad sets off an angry walkout by journalists', *New York Times*, 20 March 2004.

16 Interview with author, London, May 2007.

17 See American Civil Liberties Union, 'ACLU releases files on civilian casualties in Afghanistan and Iraq', 4 December 2007, available at *www.aclu.org/natsec/*

foia/29316prs20070412.html. The documents released by the ACLU are available online in a searchable database at *www.aclu.org/civiliancasualties*.

18 Ibid.

19 Ibid.

20 Ibid.

21 Cesar G. Soriano and Steven Komarow, 'Poll: Iraqis out of patience', *USA Today*, 28 April 2004. Findings available at *www/usatoday.com/news/world/iraq/2004-04-28-gallup-iraq-findings.htm*.

22 Douglas A. Macgregor, 'Dramatic failures require drastic changes', *St Louis Post-Dispatch*, 19 December 2004.

23 Douglas Jehl, 'Earlier jail seen as incubator for abuses in Iraq', *Washington Post*, 15 May 2004.

24 Douglas Jehl and Eric Schmitt, 'Army's report faults general in prison abuse', *New York Times*, 27 August 2004.

25 *New York Times*, 1 June 2004. The full report is available at *http://download.repubblica.it/pdf/rapporto_crocerossa.pdf*.

26 Rami Khouri, 'Abu Ghraib in the Arab mirror', 19 October 2004, available at *www.opendemocracy.net/media-abu_ghraib/article_2166.jsp*.

27 Ibid.

28 L. Paul Bremer, *My Year in Iraq* (New York: Simon and Schuster, 2006), p.350.

29 Cracknell: 'British fears on US tactics'.

30 See CPA, 'Public opinion in Iraq: first poll following Abu Ghraib revelations', Baghdad, 14–23 May 2004, available at *www.msnbc.msn.com/id/5217741/site/newsweek*.

31 Ian Fisher, 'The world: going, going …: How Iraqis see their future', *New York Times*, 23 May 2004.

VII Britain and Basra

1   T.E. Lawrence in a letter to the *Sunday Times*, London, August 1920, cited in William Polk, *Understanding Iraq* (London: I.B.Tauris, 2006), p.77.

2   Anthony Cordesman, a senior national security analyst at the Center for Strategic and International Studies (a Washington-based research organization), quoted by *Voice of America* correspondent Meredith Buel, 29 November 2006.

3   'Doomed to failure in the Middle East: a letter from 52 former senior British diplomats to Tony Blair', *Guardian*, 27 April 2004.

4   The texts of all the memos are available at Michael Smith's website at *www.michaelsmithwriter.com/memos.html*.

5   See the Downing Street Memos at *www.michaelsmithwriter.com/memos.html.*

6   Clare Short, *An Honourable Deception? New Labour, Iraq and the Misuse of Power* (London: Free Press, 2004), p.147.

7   Peter Hain, speech at Chatham House, London, 12 June 2007, full transcripts available to members of Chatham House on Chatham House website at *www.chathamhouse.org.uk/research/security/transcripts/*; redacted text available from the Northern Ireland Office at *www.nio.gov.uk/nio_conflict_speech-2.pdf.*

8   Interviews with the author, London, March 2007.

9   Christopher Segar in interview with the author, London, March 2007.

10 Interview with the author, London, March 2007.

11 Interview by James Graff and Bruce Crumley with French president Jacques Chirac, 'France is not a pacifist country', *Time* magazine, 24 February 2003, available at *www.time.com/time/europe/magazine/2003/0224/cover/story_4.html.*

12 Pierre Pean, *L'Inconnu del 'Elysee* (Paris: Fayard, 2007), p.424.

13 Ibid., p.427.

14 Telephone interview with the author, March 2007.

15 Interview for Iraq Commission, 5 June 2007, available on the Channel 4 website at *www.channel4.com/news/microsites/I/the_iraq_commission/pdfs/macshane_submission.pdf.*

16 Interview with the author, London, March 2007.

17 Interview in January 2007 for a British play on Blair entitled 'Called to Account', by Richard Norton-Taylor. Transcript in possession of the author.

18 Interview with the author, London, March 2007.

19 Sir Michael Jay in interview with the author, London, March 2007.

20 Interview with the author, London, May 2007.

21 Sir Michael Boyce in interview with the author, London, 24 April 2007.

22 Interview with the author, London, 2007.

23 Ibid.

24 William Polk, *Understanding Iraq* (London: I.B.Tauris, 2006), p.62.

25 Iraq Centre for Research and Strategic Studies. These 2003 findings are no longer on their website, but they can be contacted on icrs1@hotmail.com or *www.iraq-crss.org/contactus.html.*

26 Mark Magnier, 'People of Basra hope for trust, security', *Los Angeles Times*, 9 April 2003.

27 Colonel Ali Abdullah Najim in interview with the author, Basra, July 2003.

28 Mark Lacey, 'Plans for a British-appointed ruling council in Basra go awry', *New York Times*, 2 June 2003.

29 Sir Hilary Synnott in interview with the author, London, 17 April 2007.

30 See Michael Knights and Ed Williams, 'The calm before the storm: the British experience in southern Iraq', Policy Focus No. 66, February 2007, published by the Washington Institute for Near East Policy, 1828 L Street NW, Suite 1050, Washington, DC 20036. This is one of the most detailed studies yet available of British policy in Basra.

31 Quoted by Knights and Williams, ibid. Brigadier Moore's testimony is available online at *www.publications.parliament.uk/pa/cm200506/cmselect/cmdfence/uc 1241-i/uc124102.htm.*

32 Daniel McGrory, 'Locals predict more bloodshed in murder town', *The Times*, London, 1 July 2003.

33 Knights and Williams: 'The calm before the storm', p.10.

34 Ibid., p.15.

35 Electoral results are available from the Independent Electoral Commission of Iraq at *www.ieciraq.org/English/Frameset_english.htm.*

36 See Robin Cook, Douglas Hurd, and Menzies Campbell, 'Our troops must quit Iraq when the UN mandate ends in a year', *The Times*, 29 January 2005, available at *www.timesonline.co.uk/tol/comment/columnists/guest_contributors/article507848.ece.*

37 Rory Carroll, 'Police in Basra out of control, says chief of police: militias are the "real power" in Iraq's deceptively quiet second city', *Guardian*, 31 May 2005.

38 Knights and Williams: 'The calm before the storm', p.27.

39 See Eric Schmitt and Edward Wong, 'US study paints somber picture of Iraqi discord', *New York Times*, 9 April 2006.

40 Sabrina Tavernise and Qais Mizher, 'Oil, politics and bloodshed corrupt an Iraqi city', *New York Times*, 13 June 2006.

41 Ibid.

42 Ghaith Abdul-Ahad, 'The British officer said: "We are now just another tribe"', *Guardian*, 14 October 2006.

43 Sarah Sands, 'A very honest general', *Daily Mail*, 13 October 2006.

44 Richard Norton-Taylor, 'Defence Committee: British troops in Iraq face "nightly suicide missions"', *Guardian*, 25 July 2007.

45 See *www.number10.gov.uk/output/Page3280.asp.*

46 Knights and Williams: 'The calm before the storm', p.36.

47 Such examples appear in various media reports. See for example Steven Morris, 'First British soldier to be convicted of a war crime is jailed for ill-treatment of Iraqi civilians', *Guardian*, 1 May 2007.

48 Reidar Visser, 'Britain in Basra: past experiences and current challenges', paper presented to the Global Gulf Conference, University of Exeter, 4–6 July 2006. Originally titled 'Melting pot of the Gulf? Cosmopolitanism and its limits in the experience of Basra's British community, 1890–1940'. Published with some additional reflections on multiculturalism in contemporary Basra and the current British role in the city at *www.historiae.org*.

49 See Ghaith Abdul-Ahad, '"Welcome to Tehran"' – how Iran took control of Basra', *Guardian*, 19 May 2007.

50 Personal email communication with the author, 21 February 2007.

51 International Crisis Group, 'Where is Iraq heading? Lessons from Basra', Middle East Report No. 67, 25 June 2007, executive summary.

VIII SECTARIAN CONFLICT: WHO'S TO BLAME?

1 Ghazi Ajil al-Yawer, on NBC's *Meet the Press* in November 2004, quoted in Alissa J. Rubin, 'The conflict in Iraq: religious hostility surfacing', *Los Angeles Times*, 20 December 2004.

2 Mustafa Alani, quoted in 'Lebanese pattern is seen', Reuters, 2 September 2003.

3 Figures taken from UNHCR (*www.unhcr.org/cgi-bin/texis/vtx/iraq?page= statistics*) and Iraq Body Count (*www.iraqbodycount.org*).

4 Charles Tripp, *A History of Iraq* (Cambridge: Cambridge University Press, 2000), p.41.

5 William Polk, *Understanding Iraq* (London: I.B.Tauris, 2006), p.81.

6 See 'Democracy, Iraq, and the Middle East', 18 November 2005 at *www.opendemocracy.net/democracy-opening/iraq_3042.jsp*.

7 Ibid.

8 See for example Jane Mayer, 'The manipulator: Ahmad Chalabi pushed a tainted case for war', *New Yorker*, 7 June 2004, p.58.

9 Quoted in International Crisis Group, 'The next Iraqi war? Sectarianism and civil conflict', Middle East Report No. 52, 27 February 2006, p.8.

10 Ali Allawi, *The Occupation of Iraq: Winning the War, Losing the Peace* (New Haven, CT: Yale University Press, 2007), p.136.

11 International Crisis Group: 'The next Iraqi war?', p.10.

12 See transcript of Ambassador Bremer's weekly address, Coalition Provisional Authority, 12 July 2003, available at *http://usinfo.state.gov*.

13 Mustafa Alani, quoted in 'Lebanese pattern is seen', Reuters, 2 September 2003.

14 Michael F. Scheuer, 'Tenet tries to shift the blame. Don't buy it', *Washington Post*, 29 April 2007.

15 Buzzflash interview with Scheuer, 5 January 2005, available at *www.buzzflash. com/interviews/05/01/int05001.html*.

16 Quoted in Elisabeth Drew, 'The war in Washington', *New York Review of Books*, 10 May 2007.

17 Sami Ramadani in interview with the author, London, 13 February 2007.

18 Iraq Centre for Research and Strategic Studies. These 2004 findings are no longer on their website, but they can be contacted on icrs1@hotmail.com via *www. iraq-crss.org/contactus.html*.

19 See Brookings Institution, 'Iraq Index: tracking variables of reconstruction and security in post-Saddam Iraq', available at *www.brookings.edu/iraqindex*.

20 Rubin: 'The conflict in Iraq'.

21 Ibid.

22 Ibid.

23 Electoral results are available from the Independent Electoral Commission of Iraq at *www.ieciraq.org/English/Frameset_english.htm*.

24 Sabrina Tavernise, 'Killing off Sunnis, one by one', *New York Times*, 5 July 2005.

25 Sabrina Tavernise, 'Sunnis feel heavy hand of Shiites', *New York Times*, 7 February 2006.

26 The Zawahiri letter is available on the website of the Office of the Director of National Intelligence at *www.fas.org/irp/news/2005/10/dni101105.html*.

27 See 'Khalilzad urges divided leaders to rein in militias', Reuters, 26 March 2006.

28 Seumas Milne, 'Insurgents form political front to plan for US pullout', *Guardian*, 19 July 2007.

29 See Gary Langer, 'Iraq's own surge assessment: few see security gains', available at *http://abcnews.go.com/US/story?id=3571504*.

30 Harith al-Dhari in interview with the author in Amman, October 2007.

IX THE FARCE OF SOVEREIGNTY

1 Mahmoud Othman was a Kurdish member of the constitution drafting committee, quoted in the *Washington Post* on 13 August 2005.

2 Quoted in John F. Burns and Thom Shanker, 'US officials fashion legal basis to keep force in Iraq', *New York Times*, 26 March 2004.

3 Bob Woodward, *State of Denial* (New York: Simon and Schuster, 2006), p.447.

4 Ibid., p.462.

5 L. Paul Bremer, *My Year in Iraq* (New York: Simon and Schuster, 2006), p.300.

6 CPA Order 67 of 21 March 2004, paragraph 2 of section 4, see *www.iraqcoalition.org/regulations/20040321_CPAORD67_Ministry_of_Defence.pdf*.

7 Statement by France's permanent representative at the UN, Jean-Marc de la Sablière, 8 June 2004, available at *www.un.int/france/documents_anglais/040608_cs_france_irak.htm*.

8 Press release from the Multi-National Division's public affairs office, Baghdad.

9 Alissa J. Rubin and Jon Elsen, 'US plan to wall off Sunni area hits trouble', *New York Times*, 24 April 2007.

10 Press conference called by Ryan Crocker in the Green Zone, Baghdad, 23 April 2007. See *www.state.gov/p/nea/rls/rm/2007/84013.htm*.

11 See 'Iraq's parliament objects to Baghdad security walls', Associated Press, 13 May 2007.

12 See Jonathan Finer and Omar Fekeiki, 'US steps up role in Iraq charter talks', *Washington Post*, 13 August 2005. These and the following three quotations are contained in a detailed analysis of the constitution-writing by Herbert Docena, 'How the US got its neoliberal way in Iraq', *Asia Times*, 1 September 2005.

13 Dexter Filkins and James Glanz, 'Shiites and Kurds halt charter talks with Sunnis', *New York Times*, 27 August 2005.

14 Ellen Knickmeyer and Bassam Sebti, 'Glee and anger greet Iraq's draft charter', *Washington Post*, 24 August 2005.

15 Ashraf Khalil and Caesar Ahmed, 'Iraqis extend deadline for constitution', *Washington Post*, 13 August 2005.

16 Michael Georgy, 'Iraq parliament may back charter, Sunnis opposed', Reuters, 28 August 2005.

17 James A. Baker III and Lee H. Hamilton (Co-Chairs) with Lawrence S. Eagleburger, Vernon E. Jordan, Jr., Edwin Meese III, Sandra Day O'Connor, Leon E. Panetta, William J. Perry, Charles S. Robb, and Alan K. Simpson, *The Iraq Study Group Report: The Way Forward – A New Approach* (New York: Vintage Books, 2006).

18 Ibid., p.60.

19 Michael Gordon, 'US warns Iraq progress needs to be made', *New York Times*, 12 June 2007.

CONCLUSION

1 See Edward Wong, 'Critic of Hussein grapples with horror of post-invasion Iraq', *New York Times*, 24 March 2007.

2 Interview with the author, April 2003.

3   Bob Woodward, *State of Denial* (New York: Simon and Schuster, 2006), p.455.

4   Roger Cohen, 'The failure of Iraq captured in a sentence', *International Herald Tribune*, 28–29 April 2007.

5   Transcript in possession of author.

6   Department of Defense report to Congress, 'Measuring stability and security in Iraq', June 2007, p.23, see *www.defenselink.mil/pubs/pdfs/9010-Final-20070608. pdf.*

7   Fact sheet available from the Office of the Press Secretary, at *www.whitehouse. gov/infocus/iraq/news/20030404-1.html.*

8   Gilbert Burnham, Riyadh Lafta, Shannon Doocy, and Les Roberts, 'Mortality after the 2003 invasion of Iraq: a cross-sectional cluster sample survey', *Lancet* Vol. 368, 21 October 2006.

9   Iraq Body Count website, 'A dossier of civilian casualties in Iraq 2003–2005', Iraq Body Count, available at *www.iraqbodycount.org/analysis/reference/press -releases/12/.*

10 Tony Blair's resignation speech, at Trimdon Labour Club in his Sedgefield constituency, 10 May 2007.

11 Ibid.

12 Amit R. Paley, 'Most Iraqis favor immediate US pullout, polls show: leaders' views out of step with public', *Washington Post*, 27 September 2006.

13 Ibid.

14 Leo Shane III, 'Poll of troops in Iraq sees 72% support for withdrawal within a year', *Stars and Stripes*, Mideast edition, 1 March 2006, available at *www.es-tripes.com/article.asp?section=104&article=34538&archive=true.*

15 See 'US looking to long-term presence in Iraq, says Gates', Agence France-Presse, 1 June 2007.

Epilogue

1   Interview with the author, Tehran, October 2008.

2   Interview with the author, al-Doura, September 2008.

3   Barack Obama, *Dreams From My Father: A Story of Race and Inheritance* (New York: Three Rivers Press, 2004), p.47.

Bibliography

Books, Reports and Essays

Aflaq, Michel, 'Let us unify the leadership of the Arab struggle', in *Choice of Texts from the Baath Party Founder's Thought* (Arab Baath Socialist Party, 1977).

Ajami, Fouad, *The Dream Palace of the Arabs* (Pantheon: New York, 1998).

Al-Ali, Nadje Sadig, *Iraqi Women* (London: Zed Books, 2007).

Ali, Tariq, *Bush in Babylon* (London: Verso, 2003).

Allawi, Ali, *The Occupation of Iraq: Winning the War, Losing the Peace* (New Haven, CT: Yale University Press, 2007).

Anderson, Jon Lee, *The Fall of Baghdad* (London: Little, Brown and Co., 2005).

Baker III, James A. and Lee H. Hamilton (Co-Chairs) with Lawrence S. Eagleburger, Vernon E. Jordan, Jr., Edwin Meese III, Sandra Day O'Connor, Leon E. Panetta, William J. Perry, Charles S. Robb, and Alan K. Simpson, *The Iraq Study Group Report: The Way Forward – A New Approach* (New York: Vintage Books, 2006).

Banna, Hasan al-, *Five Tracts of Hasan al-Banna* (Cairo: Muslim Brotherhood, 1930s).

Blix, Hans, *Disarming Iraq* (London: Bloomsbury, 2004).

Blunt, Wilfred, *Gordon at Khartoum* (London: S. Swift and Co., 1911).

Bremer, L. Paul, *My Year in Iraq* (New York: Simon and Schuster, 2006).

Bullard, Reader, *The Camels Must Go* (London: Faber and Faber, 1961).

Chehab, Zaki, *Iraq Ablaze* (London: I.B.Tauris, 2006).

Cockburn, Patrick, *The Occupation* (London: Verso 2006).

Crane, Conrad C. and W. Andrew Terrill, 'Reconstructing Iraq: insights, challenges, and missions for military forces in a post-conflict situation' (Carlisle Barracks, PA: US Army War College, February 2003).

Department of Defense report to Congress, 'Measuring stability and security in Iraq', June 2007, p.23, see *www.defenselink.mil/pubs/pdfs/9010-Final-20070608.pdf*.

Diamond, Larry, *Squandered Victory: The American Occupation and the Bungled Effort to Bring Democracy to Iraq* (New York: Times Books, 2005).

Dodge, Toby, 'The causes of US failure in Iraq', *Survival* (journal of the International Institute of Strategic Studies), London, Spring 2007, pp.85–106.

Dodge, Toby, *Inventing Iraq* (New York: Columbia University Press, 2003).

Elworthy, Scilla, *Learning from Fallujah: Lessons Identified 2003–2005* (London: Oxford Research Group, 2005).

Feldman, Noah, *What We Owe Iraq: War and the Ethics of Nation Building* (Princeton, NJ: Princeton University Press, 2004).

Garrels, Anne, *Naked in Baghdad* (New York: Farrar, Straus and Giroux, 2003).

Gordon, Michael and Trainor, Bernard, *Cobra II: The Inside Story of the Invasion and Occupation of Iraq* (London: Atlantic, 2006).

Haim, Sylvia G., *Arab Nationalism: An Anthology* (Berkeley: University of California Press, 1962).

Hashim, Ahmed S., *Insurgency and Counter-Insurgency in Iraq* (Ithaca: Cornell University Press, 2006).

Heikal, Mohammed, *Illusions of Triumph: An Arab View of the Gulf War* (London: Fontana, 1993).

Hiro, Dilip, *Secrets and Lies* (London: Politico's, 2005).

Hourani, Albert, *Arabic Thought in the Liberal Age* (London: Oxford University Press, 1962).

Human Rights Watch, *Violent Response: The US Army in al-Falluja* (New York: Human Rights Watch, June 2003).

International Crisis Group, 'Where is Iraq heading? Lessons from Basra', Middle East Report No. 67, 25 June 2007.

International Crisis Group, 'Iraq's Muqtada al-Sadr: spoiler or stabiliser?', Middle East Report No. 55, 11 July 2006.

International Crisis Group, 'The next Iraqi war? Sectarianism and civil conflict', Middle East Report No. 52, 27 February 2006.

Jabar, Faleh A., *The Shi'ite Movement in Iraq* (London: Saqi, 2003).

Kampfner, John, *Blair's Wars* (London; The Free Press, 2003).

Khalil, Samir al- [Kanan Makiya], *Republic of Fear: The Inside Story of Saddam's Iraq* (New York: Pantheon Books, 1989).

Knights, Michael and Ed Williams, 'The calm before the storm: the British experience in Southern Iraq', Policy Focus No. 66, February 2007, published by the Washington Institute for Near East Policy.

Lynch, Marc, *Voices of the New Arab Public: Iraq, Al-Jazeeera, and Middle East Politicis Today* (New York: Columbia University Press, 2006).

Maalouf, Amin, *The Crusades Through Arab Eyes* (London: Al-Saqi Books, 1984).

Makiya, Kanan, *Cruelty and Silence* (London: Jonathan Cape, 1993).

Malik, Charles, 'The Near East – the search for truth', *Foreign Affairs*, 30 (January 1952).

McCarthy, Rory, *Nobody Told Us We are Defeated* (London: Chatto and Windus, 2006).

Obama, Barack, *Dreams From My Father: A Story of Race and Inheritance* (New York: Three Rivers Press, 2004).

Packer, George, *The Assassin's Gate* (London: Faber and Faber, 2006).

Pean, Pierre, *L'Inconnu del 'Elysee* (Paris: Fayard, 2007).

Philips, David L., *Losing Iraq: Inside the Post-War Reconstruction Fiasco* (Boulder, CO: Westview Press, 2005).

Polk, William, *Understanding Iraq* (London: I.B.Tauris, 2006).

Pritchard, Tim, *Ambush Alley* (New York: Ballantine Books, 2005).

Qutb, Sayyid, *Social Justice in Islam* (Kualar Lumpur: English translation by Islamic Publications International, 2000).

Qutb, Sayyid, *Dirasaat Islamiyya* (Cairo: Dar al-Shuruq, 1950s).

Ricks, Thomas, *Fiasco: The American Military Adventure in Iraq* (London: Penguin Press, 2006).

Said, Edward, *Power, Politics, and Culture: Interviews with Edward Said* (London: Bloomsbury, 2005)

Sa'id, Ali Ahmad, 'Identity and questions of modernity', in *Questions of Nationalism on the Eve of a Third Millennium – Essays in Honour of Antoun Maqdisi* (Beirut: Dar al-Nahar, 1998).

Salame, Ghassan, *American Policy for the Arabs* (Beirut: Markaz Dirasat al-Wahda al-Arabiyya, 1982).

Senate Intelligence Committee, 'Report of the Senate Intelligence Committee on Prewar Intelligence Assessments about Postwar Iraq' (Washington DC, 25 May 2007), available at *http://intelligence.senate.gov/prewar.pdf.*

Short, Clare, *An Honourable Deception? New Labour, Iraq and the Misuse of Power* (London: Free Press, 2004).

Simpson, John, *Not Quite World's End* (London: Macmillan, 2007).

BIBLIOGRAPHY

Stewart, Rory, *Occupational Hazards* (London: Picador, 2006).

Tripp, Charles, *A History of Iraq* (Cambridge: Cambridge University Press, 2000).

UN Security Council, 'Report of the Secretary-General Pursuant to Paragraph 24 of Security Council Resolution 1483 (2003), July 17 2003', available at *www.un.org/documents/repsc.htm* as s/2003/715.

Visser, Reidar, 'Britain in Basra: past experiences and current challenges', paper presented to the Global Gulf Conference, University of Exeter, 4–6 July 2006.

Woodward, Bob, *State of Denial* (New York: Simon and Schuster, 2006).

ARTICLES AND WEB RESOURCES

Abdul-Ahad, Ghaith, '"Welcome to Tehran"' – how Iran took control of Basra', *Guardian*, 19 May 2007.

Abdul-Ahad, Ghaith, 'The British officer said: "We are now just another tribe"', *Guardian*, 14 October 2006.

American Civil Liberties Union, 'ACLU releases files on civilian casualties in Afghanistan and Iraq', 4 December 2007, available at *www.aclu.org/natsec/foia/29316prs20070412.html*.

Amnesty International, 'Iraq: memorandum on concerns relating to law and order', 23 July 2003, available at *http://web.amnesty.org/library/Index/ENG-MDE141572003*.

Brookings Institution, 'Iraq Index: tracking variables of reconstruction and security in post-Saddam Iraq', available at *www.brookings.edu/iraqindex*.

Burnham, Gilbert, Riyadh Lafta, Shannon Doocy, and Les Roberts, 'Mortality after the 2003 invasion of Iraq: a cross-sectional cluster sample survey', *Lancet* 368, 21 October 2006.

Burns, John F. and Thom Shanker, 'US officials fashion legal basis to keep force in Iraq', *New York Times*, 26 March 2004.

Carroll, Rory, 'Police in Basra out of control, says chief of police: militias are the "real power" in Iraq's deceptively quiet second city', *Guardian*, 31 May 2005.

Cohen, Roger, 'The failure of Iraq captured in a sentence', *International Herald Tribune*, 28–29 April 2007.

Cook, Robin, Douglas Hurd and Menzies Campbell, 'Our troops must quit Iraq when the UN mandate ends in a year', *The Times*, 29 January 2005, available at *www.timesonline.co.uk/tol/comment/columnists/guest_contributors/article507848.ece*.

Coalition Provisional Authority, 'Public opinion in Iraq: first poll following Abu Ghraib revelations', Baghdad, 14–23 May 2004, available at *www.msnbc.msn.com/id/5217741/site/newsweek*.

Cracknell, David, 'British fears on US tactics are leaked', *Sunday Times*, London, 23 May 2004.

'Democracy, Iraq, and the Middle East', 18 November 2005, available at *www.open democracy.net/democracy-opening/iraq_3042.jsp.*

Docena, Herbert, 'How the US got its neoliberal way in Iraq', *Asia Times*, 1 September 2005.

'Doomed to failure in the Middle East: a letter from 52 former senior British diplomats to Tony Blair', *Guardian*, 27 April 2004.

Drew, Elisabeth, 'The war in Washington', *New York Review of Books*, 10 May 2007.

Filkins, Dexter and James Glanz, 'Shiites and Kurds halt charter talks with Sunnis', *New York Times*, 27 August 2005.

Finer, Jonathan and Omar Fekeiki, 'US steps up role in Iraq charter talks', *Washington Post*, 13 August 2005.

Fisher, Ian, 'The world: going, going ...: How Iraqis see their future', *New York Times*, 23 May 2004.

George, Alan, Raymond Whitaker, and Andy McSmith, 'Inside story: the countdown to war', *Independent on Sunday*, 17 October 2004.

Georgy, Michael, 'Iraq parliament may back charter, Sunnis opposed', Reuters, 28 August 2005.

Gettleman, Jeffrey, 'US detains Iraqis, and families plead for news', *New York Times*, 7 March 2004.

Gordon, Michael, 'US warns Iraq progress needs to be made', *New York Times*, 12 June 2007.

Gordon, Michael, 'Prewar planning for Iraq painted very rosy future', *New York Times*, 16 February 2007.

Graff, James and Bruce Crumley, 'France is not a pacifist country', *Time* magazine, 24 February 2003, available at *www.time.com/time/europe/magazine/2003/0224/cover/story_4.html.*

Hashim, Ahmed S., 'Iraq's chaos: why the insurgency won't go away', *Boston Review*, October/November 2004.

Iraq Centre for Research and Strategic Studies, 'The results of the public opinion poll in Iraq, field research: May 2004'. See *www.iraq-crss.org.*

Jehl, Douglas and Eric Schmitt, 'Army's report faults general in prison abuse', *New York Times*, 27 August 2004.

Jehl, Douglas, 'Earlier jail seen as incubator for abuses in Iraq', *Washington Post*, 15 May 2004.

Khouri, Rami, 'Abu Ghraib in the Arab mirror', 19 October 2004, available at *www.opendemocracy.net/media-abu_ghraib/article_2166.jsp.*

Knickmeyer, Ellen, 'Iraqi townspeople describe slaying of 24 civilians by marines in Nov. 19 incident', *Washington Post*, 27 May 2006.

Knickmeyer, Ellen and Bassam Sebti, 'Glee and anger greet Iraq's draft charter', *Washington Post*, 24 August 2005.

Lacey, Mark, 'Plans for a British-appointed ruling council in Basra go awry', *New York Times*, 2 June 2003.

Macgregor, Douglas A., 'Dramatic failures require drastic changes', *St Louis Post-Dispatch*, 19 December 2004.

Magnier, Mark, 'People of Basra hope for trust, security', *Los Angeles Times*, 9 April 2003.

McDonnell, Patrick J. and Terry McDermott, 'Mystery blast highlights US military's dilemma: an unresolved, deadly incident at a mosque points up the difficulty of managing Iraq', *Los Angeles Times*, 13 July 2003.

McGrory, Daniel, 'Locals predict more bloodshed in murder town', *The Times*, London, 1 July 2003.

Milne, Seumas, 'Insurgents form political front to plan for US pullout', *Guardian*, 19 July 2007.

Morris, Steven, 'First British soldier to be convicted of a war crime is jailed for ill-treatment of Iraqi civilians', *Guardian*, 1 May 2007.

Mortimer, Edward, 'Iraq's future lies beyond conquest', *Financial Times*, 22 August 2003.

Norton-Taylor, Richard, 'Defence Committee: British troops in Iraq face "nightly suicide missions"', *Guardian*, 25 July 2007.

Packer, George, 'Betrayed: the Iraqis who trusted America the most', *New Yorker*, 26 March 2007, pp.53–73.

Paley, Amit R., 'Most Iraqis favor immediate US pullout, polls show: leaders' views out of step with public', *Washington Post*, 27 September 2006.

Pilger, John, 'Squeezed to death', *Guardian*, 4 March 2000.

Ricks, Thomas E., 'US adopts aggressive tactics on Iraqi fighters: intensified offensive leads to detentions, intelligence', *Washington Post*, 28 July 2003.

Rubin, Alissa J., 'The conflict in Iraq: religious hostility surfacing', *Los Angeles Times*, 20 December 2004.

Rubin, Alissa J. and Jon Elsen, 'US plan to wall off Sunni area hits trouble', *New York Times*, 24 April 2007.

Sands, Sarah, 'A very honest general', *Daily Mail*, 13 October 2006.

Scheuer, Michael F., 'Tenet tries to shift the blame. Don't buy it', *Washington Post*, 29 April 2007.

Schmitt, Eric and Edward Wong, 'US study paints somber picture of Iraqi discord', *New York Times*, 9 April 2006.

Shane III, Leo, 'Poll of troops in Iraq sees 72% support for withdrawal within a year', *Stars and Stripes*, Mideast edition, 1 March 2006, available at *www.estripes.com/ article.asp?section=104&article=34538&archive=true*.

Soriano, Cesar. G. and Steven Komarow, 'Poll: Iraqis out of patience', *USA Today*, 28 April 2004.

Tavernise, Sabrina, 'Sunnis feel heavy hand of Shiites', *New York Times*, 7 February 2006.

Tavernise, Sabrina, 'Killing off Sunnis, one by one', *New York Times*, 5 July 2005.

Tavernise, Sabrina and Qais Mizher, 'Oil, politics and bloodshed corrupt an Iraqi city', *New York Times*, 13 June 2006.

Tripp, Charles, 'Militias, vigilantes, death squads', essay in the *London Review of Books*, 25 January 2007.

Weisman, Steven R. and Jeffrey Gettleman, 'An unexpected visit by Powell to Baghdad sets off an angry walkout by journalists', *New York Times*, 20 March 2004.

Wong, Edward, 'Critic of Hussein grapples with horrors of post-invasion Iraq', Saturday Profile in the *New York Times*, 24 March 2007.

INDEX

Note: Arabic names in this index follow the convention of being alphabetised by the first letter of the last name, ignoring the article 'al'. Thus *Moqtada al-Sadr* would be listed as *al-Sadr, Moqtada*, and alphabetised under *S*.